TAX HAVEN ROADMAP

RICHARD CZERLAU

UPHILL PUBLISHING LTD.

Published in 1995 by
Uphill Publishing Ltd.
190 Attwell Drive, Suite 400
Toronto, Canada
M9W 6H8

First printing
June 1995

Czerlau, Richard, 1966
Tax Haven Road Map

ISBN 0-9698432-2-4
1. Tax Havens - Canada.
K4464.5.C84 1995 343.04 C95-931674-4

Although the author has exhaustively researched all sources to ensure the accuracy and completeness of the information contained in this book, the author and publisher assume no responsibility for errors, inaccuracies, omissions or any inconsistency herein. Readers should use their own judgement and/or consult professional advisors for specific applications to their individual circumstances.

All the characters in this book are fictitious or have had their names changed. Any resemblance to actual persons, living or dead, is purely coincidental.

Editor: Uphill Publishing Ltd.
Cover Artwork: Steven Nease
Printed in Canada

I am very fortunate that many of my family and friends took the time to help me develop this book. I am especially grateful to my wonderful wife Monique, whose help and encouragement brought this book to a successful completion.

Richard Czerlau

DISCLAIMER

The information contained in this book has been developed using various research data. Such information is believed to be accurate and reliable at the time it was written. While every precaution has been taken in the preparation of this book, it must be understood that this information is very technical in nature and sometimes laws, rules, and regulations change quickly.

The author and publisher specifically disclaim any liability, loss or risk, personal or otherwise, incurred directly or indirectly as a consequence of the use and application of any of the information contained in this book. In no event will the author, editor, publisher, or any distributor of this book be liable to the purchaser for any amount greater than the purchase price of this book.

This publication is sold with the understanding that neither the author nor the publisher is engaged in rendering legal, accounting, tax, or other professional assistance or advice. If legal, accounting, tax, or other professional assistance or advice is required, you should seek the services of a competent professional with the required qualifications.

This book is being provided for your reading enjoyment and information purposes only. While some countries may consider these techniques perfectly legal, there may be some that do not. A competent professional can guide you correctly.

TABLE OF CONTENTS

PREFACE

Look to the past to learn about the future.

History does repeat. Much can be learned by studying the fall of the Roman Empire. Three successive Roman emperors, Caligula, Claudius, and Nero the Fiddler, squandered their government's reserves to pay for opulent private villas, grandiose monuments and temples, armies of civil servants, lavish ceremonial feasts, and bribes to the Praetorian Guard to ensure their loyalty. Predictably, their reserves ran low, and these foolish emperors raised taxes (*sound familiar?*), expropriated the assets of wealthy citizens, and expanded the money supply by re-minting coins using less gold and silver.

Roman commerce was destroyed by high taxes. Once proud Roman cities were reduced to ruin because of the lack of investment in infrastructure. Citizens became impoverished, plagued with riot and civil strife. History clearly shows that the foolish government policies of the Roman empire led to its bankruptcy and inevitable collapse.

A contrary explanation for the fall of the Roman empire relates to the discovery of lead. At the time, lead was very expensive, and considered a precious metal. Wealthy and powerful Romans had their table service made of lead as a status symbol. This resulted in lead poisoning, which detrimentally impacted on the quality of decisions and judgement. It is probably time for someone to check the lead content of the table service in today's government offices in Washington and Ottawa.

INTRODUCTION

This book is designed to assist in the reduction, deferral, or elimination of income reporting and the payment of income taxes, by providing information on secrecy, privacy, and confidentiality.

Tax Haven Roadmap shows you how to protect, preserve, and expand assets and income, without the tax collector standing at the front door demanding an ever increasing share.

Tax Haven Roadmap is designed to assist individuals and companies, located in countries with high and un-just tax structures tax laws that extract hard earned dollars from income producers and earners, while paying or subsidizing non-workers and non-producers.

Tax Haven Roadmap will help you understand the real meaning of financial independence and why existing tax laws make financial independence virtually impossible. The book also provides advice on how to protect your assets from confiscation by governments or individuals who may try to take away those hard earned assets.

Many of the suggestions and much of the advice contained in this book may seem extreme or unnecessary, and probably are, at least at the present time. While today, the effective use of tax havens does not necessarily require following all of the advice contained in Tax Haven Roadmap, in the future, some of the concepts discussed in this book may very well be the keys to your financial survival.

Tax Haven Roadmap is dedicated to the protection, preservation, and expansion of assets and income, and the ownership of personal private property, from which those assets are produced.

CHAPTER 1

TAX HAVENS AND THEIR APPLICATIONS

How did tax havens originate?

The twentieth century has seen income tax rates spiral higher and higher with seemingly no end in sight. The United States, founded in 1776 because of a tax revolt, functioned for nearly 137 of its first 220 years without any form of income tax. An income tax was briefly imposed during the Civil War, however, it remained in effect for only a few years.

Drastic change came in 1913, when the United States government passed a law making income tax on individuals legal. Opponents to this form of taxation feared that once the state was given power to levy income taxes, the tendency would be to continually raise taxes. At the time, the mere suggestion of a country imposing a maximum 20% rate of income tax was considered at the time "outrageous" by the advocates of such a temporary measure. Unfortunately, today a nation with a 20% rate of tax would probably be classified as a tax haven jurisdiction.

It isn't simply the ever increasing tax rates that have lead to outrage among individuals, but the fact that governments, in their constant search for new ways to generate revenue, have increased the scope of their taxation to encompass nearly every event of daily life. Today, making a gift is often seen as a taxable event, and to die is the ultimate "financial sacrifice," since estate taxes can be as high as 60% in some jurisdictions.

Supporters of tax systems that impose higher tax rates on those who earn higher incomes often argue that taxation is required to change the distribution of wealth within society. However, many individuals prefer to make their own decisions on who gets what portion of their hard earned money. Fortunately, an entire industry has developed for the sole purpose of assisting highly taxed individuals and businesses to legally avoid confiscatory taxes.

What is a tax haven?

The most compelling reason for the existence of tax havens is directly related to the fact that not every country in the world has the same need to levy taxes at punitive rates. As long as differences exist in either the types of taxes, or the rates charged, taxpayers will constantly seek to carry out their activities in jurisdictions which impose the least financial burden.

The importance of tax havens has increased dramatically within the past few decades and there seems to be no end in sight. Even the once popular misconception that tax havens existed for only the extremely wealthy has noticeably diminished. As tax havens become more commonplace, the need to understand their policies, requirements, economics, and laws also increases. Not every individual may be able to benefit from the utilization of a more friendly tax jurisdiction, but everyone should have the opportunity to make an informed decision.

Implicit in the everyday meaning of the word "haven" is a place where one is protected from something. A tax haven is traditionally viewed as a place of shelter, particularly from high income taxes and currency controls. In general, a tax haven is a jurisdiction that possesses one or more of the following characteristics:

1. either no tax or low tax is imposed;
2. a high level of bank and commercial secrecy;
3. banking and similar financial activities are significant to the country's economy;
4. modern transportation and communication facilities are available;
5. lack of currency controls on foreign deposits of foreign currency; and
6. self-promotion as a tax haven, or offshore financial centre.

No tax or low tax.

The term "tax haven" describes the concept of an absence of tax, or a lower rate of tax, as compared to the tax imposed by the country in which an individual or corporation resides. There are numerous ways that a country can achieve distinction as a tax haven. However, it is generally agreed by tax specialists that the following five main tax categories exist:

1. Countries in which there is no direct taxation at all. There is no income tax, profit tax, capital gains tax, wealth tax, or estate tax. The following jurisdictions are commonly included in this category:
    - Anguilla
    - Bahamas

- Bermuda
- Cayman Islands
- Cook Islands
- Nauru
- Turks & Caicos

2. Countries in which direct taxation is imposed at relatively low levels. The following jurisdictions are commonly included in this category:
    - Barbados
    - Channel Islands
    - Luxembourg
    - Switzerland

3. Countries that apply the territorial concept, where only domestic-source income is taxed, and foreign-source income is excluded from the tax base. The following jurisdictions are commonly included in this category:
    - Antigua and Barbuda
    - Austria
    - Belize
    - British Virgin Islands
    - Gibraltar
    - Hong Kong
    - Isle of Man
    - Liechtenstein
    - Malta
    - Monaco
    - Montserrat
    - Panama
    - St.Kitts & Nevis

4. Countries that have tax treaties with high taxing jurisdictions permitting their use as a tax haven. The following jurisdictions are commonly included in this category:
   - Austria
   - Barbados
   - Luxembourg
   - Malta
   - Switzerland

5. Countries that offer special tax privileges with respect to particular activities. A number of jurisdictions fall within the parameters of this category.

Bank and commercial secrecy.

In all countries there exists some form of commercial confidentiality, such as certain professional relationships (for instance, lawyers have what is known as client/attorney confidentiality, which prohibits a lawyer from disclosing information obtained from a client). The tax haven jurisdictions referred to in Tax Haven Roadmap also provide some level of secrecy to persons transacting business, particularly with banks. This secrecy has originated either in Common Law or through the implementation of specific secrecy legislation.

Secrecy is of such importance to the effectiveness of a tax haven that certain countries have gone so far as to enact laws making it a criminal offense to reveal any information that is protected under such secrecy legislation. For example, bank secrecy in Switzerland is governed by the 1934 Swiss Federal Law Relating to Banks and Savings Institutions, as amended in 1970, and provides for imprisonment of up to six months or a fine of up to SFr50,000, as a penalty for anyone who discloses such bank secrets or attempts to induce someone else to do so. Despite such legislation, some bank secrecy laws are not nearly as effective as tax planners are led to believe. There always exists a possibility that details of any particular financial transaction may be disclosed.

Despite such secrecy legislation, there often exist tax treaties between tax-haven countries and high taxing countries, allowing for double-taxation relief, including in certain cases the sharing of information. This exchange of information, however, generally does not grant foreign tax authorities the right to arbitrarily request information in cases that are not related to the relief of double taxation. For example, the tax treaty between Switzerland and the United States provides for the exchange of information in double-taxation cases, and this does not breach the right to bank secrecy enshrined in the Swiss Federal Constitution.

Relative importance of the financial sector.

Both the banking and financial sectors tend to be of greater importance when considering the economy of a tax haven in comparison to the economies of non tax haven countries. In fact, in many tax haven countries, the banking industry is responsible for over 40% of the country's revenues. The banking industry has a significant effect on the economy of a tax haven by producing revenues in the form of fees and modest stamp duties on certain financial transactions, such as transferring funds. For this reason, most tax havens follow the policy of encouraging offshore business. The most common way for a tax haven to achieve such a policy of encouragement is by distinguishing between resident and non-resident accounts. By providing incentives for non-resident accounts, tax haven jurisdictions draw increasing volumes of offshore banking business. Some common incentives include:

- allowing non-resident accounts to be free of foreign exchange and other currency controls;
- eliminating reserve requirements on non-resident accounts; and
- the reduction or elimination of tax on non-resident accounts.

Modern transportation and communications.

To be effective as a tax haven, strong communication facilities are required. If reliable and cost-effective communications are unavailable, individuals lose confidence in utilizing the tax haven, reducing its inherent attractiveness. Most tax haven countries have excellent transportation and communication facilities, including good telecommunication and telex services. Recent advances in computer modem technology and data communication links have also been an aid to communication.

Lack of currency controls on foreign deposits.

It is essential that individuals and corporations making use of tax havens are free to move money in and out of the country at will. Most major tax havens either impose no form of exchange controls, or they operate with a dual currency system where non-residents, or companies formed by non-residents, are exempt from exchange control regulations. The exemption of foreign exchange control restrictions is often crucial in selecting a tax haven jurisdiction. The importance of the absence of exchange controls is clearly important when considering the operation of a captive insurance company, as it is imperative to have insurance premiums exempt from exchange control restrictions, making it easier to transfer this money out of the country.

Self-promotion as a tax haven.

It is quite common for tax havens to solicit financial business and to promote themselves as tax havens. Most tax havens are typically countries with few natural resources, heavily dependent upon the uncertainties of the tourist trade. For this reason, the banking and financial industry is seen as the only relatively stable source of revenue that, otherwise may be unattainable. Tax haven countries view this self-promotion as a necessity, often advertising the advantages they offer through seminars, articles in the press, and advertisements.

What are tax havens used for?

When considering the use of a tax haven, one must remember that although tax havens may have the potential to attract illegal activity, they should not be condemned for this reason alone. Such a generalization would in essence be a condemnation of international tax planning, which has long been regarded not only as a privilege, but as a right. Mr. Justice Sutherland, speaking for the United States Supreme Court, clearly expressed this view in the following quote:

> *"The legal right of a taxpayer to decrease the amount of what otherwise would be his taxes, or altogether avoid them, by means which the law permits, cannot be doubted."* - Gregory vs. Helvering, 293 U.S. 454 (1935).

The utilization of tax havens is clearly only limited by the imagination of individuals, companies, and their respective tax planners. Tax havens openly acknowledge the needs of individuals to safeguard their assets, and to place limits on the high tax burden they are exposed to in their current country of residence. If all countries recognized these needs, or at the very least considered them, the utilization of tax havens would probably diminish over time. However, until these needs are recognized, tax havens will continue to play an ever increasing role in all facets of tax planning.

Why utilize a tax haven?

The following list provides many of the most common reasons why individuals and corporations utilize tax havens. Most tax havens have been organized to permit the following objectives to be easily achieved:

1. **Taxes on Income** - To eliminate the reporting and paying of income tax on earnings, interest, dividends, and investments.
2. **Taxes on Capital gains** - To protect against high capital gains taxes and reporting requirements.
3. **Taxes on Estates** - To prevent inheritance taxes, estate taxes, executor's fees, and probate fees.
4. **Asset Protection** - To protect assets from creditors, malpractice claims, judgements, liens, and bankruptcy, and to deter the initiation of civil litigation.
5. **Divorce and Separation** - To prevent the erosion of assets as a result of divorce or separation.
6. **Safekeeping** - To prevent any individual or government agency from locating your private documents.
7. **Public Record** - To prevent any knowledge of your assets or affairs from becoming public.
8. **Investment** - To protect the privacy of your involvement with investment houses, brokers, and securities markets.

9. **Share Holdings** - To protect the privacy of corporate ownership from becoming known to any individual or government.

10. **Cash** - To prevent any person or government from gaining access to your hard currency.

11. **Management** - To centralize the holding of securities, real estate and various other assets, which may be held and managed in several jurisdictions around the world.

12. **Active Business** - To earn tax free income through the operation of an active business. Examples include advertising, consulting, factoring, leasing, and trading.

13. **Intellectual Property** - To earn tax free income generated by the licensing of trade marks, patents, royalties, software licenses, and other rights from an offshore company.

14. **Travel** - Use offshore funds and automatic teller machines to gain immediate access to hard currency anywhere in the world.

CHAPTER 2

CONFISCATORY TAXES AND THEIR IMPACT

In countries where the government provides a minimum standard of living for its citizens, a certain amount of taxation is required to ensure that the costs of providing this standard are spread fairly among the entire population. However, once implemented, tax systems often take on a life of their own. Rather than utilizing the tax revenue to assist in providing essential services, governments often begin to see taxpayers as a never ending source of revenue.

> "*It must be nice to belong to some legislative body and just pick money out of the air.*" - Will Rogers

Projects get planned and implemented without immediate financing. Governments borrow and increase debt, with the only way out being to raise revenues by increasing taxation. Most of the high tax countries in the world have now reached the "tax wall." Citizens are at a point where increased taxation will not be tolerated. Individuals now, more than ever, must arrange their affairs to reduce their tax liabilities.

Courts have been asked to rule on whether people can plan their business and personal affairs so as to pay the minimum amount of tax possible. Decisions have been reached over the years agreeing with the statement that arranging one's affairs to pay as little tax as possible is entirely acceptable.

> "*Anyone may so arrange his affairs that his taxes to be as low as possible; he is not bound to choose that pattern which will best pay the Treasury; there is not even a patriotic duty to increase one's taxes.*" - Federal Judge Learned Hand, Gregory vs. Helvering, 69 F.2d 809, 1935.

> "*Every man is entitled, if he can, to order his affairs so that the tax attaching under the appropriate Acts is less than it otherwise would be. If he succeeds in ordering them so as to secure this result, then, however unappreciative the Commissioners of Inland Revenue or his fellow taxpayers may be of his ingenuity, he cannot be compelled to pay an increased tax.*" - Lord Tomlin, Inland Revenue vs. Duke of Westminster, 1936.

The decline of many great civilizations in history has been due to extreme levels of taxation. In fact, the United States was founded in 1776 because a significant number of early colonists revolted against unreasonable taxation.

Wealthy citizens of high tax countries have been using offshore centres to protect their assets.

Wealthy Europeans have been transferring assets to tax havens since the French Revolution. Today, citizens of the Persian Gulf countries are also protecting their assets from ruthless dictators and other financial enemies.

Not surprisingly, increasing numbers of Americans are giving up their citizenship to avoid estate taxes that in some cases can exceed 60%. Uncle Sam's power even extends beyond the border, requiring foreigners to pay estate taxes on assets such as property or business interests held within the United States. The *Foreign Investment in Real Property Tax*

Act of 1980 requires foreigners to pay a capital gains tax when they sell U.S. real estate. Can you imagine what would happen to the U.S. markets if all foreign holdings were taxed in a similar manner to real estate?

Is your government taxing away your income?

The high rate of income tax paid by citizens of the major industrialized nations will negatively impact on the continued prosperity these respective countries now enjoy. The following table shows rates of income, capital gains, and dividend taxes for 1994:

	Income Tax	Capital gains Tax	Dividend Tax
Britain	40%	40%	n/a
Canada (Ontario)	53.2%	39.9%	39.9%
France	57%	19% to 57%	57%
Germany	53%	n/a	53%
Italy	51% to 67%	25%	51% to 67%
Japan	65%	65%	35%
United States	39.6%	39.6%	39.6%

Are you taxed to the last drop?

Several jurisdictions, in addition to their high rates of tax on income, also have high taxes on the purchase of goods and services. Excessive levels of taxation have the potential to hurt all citizens. Take, for example, the taxation of distilled spirits in Canada (as of January 1, 1995):

- 83% of the retail price of distilled spirits represents direct taxes.
- This has contributed to the closure of 16 distilled spirits plants in Canada, and the loss of 4,200 jobs.

- It is estimated that at least 4 million cases of spirits are smuggled annually into Canada.

Government debt is increasing at the rate of over one billion dollars a day!

In 1980 the U.S. national debt reached one trillion dollars. By 1990, the national debt had increased to over four trillion dollars. More and more people are beginning to realize the dangers of massive government debt. The realization that such a massive debt may never be controlled has led to an unprecedented devaluation of the U.S. dollar against world currencies such as the Swiss Franc, Japanese Yen, German Deutschemark, and British Pound.

United States Government net worth.

Figures shown are in trillions of dollars.

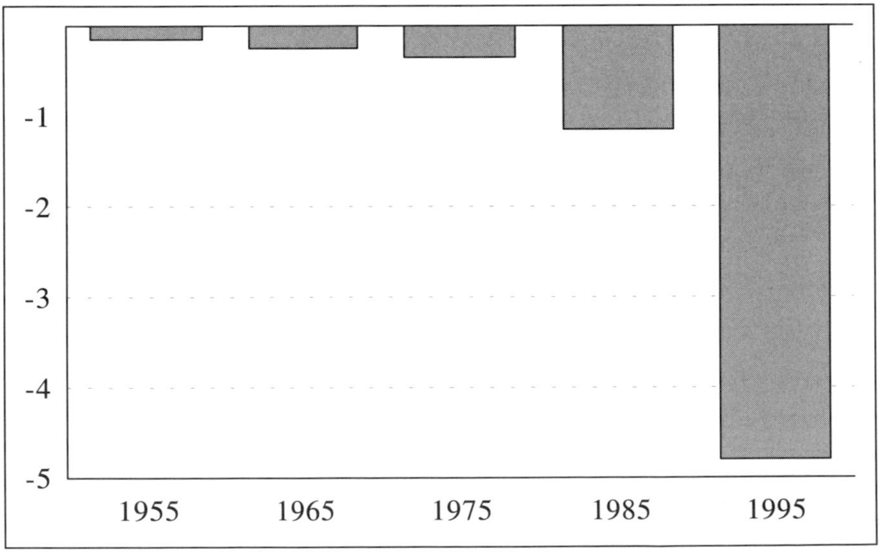

High government debt and deficits have contributed to an overall decrease in the average standard of living. Today many people work more for less. The following table indicates the dramatic growth in the U.S. annual federal deficit. A clear trend towards increasing deficits is shown. Sooner or later someone is going to have to pay for past excesses.

Annual United States deficit.

Figures shown are in billions of dollars.

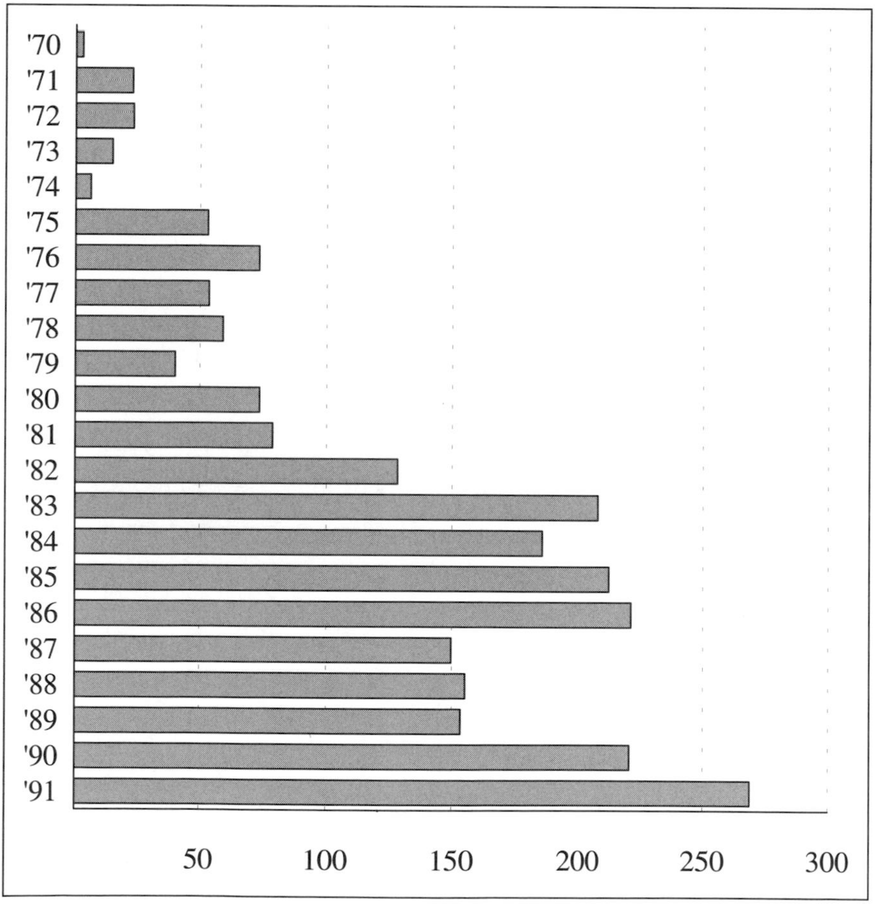

CHAPTER 3

PRIVACY AND CONFIDENTIALITY

Why are privacy and confidentiality important?

Recent headlines: A woman wins a multi-million dollar lawsuit against McDonald's because their coffee was too hot. A burglar collects from the owner of a mansion after falling on the property. Homeowners lose their entire net worth because an intoxicated man jumped off their roof and into their swimming pool, breaking his neck.

Who needs asset protection? The answer is obvious, anyone who owns assets. If you have debt-free assets, you are the prime target of frivolous lawsuits. As a successful individual, you may find yourself as a defendant of one of over 20 million civil lawsuits filed every year. Many of these lawsuits, although frivolous, result in judgements that can reduce a substantial net worth to virtually nothing. By properly structuring the ownership of your assets, a potential plaintiff may be dissuaded from commencing costly litigation.

Are your life savings in jeopardy?

Your teenage son holds a party while you're out of town. Someone drinks and drives, causing a serious accident, killing another driver. You are sued by the deceased person's family for $5 million dollars. A verdict of criminal negligence carries with it a judgement of $2.5 million dollars. Because the liability insurance you hold only covers $1 million dollars, you are now faced with losing your home, your business, and your life savings. It's all too easy to assume a lawsuit won't happen to you, but once it occurs, it's too late. If money is transferred after an incident, the law looks at it as stealing the property of the person who may sue. Of course, you think of it as protecting your lifetime of hard work, but you're too late.

Have you been harassed by the IRS?

Roger Brown (name intentionally changed), a Miami lawyer, had served as general counsel to a newspaper that had been investigating the actions of the IRS. The newspaper had found that the IRS was engaged in spying on the sexual habits of important local officials, and had reported it on the pages of the newspaper. Unfortunately for Brown, the IRS was not happy that their actions had been publicized, and the IRS was less than enthused with Brown's role as counsel for the newspaper. As a result, Brown was unfairly indicted on tax evasion charges, and forced to serve a four month sentence in a minimum security prison at Elgin Air Force base. Brown struck back, and eventually was awarded an out-of-court settlement in the amount of US$500,000, representing the largest amount ever paid by the IRS for harassing a taxpayer.

Don't send your kids to school.

The U.S. *Money Laundering Control Act* of 1986 made it a crime to conduct or transact any financial activity if you had prior knowledge that the transaction was structured to avoid reporting financial transactions over US$10,000, the legal reporting threshold.

In a true case (names withheld) a man decided to place a mortgage on his house so that he could help pay for his son's tuition. This involved several cash deposits to his son's U.S. bank account, all less than $10,000. Ignoring the reasons for the deposits, the government accused the man of "structuring," with the U.S. court maintaining that the prosecutor was not required to prove the fact that the man had prior knowledge of "structuring." This resulted in the man's arrest, and the eventual loss of his home, car, bank account, and other assets, which were sold before he had a chance to defend himself in a federal court.

The *Money Laundering Control Act* of 1986 (prohibiting the structuring of transactions to avoid reporting) is stronger than the reporting law itself. A money laundering conviction will result in a 20 year sentence and the forfeiture of your property. Federal judges are required to sentence the mandatory prison terms specified, and may not prescribe probation for first offenders.

"Big Brother" is watching you.

The United States government has recently established the Financial Crimes Enforcement Network (FinCEN) in Arlington, Virginia. FinCEN has access to all bank records, credit records, insurance and medical records, criminal records, driving records, census data, and other personal records on the majority of the U.S. population. This information is also available for much of the population residing in the G7 countries, and in most of the developed countries worldwide. In fact, former Russian President Boris Yeltsin turned to FinCEN for help in recovering funds stolen by former Russian officials.

FinCEN acts as a global database for the IRS (Internal Revenue Service), FBI (Federal Bureau of Investigation), CIA (Central

Intelligence Agency), DEA (Drug Enforcement Agency), ATF (Bureau of Alcohol, Tobacco, and Firearms), and other U.S. government agencies.

FinCEN also works with Revenue Canada, the RCMP, Inland Revenue, InterPol, and other agencies world-wide. Peter Djinis, a Treasury official aware of FinCEN's operation, said in a 1994 interview, *"It's the first ever government-wide, multi-source intelligence and analytical network brought together under one roof to combat financial crimes."*

FinCEN has access to the most private of information. For instance, FinCEN performs a real-timc analysis of all electronic currency movements into and out of the United States by utilizing data supplied by the National Security Agency. Currently, FinCEN is working on computerizing all land transfer and real estate records in the U.S. Now you can be monitored 24-hours-a-day, thanks to the U.S. government.

Don't invite the neighbors.

In 1994, Bob Jones (name intentionally changed), a man who became a quadriplegic in an accident that broke his neck, was awarded $5 million dollars in damages. His lawyer said that while Jones had consumed six alcoholic drinks, he completed three successful dives (diving eight feet from a rooftop into a 3-foot deep pool) before his ill-fated plunge. The court found the homeowners 40% responsible, requiring them to pay $2 million dollars in damages. Even though the homeowners tried to stop Jones from jumping from the roof, the court stated that "*it was stupid and dangerous and (he) shouldn't have done it, but the homeowners should have used force to stop him from doing something reckless.*"

Assets are the target.

In the mid 1980's, Congress gave law enforcement agencies the power to confiscate assets of anyone involved in drug trafficking. The intent was to prevent criminals from profiting from their illegal activities. Beginning in the late 1980's law enforcement agencies began to keep the confiscated assets, and have continued to abuse these powers, as shown by the following examples:

- Police in Florida are randomly stopping vehicles (they look for vehicles with hanging air fresheners, the theory being that the air fresheners are used to mask the smell of drugs). If they discover more than $1,000 in cash, the money is immediately confiscated. There is no due process because the police take the position that the money was acquired illegally.

- A charter airline based in Nevada flew a customer to an airport in California. The FBI was waiting for them, arresting the customer, who was carrying $2 million cash. The cash, along with the airplane, were confiscated by the FBI. Eventually, the customer was released without being charged for any crime. However, the airplane was not released, forcing the charter airline out of business.

- Mike Smith (name intentionally changed), a 61 year old multi-millionaire from Malibu, California was recovering from a cataract operation. He was awakened by the sound of people beating on the front door of his house. Before his wife could get to the door, 27 armed undercover police officers broke down the door and entered the home. Wishing to protect his wife and his property, Mr. Smith went with his gun to the front door where he was confronted by a gang of armed officers. Mr. Smith was ordered to drop his gun, but before he could comply he was shot and killed.

The police broke into the home because it was alleged they flew over his 200-acre ranch by helicopter and saw 50 marijuana plants. Supposedly an informant said his wife was "throwing around" 100 dollar bills in Malibu. It was proven afterwards that there were no marijuana plants on the ranch, and his wife could afford to "throw around" 100 dollar bills because Mike Smith was a multi-millionaire! The district attorney conducted a six month investigation and found the following:

- the police lied about the evidence presented to the judge;
- they had no evidence marijuana plants were being grown on the ranch;
- they obtained an illegal search warrant; and
- they fabricated evidence in order to confiscate property to get money for their police department.

Incredibly enough, it was ruled that the shooting was justified! Apparently, the police had the right to shoot Mike Smith because he did not drop his gun quickly enough, and was, therefore, cut down by the bullets of 27 undercover police officers who were in his home illegally.

CHAPTER 4

THE WORLD OF OFFSHORE

Global tax planning brings with it a whole host of new concepts and procedures that are not readily apparent to individuals operating in a traditional taxing jurisdiction. What follows is a brief listing of certain concepts, procedures, and protocols that anyone considering utilizing a tax haven must understand.

When selecting and utilizing a tax haven, or implementing global tax planning strategies, individuals require certain preliminary information. The following list, although not exhaustive, provides a good review of some of the major concepts, such as:

- Global Investing.
- Private Accounts.
- Transferring Funds.
- Mail Forwarding.
- Secret Safekeeping.
- Computer Privacy.
- Personal Privacy.
- Counter-Intelligence.
- Information Sources.

GLOBAL INVESTING

Why take the global approach?

Investing offshore gives you the "launching pad" to obtain direct access to many international investments not available in North America. In certain circumstances, some international investments can not be purchased by North American residents, providing another reason why one may want to utilize a foreign entity for investing globally. Investments made through your offshore investment account may be held in stable currencies such as Swiss Francs or German Deutschemarks.

Over 60% of the world's investment opportunities in stocks and bonds are found outside North American boundaries. Many economies are growing more rapidly than the world's "established" economies. Investing globally provides an opportunity to invest in higher growth regions of the world, with a greater range of investment opportunities, while reducing risk through diversification of assets over various countries.

Over the last ten years, stocks from foreign countries have outperformed U.S. and Canadian stocks when measured in U.S. dollars. Changes in global markets have allowed investors to take advantage of these higher returns.

North American global investing contacts:

Agora Inc.

Mr. William Bonner	410-234-0515	dial
Publisher	410-837-1999	fax
824 E. Baltimore Street	910250 6212	telex

Baltimore, MD, USA 21202-4799

- Primary business activity: newsletters, books, or information.
- Specific product: Newsletters - International Living, Strategic Investment, Taipan, The Oxford Club, and others.

BZW Canada Limited

Mr. Eric Mennell	416-350-3230	dial
Investment Manager	416-350-3201	fax

304 Bay Street
Toronto, Ontario, Canada M5H 4A5

- Primary business activity: fund or portfolio manager.
- Portfolio management of securities and mutual funds.

Global Mutual Fund Investor

Mr. Eric Roseman	514-989-8027	dial
Editor-in-Chief	514-932-6707	fax

PO.Box 25, Station H, Montreal, Quebec, Canada H3G 2K5

- Primary business activity: global investing information
- Specific product: Global Mutual Fund Investor newsletter.

International Research

Mr. Richard Ashworth	706-865-6602	dial
Publisher	706-865-2988	fax

16 Daybreak Road, PO.Box 2323, Cleveland, GA, USA 30528

- Primary business activity: global investing information
- Specific product: Investment Trust Report.

International Service Center
Mr. Gary A. Scott 813-261-12
Publisher 813-261-2001 fax
3106 Tamiami Trail North
Suite 264, Naples, FL, USA 33940

- Primary business activity: global investing information
- Specific product: World Reports newsletter.

Smith Barney Inc.
Mr. Larry C. Grossman 813-799-5700 dial
Financial Consultant 800-237-5232 free
311 Park Place Boulevard, Suite 100, Clearwater, FL, USA 34609-6498

- Primary business activity: fund or portfolio manager.
- Primary business activity: global investing information
- Offers private credit card backed by deposit.
- Private banking services and/or savings accounts.
- Portfolio management of securities and mutual funds.

Tropical Offshore Investment Corp.
Mr. Fred Elliott 809-543-3598 dial
EPS - C - 448 809-586-6874 fax
PO.Box 02-5553, Miami, FL, USA 33102

- Primary business activity: global investing information
- Specific product: Offshore investments in real property.

Worldwide Investment News
Mr. Jim F. Straw 404-259-6035 dial
Publisher
301 Plymouth Drive North East, Dalton, GA, USA 30721-9983

- Primary business activity: global investing information
- Specific product: Worldwide Investment News newsletter.

PRIVATE ACCOUNTS

The concept of a numbered, or "private" account began before World War II when financial institutions in Switzerland created the accounts to keep the financial assets of fleeing German Jews secret and confidential, a practice that continues to this day. Austria even permits bank accounts to be opened without a name, requiring only a code number or word to make transactions.

Private accounts can be used as part of a safe yet aggressive wealth building strategy, allowing you to invest in foreign mutual funds, stocks, and bonds. It also allows investment in stocks and mutual funds that are not registered with the U.S. Securities Exchange Commission. Private accounts also provide an extra level of protection against anyone seeking to seize your assets. A creditor is required to file a court action and get a judgement in the jurisdiction where you hold the private account, a very expensive action for the creditor to undertake. This allows you time to fight the court action, or simply move the assets to another jurisdiction.

Individuals often cite the lack of FDIC (Federal Deposit Insurance Corporation) or CDIC (Canadian Deposit Insurance Corporation) account insurance as a concern with respect to such accounts. However, most offshore banks are either insured by independent insurance companies, or are self insured, maintaining a liquidity factor of 1:1, meaning that there is $1 for every $1 held in public deposits. If you are at all concerned with the liquidity factor of 1:1, consider that most U.S. financial institutions have only 10 cents cash for every $1 on deposit.

Even with such good reserve ratios, when dealing with an offshore financial institution it is wise to inspect a copy of the bank's annual financial report before making any deposits. Be sure the report you receive is an audited annual report, stating the names of the financial institution's principals. While you're at it, maybe now would be a good time to look at the financial statements of your local United States or Canadian bank.

A private account is easily opened.

Most offshore banks will require a reference letter from your current financial institution. This is a result of the "know your customer rules" that banks are required to follow, as a preventative measure to protect against money laundering.

Sample letter of reference.

To whom it may concern,

We wish to advise that Mr. ____________ has been a satisfactory client of this Bank in excess of 3 years. He has various deposit and borrowing accounts with us, all being maintained as agreed.

We trust that the above information is satisfactory for your purposes, and if you should have any questions or require any additional information, do not hesitate to contact the undersigned.

Yours very truly,

Account Manager

Certain banks will require a personal meeting to set up a banking relationship, while many others offer the option of opening the account by mail. Once the banking relationship is established, you can conduct business by mail, telephone, fax, or telex.

Advantages and benefits of private accounts:

1. **Anonymity** - A numbered account opened in a tax haven jurisdiction with legislated bank secrecy laws ensures that the assets

held in the account will remain private, and the ownership of the account will not be disclosed to outside parties.

2. **Security** - The secrecy aspect of a numbered account will help deter frivolous lawsuits. This will help protect you from liens, bankruptcy, foreclosures, liability, and malpractice claims, as well as protection from divorce and alimony payments.

3. **Additional Protection** - A numbered account combined with a certificate of deposit in the name of an offshore corporation adds an additional layer of "protection" to your secrecy and privacy. This ensures that your personal name will never appear on any bank records, adding an additional stumbling block between you and the IRS, Revenue Canada, or Inland Revenue.

4. **Higher Earnings** - Some offshore financial institutions located in low-tax countries pay at least 10% more interest than financial institutions located in high tax jurisdictions. This is because offshore banks pay lower income, property, and payroll taxes. Taxes are one of the highest non-recoverable costs of doing business in punitive-tax countries such as the U.S. and Canada. Banks operating in low-tax jurisdictions, not burdened by those non-recoverable tax costs, can offer depositors a much higher return. However, some banks in tax haven jurisdictions pay little or no interest, so shop around.

TRANSFERRING FUNDS

It is important to reduce the paper trail when transferring funds to and from your offshore bank. When you send a personal or business check to be invested, you are leaving a very clear paper trail that can be easily audited by the IRS, Revenue Canada, or Inland Revenue. Although the transfer of funds may be perfectly legal, you may want to avoid having to explain your actions to the IRS or Revenue Canada, or anyone else for that matter.

In the United States, specific legislation (P.L. 91-508; 31 USC 5316) requires the filing of a Currency Transaction Report (CTR) that details a transaction of "currency" or certain "monetary instruments" in an amount exceeding US$10,000. Financial institutions must also file a CTR, or IRS form 4789, if a transaction under US$10,000 is considered suspicious. The IRS uses an extensive list to determine whether a transaction is to be considered suspicious. It is important to know the exact definition of Currency and Monetary Instruments:

> **Currency** - ...the coin and currency of the U.S. or any other country, which includes U.S. silver certificates, U.S. notes and Federal Reserve notes, but does not include bank cheques or other negotiable instruments not customarily accepted as money.

> **Monetary Instruments** - ...the coin and currency of the U.S. or any other country, including travelers cheques, money orders, investment securities in bearer form or otherwise if such title thereto passes upon delivery, and negotiable instruments (except warehouse receipts or bills of lading)

in bearer form or otherwise if such title thereto passes upon delivery. The term Monetary Instruments includes bank cheques, travelers cheques, and money orders which are signed, but on which the name of the payee has been omitted, but does not include bank cheques, travelers cheques or money orders made payable to the order of a named person which has not been endorsed or which bear restrictive endorsements.

Based on the exceptions, if a bank draft, bank check, travelers check or money order is made payable to an offshore entity such as a corporation, there is no requirement to report such transactions in the United States.

In Canada, Bill C-9 of 1993 reduced reporting requirements to Cdn$1,000 for the purchase of postal money orders and travelers cheques. Identification in the form of a driver's license, passport, or credit card is now required to purchase money orders and travelers cheques. Under the law, frequent transactions in excess of Cdn$1,000 are enough to spark an investigation.

Options for transferring funds.

To transfer funds to your offshore account, and to make use of the funds at a later date, you may wish to consider one of the following options:

1. **Bank Draft** - If you purchase a bank draft (or bank check, travelers check or money order) payable to an offshore corporation, there is no requirement to report this transaction. Despite this, it is still possible that an overzealous or mis-informed bank officer

may report such a transaction. Therefore, it may be wise to purchase bank drafts in denominations of less than US$3,000. The reason for recommending US$3,000 instead of US$10,000 is a result of the *Comprehensive Money Laundering Prevention Act* of 1986. The Act established guidelines that in some cases reduce bank reporting requirements to US$3,000, including the purchase of money orders, travelers cheques, and cashier's cheques. Under the law, frequent transactions in excess of US$3,000 may be enough to spark an investigation.

2. **Bank Wire Transfer** - While this method is a fast and efficient means of transferring funds back and forth from your offshore account, it leaves an easily identifiable paper trail if you use your name on the wire transfer. There are many offshore banks that allow you to wire transfer money anonymously with a code name, which is an acceptable means of transferring funds, as long as the sending bank does not ask for the sender's identification.

3. **Personal or Company Cheques** - Do not send money to your offshore account with personal or company cheques. Every check you write or deposit is scanned, entered into a document retrieval system, and retained by your financial institution. The information is then readily available to the IRS, Revenue Canada, or Inland Revenue.

4. **Personal or Company Check "Recycling"** - To prevent any type of trace on your incoming cheques, endorse them over to your creditors to make payments. You may also use a check cashing service to cash your cheques, although most charge a small fee. Do not cash cheques at any bank where you hold an account. The cheques are scanned by a document retrieval

system and linked to your account, providing an easy paper trail for investigators.

5. **Private Credit Cards** - Many offshore banks offer a private credit card (Visa, MasterCard, or American Express) backed by deposit, and commonly referred to as "debit cards." Because the card is backed by deposit, you are not required to supply credit information or personal information such as your Social Security Number or Drivers License. The credit card limit is set by the amount of money you have on deposit. You can have the private credit card issued in your own name, or in the name of your offshore company, adding to the privacy and secrecy of the card. Funds can be withdrawn from your account simply by using the card for purchases, or by cash advance from any financial institution that honors the card. You can purchase goods wherever your card (Visa, MasterCard, or American Express) is honored. You can also go to any Automatic Teller Machine (ATM) in the world and withdraw funds from your account. Because these transactions are processed offshore, your secrecy, privacy, and confidentiality are guaranteed by the issuing bank's secrecy laws.

6. **Money Market Accounts** - A legal way of getting around both the reporting requirements and the Money Laundering Control Act is to transfer funds from a Money Market Account with check writing privileges. The process involves writing a check from your personal account to the money market account, and then using a money market check to send the money to your offshore bank. Once the transaction is complete, the money market account may be closed to avoid the issue of structuring under the *Money Laundering Control Act*. Although this creates a minimal paper trail, it is a paper trail that is difficult to uncover.

7. **Postal Money Orders** - Believe it or not, this is still a very good method. Shop around for the best price, trying postal outlets, packaging and postage services, banks, and trust companies. Be sure not to purchase money orders from a bank where you have an account, because the institution may file money order records with your account records. For additional security, use an alias name for purchasing postal money orders. This privacy step has no effect on the transfer of funds. Be sure to retain your copy of the money order if a trace is required. It is possible to send a maximum of $1,000 without any easily identifiable paper trail.

8. **The Western Union** - A safe form of transferring funds if you use a code word or name. Simply pay for the Western Union money transfer, stating the name or company it is to be made payable to, and the address of the receiving agent. The fee for a Western Union money transfer is usually 3% to 5%, depending on amount. There is also a fee to have it delivered to your offshore agent.

9. **Travelers Cheques** - It is possible to purchase travelers cheques in denominations of up to $1,000 each. By spreading your purchases of travelers cheques among several financial institutions, and keeping the total amount purchased less than US$3,000 or Cdn$1,000, you can transfer a virtually unlimited amount of funds without any of the financial institutions reporting currency transactions. Travelers cheques are an efficient means of transferring large amounts of money without creating an easily traceable paper trail.

MAIL FORWARDING

Mail forwarding services fulfill a necessary need in providing secrecy, privacy, and confidentiality.

A mail forwarding service will forward mail for individuals and companies virtually anywhere in the world. Who uses mail forwarding services?

1. Individuals or companies who wish to eliminate a "paper trail" for offshore accounts and investments, securities trading, and ownership of foreign companies.
2. Individuals, investors, and shareholders who require an address in another city or country.
3. Foreign firms requiring an address in another city or country to pose as a branch office or local address.
4. Individuals who require an address other than their own due to separation or divorce, alimony, support payments, job transfers, or military service.
5. Individuals or companies that require a confidential storage safety deposit box or vault.
6. Individuals who wish to eliminate a "paper trail" to protect themselves from creditors, liability suits, malpractice claims, judgements, liens, and bankruptcy.
7. Individuals or companies wishing to keep the ownership and location of assets confidential.

When choosing a mail forwarding service, look for one that guarantees secrecy, privacy, and confidentiality. A mail forwarding service may receive inquiries from banks, trust companies, finance companies, insurance companies, the IRS, Revenue Canada, wives, husbands and friends to divulge your real address. Establish guarantees to ensure your address will not be given to anyone who telephones, writes, or visits the mail forwarding service.

Why be so concerned about your re-mailing services' integrity? Consider the following example. Suppose you have made a decision to keep your financial affairs totally secret, private, and confidential. You decide to use a mail forwarding service you feel you can trust. Two years later someone contacts your re-mailing service claiming to be your brother. He explains that your uncle has died and would like to get in touch with you. Your re-mailing service decides on "compassionate grounds" to provide the brother with your real address. Unfortunately, the person calling you is not your brother, it is an unauthorized person trying to gain a better understanding of your "private financial affairs." You are now back at square one trying to deal with disruptions to your secrecy, privacy, and confidentiality. This incident will cost you in both time and money, having to once again find a reliable re-mailing service. Please choose your re-mailing service carefully.

Consider this next example. In the late 1960's, the IRS began intercepting private mail from Switzerland. Even though bank statements were sent in plain envelopes, the IRS was able to penetrate this secrecy without unlawfully opening any of the mail. Most of the envelopes from Swiss banks used metered postage, instead of postage stamps. IRS agents copied the fronts of these envelopes to record the postal meter number and the addressee of the envelope. Agents then contacted the Swiss banks for information, recording the postal meter number on the reply envelopes. They then matched the envelopes to the Swiss postal meter numbers, compiling a list of possible tax evaders, who were then audited by the IRS.

Most mail forwarding services will also send mail for you from their location. This works by placing your correctly addressed mail in a larger envelope, and sending it to the mail forwarding service with instructions to mail it from their address. The postmark will be from the area that your mail forwarding service is located. This service may be a necessary part of your outgoing correspondence.

Private courier services.

Some mail forwarding services will offer private courier services that allow you to send and receive couriered material virtually anywhere in the world, while maintaining your secrecy, privacy, and confidentiality.

Private communication services.

Some mail forwarding services offer voice mail and paging services. For sensitive fax communications, they may also offer a confidential fax service.

Postal money orders and bank drafts.

You may require a money order from your mail forwarding services' local post office. For larger amounts of money, you may require an international bank draft drawn on a bank in the area of your "phantom address." An international bank draft has the advantage of being available in any amount and in any currency. A few of the mail forwarding services can do this for you for a reasonable fee. Having your mail forwarding service prepare postal money orders and international bank drafts offers you an opportunity to gain an extra degree of secrecy, privacy, and confidentiality.

Private printing services.

Some mail forwarding services also offer related printing services, such as business forms, business cards, letterhead and stationery. You may also wish to have personalized mailing labels printed for your "phantom address."

Mail forwarding services:

David Lewis Associates
Mr. David Lewis — 441-705-592255 dial
President — 441-705-591975 fax
Waterlooville, UK P08 9JL

- Primary business activity: mail forwarding service

Financial Engineering Consultants Inc.
Mr. R. Gonzalez — 506-31-6575 dial
Director of Marketing — 506-20-3470 fax
PO.Box 959, Centro Colon Towers 1007, San Jose, Costa Rica

- Primary business activity: company and trust formation services.
- Primary business activity: mail forwarding service

Private Postman
PO.Box 87210, San Diego, CA, USA 92138

- Primary business activity: mail forwarding service

PS (Postal Services)
PO.Box 29656, San Antonio, TX, USA 78229-0656

- Primary business activity: mail forwarding service

Scope International Ltd.

Dr. W.G. Hill 441-705-592255 dial
Author 441-705-591975 fax
62 Murray Road, Waterlooville, UK P08 9JL

- Primary business activity: discrete camouflage passports.
- Primary business activity: mail forwarding service
- Primary business activity: newsletters, books, or information.

Scope International Ltd.

Mr. Nicholas J. Pine 441-705-631751 dial
Publisher 441-705-631322 fax
Forestside House, Forestside Rowlands, Castle Hants, UK P09 6EE

- Primary business activity: mail forwarding service
- Primary business activity: newsletters, books, or information.

The Mail Post

Mr. Gary Pace 312-764-0100 dial
President
2421 West Pratt Boulevard, Chicago, IL, USA 60645

- Primary business activity: mail forwarding service
- Corporate services such as registered agent services.

Wayne Budd Incorporated

Mr. Wayne Budd 613-473-4838 dial
Proprietor 613-473-4443 fax
RR#1, Box 63, Eldorado, Ontario, Canada KOK 1Y0

- Primary business activity: mail forwarding service
- Safekeeping and custodian services.

SECRET SAFEKEEPING

Many individuals find it important to have cash or other assets safely stored, yet available for easy access. Where you physically store your cash and assets is a significant consideration. If there is a major natural disaster, is it going to destroy the depository you use for your safekeeping? It may be worth having more than one safekeeping depository for that reason alone.

Some of the best safekeeping depositories are:

1. **Safety Deposit Boxes** - Renting a safety deposit box has certain limitations in protecting your assets and important documents. First, your access is limited by the bank's hours of operation. Second, and more importantly, government investigators have the authority to search and seize the contents of your safety deposit box. Third, bank employees may also have access to your safety deposit box. To protect yourself, your financial institution may offer insurance for the contents of the safety deposit box. Fourth, video surveillance systems and increased monitoring help protect the security of your safety deposit box, but they also reduce your privacy. Records are kept of your visits, and some banks require photos of renters. And finally, although the cost can be deducted as a business expense, you are providing a tip-off as to the location, and possibly the contents of the safety deposit box.

2. **Offshore Safety Deposit Boxes** - An advantage over a local safety deposit box is that government investigators do not have the authority to search and seize the contents of your safety deposit box, provided it is located in a country that offers bank

secrecy. Of course, your access is limited by your ability to physically travel to the location of your offshore safety deposit box.

3. **Private Security Vaults** - It is possible to rent space in security vaults operated by privately run companies. If you decide on this option, be sure the vault provides extensive security measures, and access 24 hours a day. Standards are set by the National Association of Private Security Vaults. However, because these companies are privately run, company stability and integrity should be the primary concerns.

4. **Home Safes** - Fireproof safes in your home are excellent for maintaining your secrecy, privacy and confidentiality. Keep the safe well hidden, and keep quiet about it. It is best to mount the safe in a concrete foundation to prevent it from being removed. A good idea is to have two safes, one that is extremely well hidden, and another "dummy safe" in an ordinary location. If, for any reason, someone was to gain access to your home, the dummy safe should contain fake papers and a small amount of cash, in order to convince the intruder that he's got the real thing.

Secret safekeeping contacts:

Alternative Inphormation
Mr. James B. Fuller 903-693-7824 dial
President 903-693-7824 fax
PO.Box 4, Carthage, TX, USA 75633-0004

- Primary business activity: newsletters, books, or information.
- Secret safekeeping information.

Beekins Archival Service

619 W. 51st Street, New York, NY, USA 10019

- Primary business activity: protection and security product or service.
- Secret safekeeping information.

Delta Press Ltd.

PO.Box 1625	501-862-4984	dial
215 South Washington Street	501-862-9671	fax
El Dorado, AR, USA 71731	800-852-4445	free

- Primary business activity: newsletters, books, or information.
- Secret safekeeping information.

Eden Press

PO.Box 8410, Fountain Valley, CA, USA 92728

- Primary business activity: newsletters, books, or information.
- Secret safekeeping information.
- Specific product: Books on every aspect of protection, security, and survival.

Paladin Press

PO.Box 1307	800-872-4993	free
Boulder, CO, USA 80306	303-442-8741	fax

- Primary business activity: discrete camouflage passports.
- Primary business activity: newsletters, books, or information.
- Secret safekeeping information.

COMPUTER PRIVACY

Computers have been an incredible aid to "Big Brother," providing agencies such as FinCEN the power necessary to do real-time monitoring of financial accounts. Computers have also given the individual concerned about secrecy, privacy and confidentiality the ability to "encrypt" personal and financial information, making a breach of security virtually impossible.

Computer data encryption.

The phenomenon of Public/Private-key encryption was first discovered by mathematicians Whitfield Diffie and Martin Hellmann in 1976. Public-key encryption is based on the principle that it is relatively easy for a computer to multiply two very large prime numbers, while it is virtually impossible to work backwards and derive the numbers from the sum without knowing either of the two numbers. Powerful personal computers are able to encrypt any message with the "Public-key," and decrypt the message with the "Private-key." The first commercial implementation of this technology was known as the RSA encryption technique. At the same time, similar development was taking place at the National Security Agency.

The RSA encryption technique was patented in the United States by RSA Data Security Inc. It is this company that licenses the technology for products such as Lotus Notes. RSA Data Security Inc. also markets a product called Ripem. An American underground programmer and computer privacy advocate, Philip Zimmerman, has developed an E-mail encryption program called PGP (Pretty Good Privacy) and has released it onto the Internet, making it available world-wide.

...994, Philip Zimmerman was targeted in a federal crimi- ... to determine whether he violated a U.S. law prohibiting ... ryption software. He has also run into trouble with RSA Data Security Inc., the owner of the patent on the mathematical algorithm used in PGP. If Zimmerman is indicted and convicted of the export law violation, he could be sentenced to 51 months in federal prison. In a 1994 interview, Zimmerman summed up the concept behind data encryption:

> "*Two hundred years ago, when they wrote the Constitution, they never thought it was necessary to put a special amendment in the Bill of Rights for the right to have a private conversation. You could just go behind the barn and talk. But today, you have copper wires and glass fibres carrying our conversations. So, do we want to sacrifice our privacy because of that? Our civil liberties are eroding because of the Information Age. Cryptography will bring them back.*"

Two companies involved in PGP distribution, ViaCrypt and Austin Codeworks, have received grand jury subpoenas to investigate potential export law violations. Encryption techniques are on the State Department's list of restricted technologies, along with military and space technologies. As mentioned above, even though it is supposedly restricted, PGP is available world-wide through the Internet. PGP (pgp262.zip in the /pub/PGP directory) can be obtained from *net-dist.mit.edu* via FTP or telnet, and further information about PGP can be obtained at *http://www.mantis.co.uk/pgp/pgp.html.*

Why are governments world-wide so concerned about data encryption technologies? Because RSA encryption technologies will soon make investigative techniques that are dependent on the surveillance of data communications virtually obsolete. Imagine being able to easily complete an anonymous (but verifiable) E-mail transaction with your offshore bank by using Public-key encryption. The Public-key encryption guarantees to both parties that they can correspond with complete secrecy and privacy, and that they can verify that it is the same party they dealt with before, rendering electronic financial transactions virtually impossible to monitor.

E-mail privacy.

E-mail is a technology that has become a standard form of business communication. When E-mail is used to transmit confidential information, it is no longer confidential. E-mail isn't really erased when you use your computer's delete function. First, experts can often recover old data, despite it being erased from a hard drive or computer network. Second, a copy of the message may still exist in the E-mail transmission log. Finally, copies often exist on backup tapes.

The lack of laws protecting the privacy of E-mail, combined with the easy access to E-mail files, makes this form of communication a mistake for people interested in secrecy, privacy, and confidentiality. Several examples of E-mail snooping have been documented:

- In one case, a U.S. firm called Drug Company (name intentionally changed) monitored discussions by female employees about setting up an E-mail conference for professional women, assuming that the discussions were being used to start a unionization drive.

- In another case, two former employees working for the American head office of a major Japanese auto maker launched a lawsuit against the auto maker, because they were fired when supervisors read their E-mail.

- Copies of E-mail messages between former national security advisor John Poindexter and Colonel Oliver North were ruled to be admissible evidence in the Iran-Contra court proceedings against Poindexter.
- During an investigation by the Los Angeles police force into the beating of motorist Rodney King, investigators were able to find more than 700 offensive slurs in the officers' E-mail, some of which were used by the commission in its findings.

Personal computer data encryption.

Several products are available to keep both your personal computer and your local area network secret, private, and confidential. When evaluating a data encryption product, you should look for the following features:

- access control requiring the entry of a user ID and password;
- audit trails to monitor and record attempted security violations and users logging on and off;
- virus protection to check the integrity of system files;
- keyboard lock feature to blank the screen and lock the keyboard when the system is unattended; and
- compatibility with network systems if required.

Internet Usenet newsgroups devoted to PGP and other computer security issues can be found at *alt.security.pgp*, *alt.security*, *alt.security.index*, *comp.risks*, and *comp.security.announce*.

Data encryption contacts:

Fischer International Systems Corp.

Mr. Brian E. Bath	813-643-1500	dial
Regional Account Manager	813-643-3772	fax
4073 Mercantile Avenue	800-237-4510	free
Naples, FL, USA 33942		

- Primary business activity: data encryption
- Specific product: Watchdog PC Data Security Software, Watchdog Armor, and MailSafe, products based on the RSA Public Key Cryptosystem.

Scrambler Systems Corporation

Mr. Ron Bredehoeft	206-820-7117	dial
VP Sales and Marketing	206-821-3961	fax

13625 NE 126th Place, Suite 400, Kirkland, WA, USA 98034

- Primary business activity: data encryption

PERSONAL PRIVACY

The greatest violator of personal secrecy, privacy, and confidentiality in the United States is the United States government, and similarly in Canada, the Canadian government. The same is true in many other countries throughout the world. Even though governments claim that the breaches of privacy are necessary to uphold or enforce laws, you should still be concerned about your personal privacy.

Maintaining telephone privacy.

You may have noticed that your long-distance telephone bill details the date, time, duration, location, and telephone number of every long-distance call you make. In an IRS or Revenue Canada investigation, or in a lawsuit, these records can be easily obtained by investigators, revealing the location of your "secret" bank account.

So how do you contact your offshore bank without leaving a long-distance paper trail? The first, and simplest option is to use a pay phone. It may not be very convenient, but at least it works. The second option is to use a traceless long distance debit card. By using a long distance debit card, your card is debited for the cost of the call. No records are added to your phone bill, keeping all of your telephone conversations secret and private. To use the card, you dial a local or toll-free number, input the number on your debit card, and input the long distance telephone number you wish to call. The card is debited for the cost of the call.

If you have a personal situation that requires secrecy, don't forget about Caller Identification. Caller ID can capture your phone number, along with your name and address. Imagine calling a phone sex hotline, then being bombarded in the next few weeks with junk mail and phone calls from other hotlines. Now consider the fact that your government may believe that calling a sex line must mean that you lack moral values, and you are now a good target for a tax investigation. The technology is already available for this to happen.

Some general tips are:

- use a pay phone (or debit card) for sensitive calls;
- rotate calls among several locations;
- do your calling from outside the neighborhood;
- send and receive sensitive faxes from third-party locations; and
- try to use code words.

Maintaining cellular privacy.

Cellular phones compromise your privacy by broadcasting your conversation on an open radio frequency that can be listened to by anyone. Remember the scandal that erupted when Prince Charles and Lady Diana had their cellular telephone conversations monitored?

Cellular bills detail the date, time, duration, and telephone numbers of both incoming and outgoing calls. When using a cellular phone, follow these common-sense rules:

- never use a cellular phone for confidential conversations (either to receive calls or to make calls);
- never register a cellular phone in your own name. Put it in the name of a corporation, or better yet, in the name of an offshore corporation; and

- keep an eye out for the new digital cellular telephone technology that will be coming on-line within the next few years.

Maintaining fax privacy.

Fax transmissions work over ordinary telephone lines, and represent a security risk due to the simplicity of tapping into a fax line. Fax lines can be easily intercepted, producing a beautiful hard copy for persons intercepting your fax transmissions. Use codes if possible, and remove the fax header from your fax transmissions. Remember to delete any information identifying yourself as the sender or receiver.

One of the best ways of making your fax transmissions as secure as possible is to use a notebook computer for sending and receiving sensitive documents. You can transport your notebook computer anywhere there is a phone jack, plug it in, and use it as a secure fax device.

Credit card privacy.

Cut down or completely discontinue use of credit cards issued by banks that do not offer bank secrecy. Credit card statements provide a complete picture of your whereabouts and purchasing patterns. Any information available to a credit card company is available to the IRS, Revenue Canada, Inland Revenue, or other government agencies.

Eliminate the use of credit cards issued in your home country. Credit records give investigators an accurate picture of where you have been, and how much you have spent on what. How many times have you returned home from another country without declaring your purchases? Next time, you may not be so lucky. Customs officials inspect the credit card statements of citizens to determine if they have purchased goods and imported them into the country without paying import duties. An offshore credit card would eliminate this invasion of privacy.

Personal financial discretion.

Which investments have your social security number or other identification numbers attached? If your financial privacy is compromised by some of your current investments, consider new investments in "tax haven" countries.

Consider it a priority to establish a credit card from a country with bank secrecy laws. Have the statements either held at the bank for pickup, or sent to a re-mailing service in a country other than your country of residence. Conduct as much of your business in cash as possible.

Use a complicated single stroke signature if possible that is consistent, but unreadable. This allows for greater privacy on documents you may be required to sign.

Do not have your address printed on checks. There is no reason for anyone to know where you live. This is good advice to help reduce financial crime as well.

If you are well known in your community, or if you live in a small town, consider using a bank in another town. This will reduce the possibility of bank employees connecting you with your money.

Secure garbage disposal.

Use a paper shredder to prevent unauthorized individuals from gaining any personal information from your garbage. Burn your shreddings if possible. If your information is important enough, someone will take the time to piece it together.

Personal identification numbers.

Personal identification numbers are very powerful because they are unique, accurate, and widely used. Computer technology makes it possible to use your personal identification number to find and match your information from one database to another. This amounts to "data surveillance," which can pose a serious threat to your secrecy, privacy, and confidentiality.

Stores, financial institutions, and landlords may request your personal identification number to check your credit rating. If you refuse to provide your personal identification number, the organization may deny you the service. If asked for your personal identification number when not required by law, tell the person you prefer not to use your personal identification number and offer an alternate form of identification. Protect yourself from "data surveillance."

United States - Social Security Number - Protect your social security number very carefully. You are required to supply your social security number only to your employer, your bank, savings & loan company, trust company and stock broker when buying financial products or services that report your interest earnings to the government. No one else may demand it.

Canada - Social Insurance Number - Canada's *Privacy Act* sets out strict rules limiting other people's access to your personal information in federal data banks. The law does not prevent provinces or local governments from using your Social Insurance Number (SIN). However, all provinces (except Alberta and PEI) have privacy laws to protect personal information, including SINs, in government files.

Using camouflage passports.

A camouflage passport is a document identical to a legally issued passport, with your photo, personal information, and entry/exit stamps. The only difference between a camouflage passport and a real one is that the camouflage passport is issued from a country that has changed its name, such as British Honduras (now Belize). Why consider carrying an imitation passport? The following are two very good reasons:

- Have you ever checked into a foreign hotel, only to find that the passports of guests are kept in an unlocked drawer by the hotel staff? Any thief can grab the passport of his choice without too much trouble. You can protect yourself with a camouflage passport. The hotel staff certainly don't know the difference between a camouflage passport and a real one, allowing you to keep your legitimate passport with you at all times.

- Imagine yourself on an international flight that is hijacked by terrorists. The first thing the terrorists do is identify their expendable hostages, knowing that they will get an immediate response by threatening to kill an American, Israeli, or British citizen. You feel lucky that you have a camouflage passport, that identifies you as being a tourist from some small nation that they have never heard of, potentially helping you avoid a nasty situation.

Many international travelers have found camouflage passports to be extremely valuable. An added bonus is that you can travel under cover, assuming an alternate identity once you arrive at your destination. It should be noted that, camouflage passports should never be used for crossing international borders.

Private telephone calling card sources:

Canquest Communications Inc.

Ms. Nancy Estrella	416-364-2406	dial
20 Toronto Street	416-364-9636	fax
Suite 1210	800-678-2211	free
Toronto, Ontario, Canada M5C 2B8		

- Primary business activity: surveillance and intelligence products.
- Offers private telephone calling cards.
- Specific product: Coin Free Prepaid Long Distance Card.

Commsen Communications

Mr. John McGowan	905-332-8810	dial
General Manager	905-332-4988	fax
1200 Burloak Drive	800-461-3576	free
Burlington, Ontario, Canada L7L 6B3		

- Primary business activity: surveillance and intelligence products.
- Offers private telephone calling cards.
- Specific product: Callsaver Prepaid Long Distance Card.

Incomm / U.S. South Communications

Debbie Stamp	404-953-1520	dial
3200 Professional Parkway, Unit 210		
Atlanta, GA, USA 30339		

- Primary business activity: surveillance and intelligence products.
- Offers private telephone calling cards.
- Specific product: Domestic and International Calling Card.

Camouflage passport sources:

Privacy Reports Inc.
Mr. Gerhard Kurtz 852-2-850-5502 fax
Publisher
26A Peel Street, Ground Floor, Central, Hong Kong

- Primary business activity: discrete camouflage passports.
- Primary business activity: newsletters, books, or information.

Paladin Press
PO.Box 1307 800-872-4993 free
Boulder, CO, USA 80306 303-442-8741 fax

- Primary business activity: discrete camouflage passports.
- Primary business activity: newsletters, books, or information.
- Secret safekeeping information.

Safeguard Services
PO.Box 689-A 702-289-4229 dial
Ely, NV, USA 89301 702-289-4229 fax

- Primary business activity: discrete camouflage passports.
- Specific product: Camouflage Passports.

Scope International Ltd.
Dr. W.G. Hill 441-705-592255 dial
Author 441-705-591975 fax
62 Murray Road, Waterlooville, UK P08 9JL

- Primary business activity: discrete camouflage passports.
- Primary business activity: mail forwarding service
- Primary business activity: newsletters, books, or information.

Sources for travel products and services:

Georgetown University School of Medicine
Vaccination requirement hot-line 202-687-8672 dial
Washington, DC, USA 20007

- Primary business activity: travel services or information.

Johns Hopkins University
Hampton House, Room 113 410-955-8931 dial
624 N. Broadway, Baltimore, MD, USA 21205

- Primary business activity: travel services or information.
- Specific product: Offers complete range of vaccines, specialization in tropical diseases.

Magellan's
Mr. John McManus 800-962-4943 free
President 805-568-5406 fax
PO.Box 5485, Santa Barbara, CA, USA 93150-5485

- Primary business activity: travel services or information.
- Specific product: Travel Essentials Catalog.

U.S. Center for Disease Control
Vaccination requirement hot-line 404-332-4559 dial
USA 404-332-4565 dial

- Primary business activity: travel services or information.

U.S. Government Printing Office
8660 Cherry Lane 410-792-0262 dial
Laurel, MD, USA 20707-4980

- Primary business activity: travel services or information.
- Specific product: Vaccination certificate: stock # 017-001-00483-9. Cost is two dollars.

INFORMATION SOURCES

There are many excellent books and newsletters that provide information on tax havens, offshore investing, and personal privacy issues. The following companies offer a wide range of publications.

Information sources and contacts:

Agora Inc.

Mr. William Bonner	410-234-0515	dial
Publisher	410-837-1999	fax
824 E. Baltimore Street	910250 6212	telex
Baltimore, MD, USA 21202-4799		

- Primary business activity: newsletters, books, or information.
- Specific product: Newsletters - International Living, Strategic Investment, Taipan, The Oxford Club, and others.

Alternative Inphormation

Mr. James B. Fuller	903-693-7824	dial
President	903-693-7824	fax
PO.Box 4, Carthage, TX, USA 75633-0004		

- Primary business activity: newsletters, books, or information.
- Secret safekeeping information.

Butokukai

PO.Box 430	800-747-6280	free
Cornville, AZ, USA 86325	602-634-1203	fax

- Primary business activity: newsletters, books, or information.
- Primary business activity: protection and security product or service.

Delta Press Ltd.

PO.Box 1625	501-862-4984	dial
215 South Washington Street	501-862-9671	fax
El Dorado, AR, USA 71731	800-852-4445	free

- Primary business activity: newsletters, books, or information.
- Secret safekeeping information.

Eden Press

PO.Box 8410, Fountain Valley, CA, USA 92728

- Primary business activity: newsletters, books, or information.
- Secret safekeeping information.
- Specific product: Books on every aspect of protection, security, and survival.

Expat World

Mr. Gene Gene	65-466-3680	dial
PO.Box 1341	65-466-7006	fax
Raffles City, Singapore		

- Primary business activity: newsletters, books, or information.

Financial Privacy Reporter

Mr. Richard Czerlau	905-549-8094	dial
Publisher	905-549-5700	fax

1575 B-13 Military Road, Unit 301, Niagara Falls, NY, USA 14304
136 Cumberland Road, Hamilton, Ontario, Canada L8M 1Z4

- Primary business activity: newsletters, books, or information.
- Specific product: Financial Privacy Reporter newsletter.

Global Consulting Group, Inc.

Dr. Stephen O. Williams	506-296-1525	dial
International Consulting	509-296-1511	fax

PO.Box 945, Suite 922, Centro Colon Tower 1007, San Jose, Costa Rica

- Primary business activity: newsletters, books, or information.
- Specific product: Financial Privacy News newsletter.

Global Money Consultants
2 Perikleous Street — 30-1-896-2118 dial
Vouliagmeni — 30-1-896-2152 fax
Athens, Greece 16671

- Primary business activity: newsletters, books, or information.

International Bank Research
27 Lamar Park Center — 512-242-3170 dial
Unit A — 512-242-9768 fax
Corpus Christi, TX, USA 78411

- Primary business activity: newsletters, books, or information.

International Employment Hotline
PO.Box 3030, Oakton, VA, USA 22124

- Primary business activity: newsletters, books, or information.

Johnson Smith Company
4514 19th Street Court East — 813-747-2356 dial
PO.Box 2500 — 813-746-7896 fax
Bradenton, FL, USA 34206-5500

- Primary business activity: newsletters, books, or information.
- Primary business activity: surveillance and intelligence products.

LPP, Ltd.
Mr. Mark Nestmann — 800-528-0559 dial
Publisher — 602-943-2363 fax
1280 Terminal Way, Suite 15, Reno, NV, USA 89502

- Primary business activity: newsletters, books, or information.

Men's Defense Association
Mr. Richard F. Doyle — 612-464-7887 dial
President — 612-464-7135 fax
17854 Lyons Street, Forest Lake, MN, USA 55025-8107

- Primary business activity: newsletters, books, or information.
- Specific product: The Liberator Newsmagazine.

Paladin Press

PO.Box 1307 800-872-4993 free
Boulder, CO, USA 80306 303-442-8741 fax

- Primary business activity: discrete camouflage passports.
- Primary business activity: newsletters, books, or information.
- Secret safekeeping information.

Privacy Reports Inc.

Mr. Gerhard Kurtz 852-2-850-5502 fax
Publisher
26A Peel Street, Ground Floor, Central, Hong Kong

- Primary business activity: discrete camouflage passports.
- Primary business activity: newsletters, books, or information.

S.W.M.R., Inc.

2160 W. Charleston #334, Las Vegas, NV, USA 89102

- Primary business activity: newsletters, books, or information.
- Specific product: Lawsuit and Asset Protection Kit.

Scope International Ltd.

Dr. W.G. Hill 441-705-592255 dial
Author 441-705-591975 fax
62 Murray Road, Waterlooville, UK P08 9JL

- Primary business activity: discrete camouflage passports.
- Primary business activity: mail forwarding service
- Primary business activity: newsletters, books, or information.

Scope International Ltd.

Mr. Nicholas J. Pine 441-705-631751 dial
Publisher 441-705-631322 fax
Forestside House, Forestside Rowlands, Castle Hants, UK P09 6EE

- Primary business activity: mail forwarding service
- Primary business activity: newsletters, books, or information.

The Private Planner

Mr. Maurice Smith	509-325-9167	dial
Editor	509-326-8690	fax
9986 N. Newport Highway	800-821-6075	free
Suite 286, Spokane, WA, USA 99218		

- Primary business activity: newsletters, books, or information.
- Specific product: The Private Planner newsletter.

The Survival Center

PO.Box 234	206-458-6778	dial
McKenna, WA, USA 98558	800-321-2900	free

- Primary business activity: newsletters, books, or information.
- Primary business activity: protection and security product or service.

Travel Document Advisors (UK) Ltd.

28 Grosvenor Street	441-71-917-9624	dial
London, UK W1X 9FE	800-844-9994	free

- Primary business activity: newsletters, books, or information.

COUNTER-INTELLIGENCE

There are some incredible products available to help you protect your privacy. These products range from bug detection and surveillance equipment to military and law enforcement technology. These contacts will help you find what you're looking for.

Counter-intelligence contacts:

Alizes Group
Atlanta, GA, USA 30319 — 800-766-6179 dial

- Primary business activity: surveillance and intelligence products.
- Specific product: Night vision equipment, bug detection products.

Butokukai
PO.Box 430 — 800-747-6280 free
Cornville, AZ, USA 86325 — 602-634-1203 fax

- Primary business activity: newsletters, books, or information.
- Primary business activity: protection and security product or service.

Cabela's
Mr. Dick Cabela — 800-237-4444 dial
President — 308-254-2200 fax
812 13th Avenue — 800-237-8888 free
Sidney, NE, USA 69160

- Primary business activity: newsletters, books, or information.
- Primary business activity: protection and security product or service.

Canadian Alarm & Security Assoc.
610 Alden Rd. — 905-513-0622 dial
Suite 201, Markham, Ontario, Canada L3R 9Z1

- Primary business activity: protection and security product or service.

Cold Steel High Performance Knives

2128-D Knoll Drive	800-255-4716	dial
Ventura, CA, USA 93003		

- Primary business activity: protection and security product or service.

Communication Control Systems of NY

675 Third Ave.	212-557-3040	dial
Suite 408	212-983-1278	fax
New York, NY, USA 10017		

- Primary business activity: surveillance and intelligence products.
- Specific product: Truth phone, recording system, hidden video, and scrambling systems.

Counter Spy Shop

444 Madison Ave.	800-722-4490	free
New York, NY, USA 10022	212-888-6460	fax

- Primary business activity: protection and security product or service.
- Primary business activity: surveillance and intelligence products.

Dynamark Security Centers, Inc.

Mr. Ron Polesky	301-797-2124	dial
Franchise Development Executive	301-797-2189	fax
19833 Leitersburg Pike, PO.Box 2068		
Hagerstown, MD, USA 21742-2068		

- Primary business activity: protection and security product or service.

Eavesdropping Detection Equipment

2480 Niagara Falls Boulevard	716-691-3476	dial
Tonawanda, NY, USA 14150	716-691-0604	fax

- Primary business activity: surveillance and intelligence products.

Guardian Personal Security Products

Phoenix, AZ, USA 85027

- Primary business activity: protection and security product or service.

HiTek
490 El Camino Real — 800-546-4448 dial
Redwood City, CA, USA 94063

- Primary business activity: surveillance and intelligence products.
- Specific product: Bug detection equipment.

Information Unlimited
PO.Box 716 — 800-221-1705 free
Amherst, NH, USA 03031-0716 — 603-672-5406 fax

- Primary business activity: surveillance and intelligence products.
- Specific product: Night vision equipment.

Johnson Smith Company
4514 19th Street Court East — 813-747-2356 dial
PO.Box 2500 — 813-746-7896 fax
Bradenton, FL, USA 34206-5500

- Primary business activity: newsletters, books, or information.
- Primary business activity: surveillance and intelligence products.

Major Surplus & Survival Inc.
435 W. Alondra — 800-441-8855 free
Gardena, CA, USA 90248 — 310-324-8855 dial

- Primary business activity: protection and security product or service.
- Primary business activity: surveillance and intelligence products.

Miller Publishing Co.
7850 White Lane, Suite E-330, Bakersfield, CA, USA 93309

- Primary business activity: surveillance and intelligence products.
- Specific product: Official I.D. documents.

Quark Spy Centre
537 Third Ave. — 800-343-6443 free
New York, NY, USA 10016 — 212-447-5510 fax

- Primary business activity: protection and security product or service.
- Primary business activity: surveillance and intelligence products.

Scanner Master

Mr. Richard Barnett	508-655-6300	dial
Editor	508-655-2350	fax
PO.Box 428	800-722-6701	free

Newton Highlands, MA, USA 02161

- Primary business activity: surveillance and intelligence products.

Sherwood Communications Associates

PO.Box 535, South Hampton, PA, USA 18966

- Primary business activity: surveillance and intelligence products.

Southern Ordnance

PO.Box 279	813-638-2486	dial
Babson Park, FL, USA 33827	813-638-2499	fax

- Primary business activity: protection and security product or service.
- Primary business activity: surveillance and intelligence products.

Spy Supply

7 Colby Court	617-327-7272	dial

Suite 215, Bedford, NH, USA 03110

- Primary business activity: protection and security product or service.
- Primary business activity: surveillance and intelligence products.

The Edge Company

PO.Box 826	800-732-9976	free
Brattleboro, VT, USA 05302	802-257-2787	fax

- Primary business activity: protection and security product or service.
- Primary business activity: surveillance and intelligence products.

Sportsman's Guide

Mr. Gary Olen	800-888-3006	dial
President	800-333-6933	fax
411 Farwell Avenue	800-888-5222	free

PO.Box 239, St.Paul, MN, USA 55075-0239

- Primary business activity: newsletters, books, or information.
- Primary business activity: protection and security product or service.

The Survival Center

PO.Box 234	206-458-6778	dial
McKenna, WA, USA 98558	800-321-2900	free

- Primary business activity: newsletters, books, or information.
- Primary business activity: protection and security product or service.

U.S. Cavalry

Mr. Randy Acton	502-351-1164	dial
President	502-352-0266	fax
2855 Centennial Ave.	800-777-7732	free
Radcliff, KY, USA 40160-9000		

- Primary business activity: protection and security product or service.
- Primary business activity: surveillance and intelligence products.
- Specific product: military and adventure catalog.

USI Corporation

PO.Box 2052	407-725-1000	dial
Melbourne, FL, USA 32902	407-727-1179	fax

- Primary business activity: surveillance and intelligence products.
- Specific product: Electronic lockpicks and tools.

CHAPTER 5

STRUCTURING OFFSHORE

There are several effective methods to utilize offshore tax havens for a wide variety of reasons. The following provides an outline of the most common methods. However, care must be taken to ensure that using these structures does not violate the laws of the country in which you reside, or of which you are a citizen. The concepts discussed in this section are very general, and legal or tax professionals in your area should be able to modify them to comply with applicable legislation.

Simple Offshore bank account.

The simplest, and least effective method of structuring your offshore activities is to open an offshore bank account in your own name. Although there is some degree of secrecy and confidentiality associated with such an account, provided the account is opened in a jurisdiction with bank secrecy, your only layer of "protection" is that jurisdiction's bank secrecy legislation.

In this example, an individual opens an offshore bank account. Through this account, investments can be made in mutual funds, stocks, bonds, precious metals, and other investments. A debit card may be issued by the offshore bank, providing the account holder with immediate access to funds.

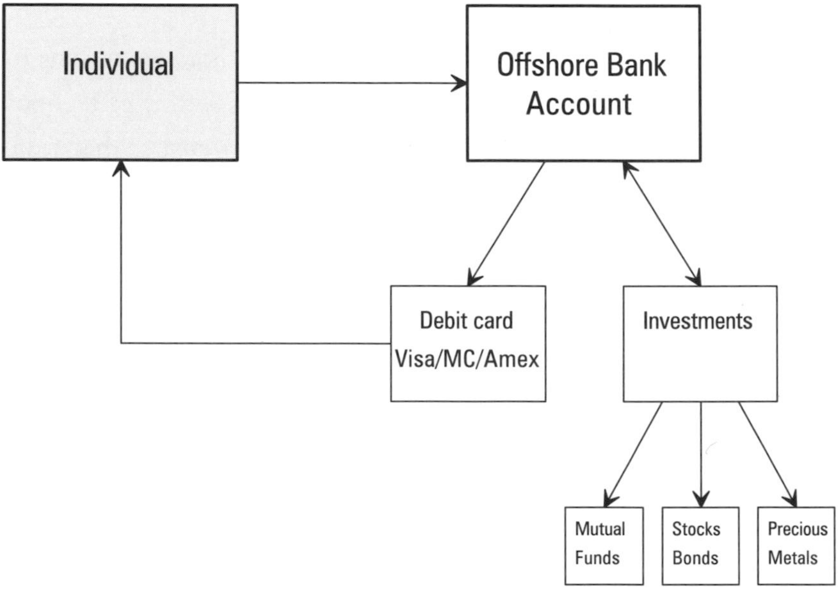

OFFSHORE COMPANIES

Historically, the primary attraction of an incorporated company was to limit the liability of the investors to the extent of their investment. Limited liability is based on the principle that the company is a distinct legal entity from its shareholders. Creditors are, therefore, only able to attack the assets of the company, rather than the assets of the company's investors. Because the company is legally distinct from its shareholders, tax planning possibilities are immediately established.

In many countries, tax rates vary between individuals and corporations. It is possible that a shareholder resident in a high tax jurisdiction may hold an interest in a company incorporated in a low tax jurisdiction. Taking advantage of low tax jurisdictions allows certain opportunities for tax avoidance and tax deferral.

Offshore Limited Companies offer numerous advantages and benefits when formed in a jurisdiction with strict bank secrecy laws. Factors to consider when choosing a jurisdiction include:

1. Taxation. Low tax is good, no tax is better.
2. Confidentiality is very important. It is best to choose a jurisdiction with formal bank and commercial secrecy laws in place.
3. Legal System. English Common Law avoids forced-heirship laws, although some jurisdictions have modified statutes to avoid forced-heirship laws.
4. Look for a statute in place that prevents a new government or political party from implementing a sudden "new tax" within a certain limitation period.

5. Government stability is important. The jurisdiction chosen should be free from violent political swings or possible military coup.
6. There should be a good selection of qualified lawyers, accountants, investment advisors, and bankers. Be sure they can speak your language.
7. A developed infrastructure is necessary. It is helpful to use a jurisdiction in a time zone close to your own.
8. There should also be good telecommunications links and travel connections.

Advantages and benefits of forming an offshore limited company.

1. **Secrecy** - The beneficial ownership of an offshore company incorporated in a jurisdiction with secrecy laws can not be disclosed. Shares may be held by nominees representing the beneficial owners under a management agreement. This ensures that the names of the beneficial owners never become a matter of public record, nor are they divulged to third parties.
2. **Security** - The ownership of assets by an offshore company guarantees that these assets will be protected by the courts in that jurisdiction. This helps to protect the offshore company's assets against attack by foreign courts or government expropriation and confiscation.
3. **Financial** - The absence of income, corporate or capital gains taxes ensures that the assets of the company will enjoy maximum growth.

4. **Professional Management** - The companies laws in most jurisdictions require compliance with certain formalities to safeguard the assets. Many offshore banks and trust companies have professional staff ensuring these requirements are met, providing you with professional portfolio management.

5. **Investment Holding Company** - Many diverse assets, such as stocks, bonds, precious metals, and mutual funds can be consolidated in an offshore investment holding company to be managed under one corporate name. The investments may also consist of real estate or any other assets, movable or immovable.

6. **Sales/Re-Invoicing Company** - An offshore company acting as a "middleman entity" may sell goods for related or unrelated parties throughout the world, accumulating profits in a tax free area for working capital or reinvestment.

7. **Trading Companies** - When an organization trades outside its own country, opportunities arise whereby the trading can be conducted through an offshore company, resulting in tax savings or tax deferral in the home jurisdiction.

8. **Leasing Company** - Capital equipment may be purchased and leased by an offshore leasing company, taking advantage of deductible tax write-offs on lease payments. Lease payments are deductible under United States and Canadian tax law.

9. **Advertising Company** - Offshore companies can act as advertising agencies, retaining the standard 15% ad agency commission, which can be invested through the offshore company tax-free. The fees paid to the advertising company are deductible under U.S. and Canadian tax law.

10. **Intellectual Property** - Royalties and licensing fees for patents, trademarks, copyright, and trade secrets may be directed to an offshore company in a tax-free environment.

11. **Professional Services** - An offshore company could acquire the exclusive rights to professional services conducted by an individual and receive payments for such services. The individual would be paid by the offshore company, with the profits being invested in a low or no-tax environment.

12. **Consulting and Employment Companies** - Experts in many fields undertake short term contracts in different countries which can cause taxation and pension fund difficulties. By forming an offshore company the expert can be employed directly by that company, with fees paid to the company rather than directly to the expert. Similar arrangements are suitable for sports and media professionals.

13. **Property Companies** - Owning property through an offshore company is a well established practice that can help reduce capital taxes, inheritance taxes, and complex probate procedures in various jurisdictions.

14. **Management Services Company** - An offshore corporation can perform various management and administration services for individuals or companies in the U.S. and Canada, taking advantage of deductible tax write-offs on management and administration expenses.

Investment holding company.

An Investment Holding Company appeals to an investor who wishes to establish an offshore company simply to hold investments, real estate, and other assets. By using one jurisdiction for the investment holding company, and a second jurisdiction for the offshore bank, an extra layer of protection is added. For instance, if the investment holding company was in the Turks & Caicos Islands, and the offshore bank was in Liechtenstein, investigating authorities would have to first breach the secrecy laws of the Turks & Caicos Islands to find out who owns the company, and then breach the secrecy laws of Liechtenstein to obtain banking information.

Simple corporate structure.

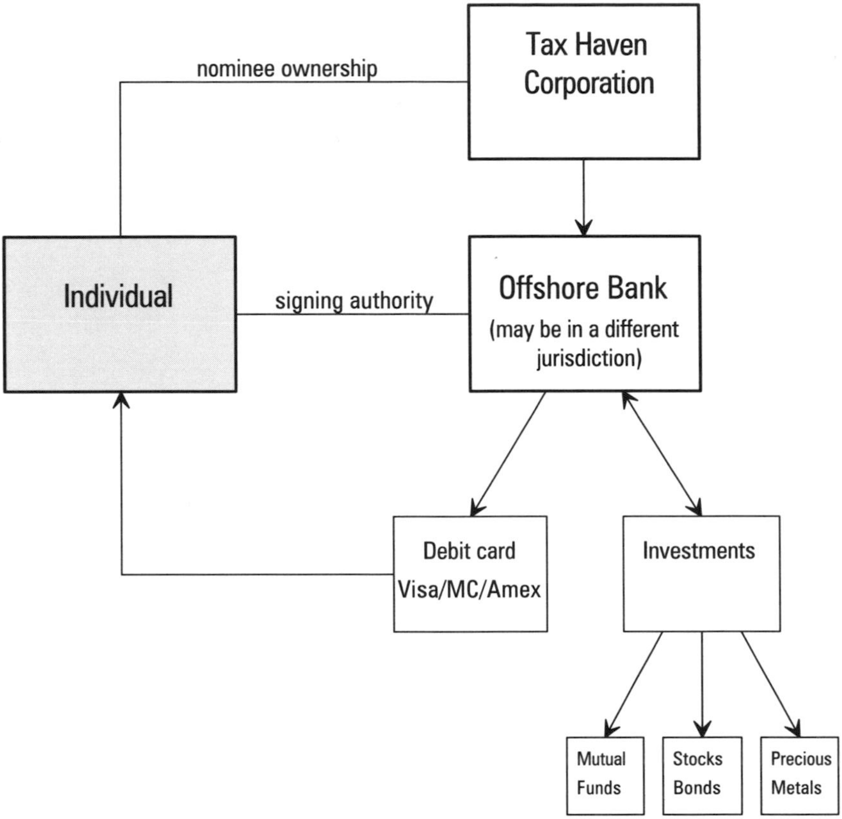

INTERNATIONAL TRUSTS

The Trust concept was developed in the British Isles around the Middle Ages, as a means of avoiding feudal taxes on property transfers and inheritance. It was the Court of Chancery (the King's "Court of Conscience" overseen by Churchmen) that developed the Trust to avoid the application of rigid laws relating to the succession of property. The Trust allowed the owner to pass legal title to a Trustee on behalf of his wife, child, or other person as Beneficiary. Trusts were not known in Roman or Civil Law, although they are becoming increasingly more popular, thanks to the Hague Convention of July 1, 1985. The Trust is a concept conceived and developed as a means of separating legal ownership from beneficial ownership. Trust law is found in all countries whose law is based on British common law, and in civil-law countries that have passed laws recognizing Trusts.

Components of a Trust.

A Trust is a right of property (real or personal), held by one party for the benefit of another.

There are four principal components to a Trust:

- The "Settlor" of a Trust is a person who creates the Trust by providing the initial property of the Trust. A Trust is created usually by means of a Declaration of Trust.

- The "Trustee" is the person who holds title for the benefit of another person. The Trustee may be an individual or a corporation.

- The "Beneficiary" is the person or persons who will benefit from the assets held by the Trust.
- The "Trust Asset" is the property being held by the Trust.

Occasionally there is a fifth component:

- The "Protector" who ensures the Settlor's wishes are carried out. The Protector may be an individual or a corporation.

Under a Trust, the original owner (Settlor) of the assets places the assets in the Trust, which is administered by the Trustee, who may be an individual, bank, trust company, etc. The Trustee becomes legal owner of the assets while the Beneficiary becomes the beneficial owner. Therefore, the ownership of the Trust Asset is vested in the Trustee who has no right or ability to enjoy the property, while those who do enjoy the property (the Beneficiaries) do not legally own it.

Types of Trusts.

Depending upon the result required, there are several types of Trusts that can be used to accomplish various goals, such as:

1. **Asset Protection Trust -** A form of Trust which provides the Settlor and the Beneficiaries with protection from creditors. To ensure creditor protection, an Asset Protection Trust should be established in a jurisdiction with specific asset protection legislation.
2. **Non-Discretionary (Fixed) Trust -** A form of Trust where the interest of the Beneficiaries is fixed, leaving the Trustee with no discretion as to how to distribute the income and/or capital of the Trust.

3. **Discretionary Trust -** A form of Trust where the interest of the Beneficiaries is not fixed, leaving the Trustee with the discretion as to how to distribute the income and/or capital of the Trust.

4. **Protective Trust -** A form of Trust where the object of the Trust is to provide income and/or capital to a Beneficiary suffering from some form of disability.

5. **Charitable Trust -** A form of Trust where one of the Beneficiaries is a charity or a charitable foundation.

6. **Spousal Trust -** A form of Trust where the only Beneficiary is the spouse of the Settlor.

7. **Revocable Trust -** A form of Trust where the Settlor has the ability at any time to revoke the Trust and, as a result, have title in the Trust Assets revert back to the Settlor.

8. **Irrevocable Trust -** A form of Trust where once the Settlor has transferred the property to the Trust, the Settlor has no ability to have the property transferred back to the Settlor.

A valid Trust requires at least two separate and distinct parties. It is not possible for the same person to be both the sole Trustee and the sole Beneficiary, since it is an established point of law that an individual cannot be under an equitable obligation to himself.

How does a Trust eliminate estate and inheritance taxes?

If a Trust is properly established, all Trust property belongs to the Trustee. Therefore, it does not form part of one's estate for estate tax purposes, or part of ones assets for wealth tax purposes. The death of the

Settlor or the Trustee does not affect the ownership of the Trust assets. It cannot be included in an estate until the Trust terminates and the Trust assets are distributed to the Beneficiaries.

Can a Trust protect against creditors?

In most jurisdictions that offer bank secrecy, the Trustee is not allowed to disclose to creditors (or anyone else) what assets are held by the Trust, nor can the Trust be required to transfer assets to foreign creditors. An attack on the assets held by your foreign Trust will allow time to move the assets to another jurisdiction. Offshore Trusts do not, however, protect assets located in your home country, such as business holdings or real estate. There is nothing a foreign Trustee can do to keep assets away from creditors in your home country.

Fraudulent conveyance statutes prevent transfers to Trusts with the explicit intention to defraud current or anticipated creditors. The statute of limitations varies with the jurisdiction where the Trust was formed, but usually it is 2 years. After this time, the Trust will protect the assets from judgements, divorce, creditors, malpractice claims, lawsuit, and bankruptcy. If the establishment of a Trust contributes to bankruptcy, the Trust may be terminated as a fraudulent transfer to defraud creditors.

Trust assets are not liable for the personal debts of the Trustee. If the Trust funds are used to pay personal expenses of the Settlor or Trustee, or if Trust funds are commingled with personal funds, a court may rule that the Trust should be terminated. Proper management is critical to the effectiveness of the Trust.

Advantages and benefits of using a Trust.

International Trusts offer several advantages and benefits when formed in a country with strict bank secrecy laws. To ensure complete compliance, research the following points with the offshore bank or trust company you wish to deal with. Advantages and benefits are as follows:

Holdings - The Trust may be used to hold any assets, such as cash, stocks, bonds, mutual funds, property (usually held through a company), or other assets.

Anonymity - The Trust deed is not a public document (unless it is registered, such as certain Asset Protection Trusts) and the Beneficiaries are known only to the Trustee. This ensures that the names of the Settlor and Beneficiaries will not be divulged to outside parties. Naturally, the use of an underlying investment company will provide even greater secrecy.

Security - Since your assets have to be delivered to the Trustee, you must have complete confidence in your chosen Trustee. The assets of the Trust may be held either directly by the Trustee or through an underlying investment company anywhere in the world. The assets may be held in the name of the Trustee or through nominees, ensuring greater security and anonymity. Provisions are also usually made for the Trust to be moved to another jurisdiction in the event of war, riot, or civil strife. While it may not be necessary to use these powers, they do give added security.

Planned Distribution - The Trust ensures that your assets will be administered in accordance with your wishes and will eventually be distributed as required. This will also prevent any forced heirship distribution. Therefore, it is not necessary for you to use any other estate planning techniques, such as wills, making periodic gifts, arranging for assets to be held in joint tenancies or leaving informal instructions. All these methods are complex, unreliable, or not legally enforceable and result in a loss of confidentiality and control.

The Trust mechanism also enables the Settlor to lay down specific instructions for the management and/or distribution of the assets after his death. For example, he may specify the following:

- income to his widow during her lifetime with no access to capital;
- income to the children when they reach the age of 21 and restricted access to capital when they reach age 25; and
- on their death before age 25, income to grandchildren, or distributions to other parties.

There are no stipulations as to distribution of assets on death, so the Settlor may specify any criteria he wishes.

Financial - The use of a completely tax free jurisdiction ensures that the value of the assets will not be eroded by probate costs and inheritance taxes. In addition, the income and capital of the Trust will also accumulate without suffering any additional income or capital gains taxes.

Flexibility - The Trust may be tailored to your specific needs and may even be varied as personal circumstances change. When the Settlor creates a Trust, he writes a "Letter of Wishes" to the Trustee, which describes the Settlor's intentions, the objects of the Trust, and his requirements as to the distribution of the assets. It is important to note that the Settlor may at any time vary the terms of the Trust or create an entirely new set of requirements of distribution. The Settlor may also wind up the Trust or replace the Trustee.

Control - While it is necessary that the assets must be delivered to the Trustee, you may retain a right to direct investment strategy and may also retain a degree of control through a beneficial interest in the Trust or through the powers of a Trust Protector.

Political - The Trust may be used to protect the wealth of individuals residing in politically sensitive areas of the world. Passing the legal control of the assets to a Trust can allow the preservation and accumulation of wealth without exposure to adverse political risk.

Probate Disclosure - By placing the ownership of assets in a Trust, you can determine how and to whom these assets are to transfer to at death, avoiding public disclosure during probate.

Taxation - Business owners may find it beneficial to place some of their shares in developing companies into a Trust, in such a way that capital gains tax would be avoided on a future disposition of those shares (for example, if the business is successful and is acquired or goes public).

Currency Controls - Assets can be protected from confiscation, enforced repatriation, or loss of freedom of choice if currency controls are introduced in your home country.

Sample letter of wishes.

A typical Letter of Wishes, provided by Standard Private Trust Ltd. in Providenciales, Turks & Caicos Islands, reads as follows:

Standard Private Trust Ltd.
Caribbean Place
Leeward Highway
Providenciales, Turks & Caicos Islands, BWI

Dear Sirs,

You are the Trustees of the settlement dated _______ and known as the "Trust". Under the terms of the Trust you are empowered to administer the assets of the Trust and to distribute them to the beneficiaries as you in your sole and absolute discretion think fit. In the exercise of your duties it will assist you to know of my wishes with regard to the administration of the assets of the Trust.

During my lifetime I request that you consider my wishes relevant to any action you propose in the administration of the Trust or the distribution of its assets. In the event of my death I propose that the Trust assets be administered in accordance with the wishes of _______.

In the event of the death of _______, or if _______ should predecease me then, upon my death, I propose that the Trust assets be divided equally between my children. Each child who survives both _______ and myself should receive his or her portion upon attaining the age of 25.

In the event of any child predeceasing _______ and myself, without leaving issue, his or her portion should be divided equally among the other children or other issue per stirpes. In the event of any child predeceasing _______ and myself, leaving issue, such child's share should be distributed to his or her children or other issue per stripes.

Yours faithfully, _______.

Simple Trust Structure.

The following is a simple Trust structure that can shelter and retain family assets by providing the following benefits:

- protect against unreasonable income and capital gains tax;
- provide confidentiality and anonymity;
- avoid possible forced heirship regulations; and
- provide protection against claims that may be made against Trust assets.

This simple Trust structure provides an ideal asset protection vehicle, allowing you to take steps to safeguard your estate.

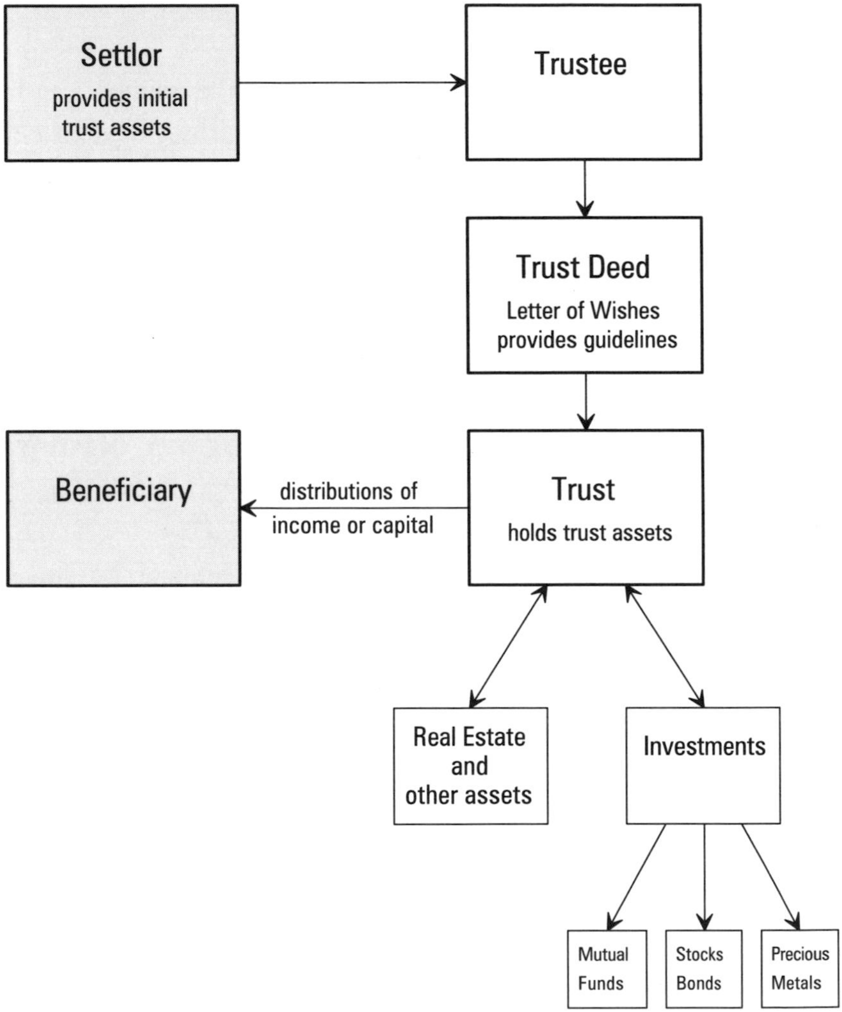

OFFSHORE CAPTIVE INSURANCE COMPANIES

Many benefits, including substantial savings in premiums, can be achieved by the risk management technique of establishing a captive insurance company. Internationally, there has been substantial growth in this industry since the mid-1970's, with thousands of captive insurance companies formed world-wide. Captive insurance companies now play a significant role in the international insurance market. Several offshore locations have developed into established insurance centres.

Advantages and benefits of establishing an offshore captive insurance company.

The advantages and benefits of industrial or commercial groups forming a captive insurance company to underwrite some or all of their risk include:

- insurance at a lower cost;
- turning a cost centre (insurance expenditure) into a profit centre;
- gaining access to the more cost effective reinsurance market;
- having the ability to build reserves from pre-tax earnings;
- enhancing group cash flow;
- providing coverage not otherwise available;
- consolidation of group insurance programs; and

- acquiring the operations of other insurance companies to increase assets and reduce risk.

Premiums paid to insurance companies include a significant mark-up to meet the insurer's general expenses such as marketing overheads, profits, and commission payments to brokers. Premiums are usually paid annually in advance, with the insurance company retaining the premium until claims are paid, earning investment income that is not usually passed back to the client company.

Creating a captive insurance company enables the industrial or commercial group to "capture" the profits obtained by the insurer from pure underwriting and investment income, without the loss of coverage. Effectively this allows the captive insurance company to have direct access to the reinsurance markets where it will have the opportunity to secure coverage at more favorable rates.

A captive insurance company can also build up reserves to fund claims on a tax deductible basis with insurance premiums, rather than out of after-tax profits. Insurance costs can also be related to the claims' experience of the group, which can often lead to lower rates than are available on the open market.

In some cases, traditional insurance companies have been unable or unwilling to provide corporate insurance buyers with the coverage they need, or are unable to provide the required policy wordings. A captive insurance company can produce an insurance policy with the wording specifically designed to suit the parent and its affiliates, or to cover risks that conventional insurance companies may find unacceptable.

Finally, the establishment of a captive insurance company provides the industrial or commercial group with an opportunity to diversify its operations into insurance services. The choice of a tax-efficient offshore location also enables the reserves of the captive insurance company to accumulate at a faster rate than those of a domestic insurance company.

CHAPTER 6

SELECTING A TAX HAVEN

The surest way to avoid confiscatory taxes is to not own assets or receive any income. Choosing the wrong jurisdiction may grant you this wish when you find out all of your assets have disappeared, or have been "nationalized" by a new government or political party.

Tax Haven Roadmap explores each of the following tax haven jurisdictions in full detail to ensure that you can make an informed decision:

- Anguilla
- Antigua & Barbuda
- Austria
- Bahamas
- Barbados
- Belize
- Bermuda
- British Virgin Islands
- Cayman Islands
- Channel Islands - Guernsey and Jersey
- Cook Islands
- Gibraltar
- Hong Kong
- Isle of Man
- Liechtenstein
- Luxembourg
- Malta
- Monaco
- Montserrat
- Nauru
- Panama
- St.Kitts & Nevis
- Switzerland
- Turks & Caicos Islands

For each tax haven the following questions will be reviewed in detail:

- Does the country have a secrecy law?
- Is there any situation where bank secrecy can be lifted?
- Can foreign tax authorities obtain information on the country's bank accounts?
- Is the country an independent country?
- Is the legal system based on English Common Law?
- Is there an income tax in the country?
- Are there any other taxes in the country?
- Are there any exchange controls in the country?
- Is there a tax treaty between the U.S. and the country?
- Is there a tax treaty between Canada and the country?
- Does the country allow the formation of Limited Companies?
- Does the country allow the formation of International Trusts?
- Does the country allow the formation of Captive Insurance Companies?

A comprehensive list of contacts is also provided to guarantee that your information will be accurate and up-to-date.

Financial secrecy, privacy, and confidentiality begins with proper goal setting, planning, and implementation of a program that will best suit your needs.

ANGUILLA

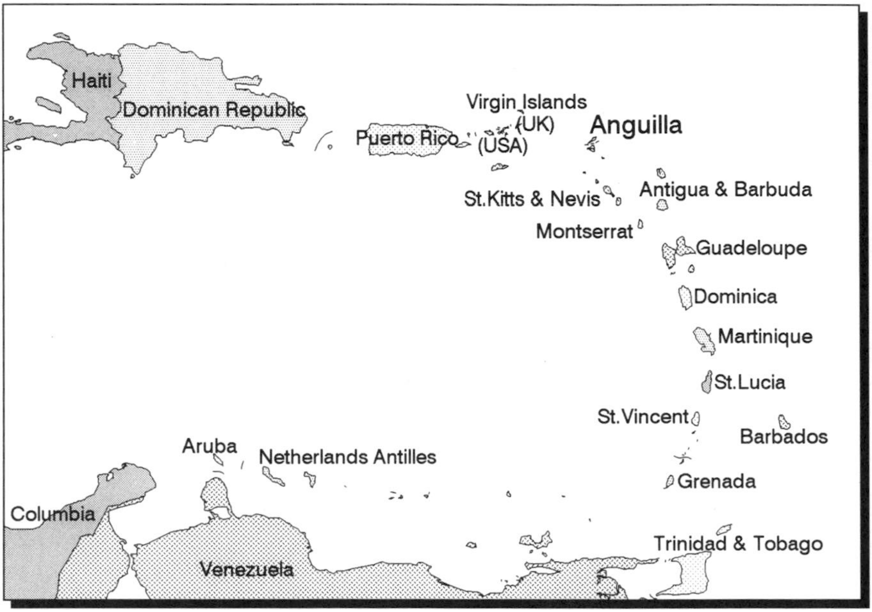

In the Caribbean (Leeward Islands). Caribbean island, 272 km southeast of Puerto Rico, 1,920 km south of Miami, population of approximately 8,000. Main language is English. Climate is tropical with relatively low humidity, average temperature 28°C.

Rich in pre-Columbian history. Archaeologists have determined there was a large settlement of Arawak Indians living on Anguilla. They called the island Malliouhana. The Spaniards who followed Christopher Columbus to the New World are said to have given the island its present name of Anguilla, because of its long eel-like shape.

The government of Anguilla is actively promoting the offshore banking and financial sector. A computerized filing system has been developed for the Anguilla Companies Registry allowing remote access filing and registration of companies by both local and overseas agents. The Companies Registry is scheduled to operate 24 hours a day, 365 days a year. In a determined effort to encourage offshore professionals to relocate to Anguilla, the government is offering multi-year renewable work permits and other financial incentives.

Does Anguilla have a secrecy law?

YES. Anguilla's strict confidentiality laws prohibit the unauthorized disclosure of information pertaining to a clients affairs to a third party, providing for criminal penalties of up to US$50,000 and a prison term of up to one year for any disclosure concerning the business affairs of a client. A bank would receive the maximum penalty.

Is there any situation where bank secrecy can be lifted?

YES. Information needed for a criminal proceeding that would be a triable offense in Anguilla can be legally disclosed. Triable offenses include drug trafficking, money laundering, theft and fraud.

Can foreign tax authorities obtain information on Anguillan bank accounts?

NO. Information cannot be released to foreign tax authorities because of Anguilla's confidentiality laws, although under the Caribbean Basin Initiative, Anguilla is considering an exchange of information treaty with the United States.

Is Anguilla an independent country?

NO. Anguilla is a stable British colony administered by the Anguilla Constitution Order of 1982, a self-governing constitution that went into effect on April 1, 1982.

Is the legal system based on English Common Law?

YES. The legal system is administered by the Eastern Caribbean States Supreme Court, and is based on English common law supplemented by local statutes.

Is there an income tax in Anguilla?

NO. There is no income tax in Anguilla. Specific statutes have been enacted to ensure a perpetual tax exemption on IBCs, LLs, and Trusts. To qualify for this exemption, the IBC or LLC must not carry on business in Anguilla. To qualify as an exempt Trust, the Settlor and Beneficiaries may not be residents of Anguilla.

Are there any other taxes in Anguilla?

NO. There is no capital gains tax, gift tax, or estate tax in Anguilla. Historically, Anguilla has always been a no-tax jurisdiction with no personal or corporate taxation.

Are there any exchange controls in Anguilla?

NO. There are currently no exchange controls in Anguilla.

Is there a tax treaty between the U.S. and Anguilla?

NO. Currently there is no tax treaty between the U.S. and Anguilla. Note that under the Caribbean Basin Initiative, Anguilla is considering an exchange of information treaty with the United States.

Anguilla maintains the UK Tax Convention with Denmark, New Zealand, Norway, Sweden, and Switzerland, allowing for a 15% withholding tax on dividends. Anguilla maintains double-taxation agreements with Barbados, Guyana, Jamaica, and Trinidad and Tobago.

Is there a tax treaty between Canada and Anguilla?

NO. Currently there is no tax treaty between Canada and Anguilla.

Does Anguilla allow the formation of Limited Companies?

YES. Limited Companies are governed by the Companies Ordinance of 1994 and the International Business Companies Ordinance of 1994. Both Ordinances were passed by the Anguilla House of Assembly on November 3, 1994, and proclaimed in force on January 1, 1995. Offshore companies can continue to be formed under the domestic Companies Ordinance as Anguillan private companies, or as offshore International Business Companies under the IBC legislation.

Companies Ordinance - The Companies Ordinance is based on the Caribbean Law Institute Draft Bill, based upon Ontario, Canada legislation. A prescribed three page Articles of Incorporation is used. Requirements and related benefits include:

- Only one shareholder and one director are required.
- Shareholder and director may both be nominees.
- Shareholders and directors may be of any nationality.
- All shares are of no par value.
- Companies must have a registered agent in Anguilla.
- Annual meetings need not be held in Anguilla.
- Annual returns listing shareholders, directors, registered office, and registered agent must be filed annually.

The Ordinance exempts a class of company called Specified Private Company (SPC) from certain financial recording requirements. To qualify as an SPC, the following conditions must be met:

- Maximum number of shareholders is 11.
- Restrictions on share transfers must be imposed.

- Shares may not be offered to the public.

International Business Companies Ordinance - The IBC Ordinance is based on the British Virgin Islands and revised Bahamas Acts, permitting the formation of an International Business Company by filing brief articles of incorporation.

Advantages of incorporating an IBC in Anguilla include:

- One person may incorporate.
- IBC's are exempt from filing accounts, although this information can be provided on an optional filing basis.
- Nominee shareholders and directors may be used.
- No par value shares are permitted.

The words Incorporated, Limited, Société Anonyme and their abbreviations indicate limited liability.

Limited Liability Company Ordinance - Anguilla also offers the option of forming a Limited Liability Company (LLC), similar to American LLCs first formed in 1977 in the state of Wyoming. LLCs formed in Anguilla can be of limited duration or have a perpetual life. A Limited Liability Company is a hybrid company with the characteristics of both a company and a partnership, offering the following advantages:

- It is a separate legal entity, as a company.
- Limited liability is offered to shareholders.
- Has status as a "pass-through" entity for U.S. income tax purposes.

Limited Liability Companies are commonly used in joint ventures, venture capital investments, and real estate syndication.

Does Anguilla allow the formation of International Trusts?

YES. International Trusts are governed by the Trusts Ordinance, passed by the Anguilla House of Assembly on November 3, 1994, and proclaimed in force on January 1, 1995. Anguilla's new trust legislation uses the most current and innovative provisions found in the Bahamas, Belize, Bermuda, Cayman Islands, and Cook Islands Trusts Acts, and the Turks & Caicos Trusts Ordinance.

Under Section 6 of the Ordinance, the rule against perpetuities has been abolished, allowing the formation of trusts of perpetual duration. Under Section 14, the definition of Charitable Trusts has been expanded to include "any other purposes which are beneficial to the community." The new Trust legislation has made it possible to create a Commercial Purpose Trust, which is a non-charitable Trust created for a specific purpose, and has also allowed for the creation of Spendthrift Trusts.

Under Section 16 of the Ordinance, a Trust Protector may be appointed for any type of Trust, and is a mandatory requirement for a Commercial Purpose Trust. The Trust Protector has the power to enforce the trust, and under the terms of the Trust can also be authorized to remove and appoint Trustees.

Under Part IX, Choice of Governing Law, "a term of the Trust expressly selecting the laws of Anguilla to govern the Trust is valid, effective and conclusive regardless of any other circumstances." Under Part XII, an optional facility to file and register a Trust with the Registrar of Companies is provided.

A Trust formed with the Settlor and Beneficiaries not resident in Anguilla is declared to be an Exempt Trust, specifically exempt from any form of taxation for an indefinite period. Exempt Trusts may not hold land in Anguilla.

The Fraudulent Dispositions Ordinance is similar to the Cayman and Bahamas Acts, which prevents transfers to Trusts with the explicit intention to defraud current or anticipated creditors. The burden of proof of establishing such an intent to defraud is upon the creditor who has a period of 3 years to make an application from the date of relevant disposition. After this time, the Trust will protect the assets from creditors. The statute of limitations is 3 years.

Does Anguilla allow the formation of Captive Insurance Companies?

YES. The statute governing the licensing and operation of insurance companies in Anguilla is the Insurance Ordinance of 1994.

To form an insurance company, the applicant must complete an Application for Registration, Certificate of Solvency, Balance Sheet, Profit and Loss Account, and Appointment of Agent. Additionally, the Application for Registration must include:

- Confirmation shareholders not involved with an insolvent company.
- 2 references for each shareholder, 1 from a banker.
- Qualifications and experience of each director.
- Clean record and financial background for each director.
- Details of all directorships in the past 5 years.
- The insurance company's auditors, bankers and lawyers must confirm in writing that they are willing to act on behalf of company.
- Details of all reinsurance arrangements.
- Copies of audited accounts for the past 5 years.
- Business plan and investment strategy for the next 5 years.

Does Anguilla allow the formation of Banking Companies?

YES. Anguilla is a suitable jurisdiction for the formation of Banking Companies.

Financial institutions and contacts:

Caricom Management Services Limited
Mr. Edmund W. Lawrence 809-497-3591 dial
Managing Director 809-497-2050 fax
PO.Box 147, The Valley, Anguilla, British West Indies

- Primary business activity: company and trust formation services.
- Company formation services are offered.

Charter Bank & Trust Ltd.
PO.Box 197 809-497-5082 dial
The Valley, Anguilla, British West Indies 809-497-5138 fax

- Primary business activity: banking services.

Government of Anguilla
Mr. Ralph Hodge 809-497-3881 dial
Director of Finance 809-497-5872 fax
The Secretariat, The Valley, Anguilla, British West Indies

- Primary business activity: government services.

IPS (Anguilla) Ltd.
Mr. Garrett Sutton 809-497-4053 dial
Barrister-at-Law
Box 801, The Valley, Anguilla, British West Indies

- Primary business activity: company and trust formation services.
- Company formation services are offered.
- Trust formation services are offered.

Mitchell's Chambers - Barristers at Law and Solicitors

Mr. I.D. Mitchell 809-497-2391 dial
Barrister-at-Law 809-497-2050 fax
PO.Box 174, The Valley, Anguilla, British West Indies

- Primary business activity: law office.
- Company formation services are offered. Minimum formation fee US$1,050 including US$250 government fee. Minimum annual fee US$500.
- Trust formation services are offered.
- Captive insurance company formation. Minimum formation fee US$4,089. Minimum annual fee US$3,038.

Swiss Arab Bank & Trust Co.

PO.Box 100, The Valley, Anguilla, British West Indies

- Primary business activity: banking services.

ANTIGUA & BARBUDA

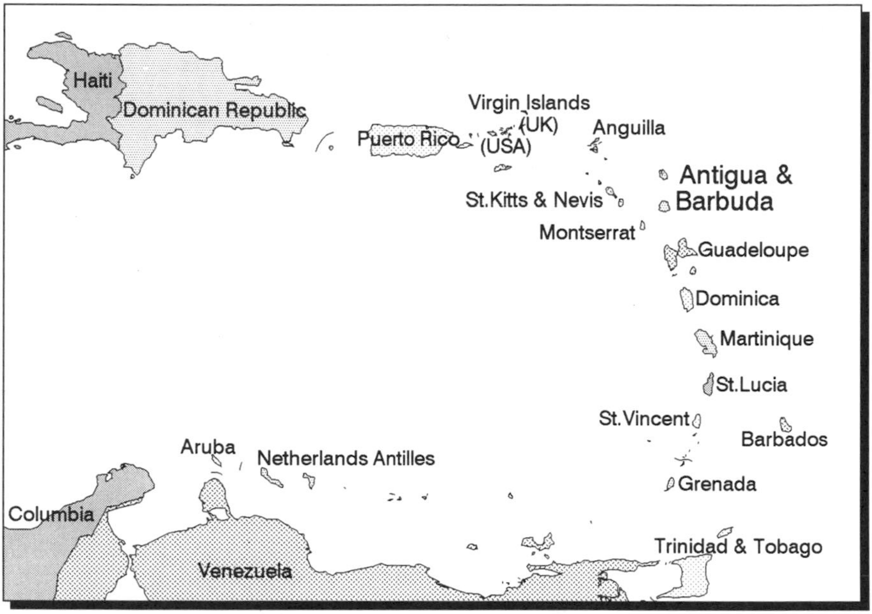

In the Caribbean. 108 square miles, 320 km southeast of Puerto Rico in the Leeward Islands. Population is approximately 65,000, with approximately 20,000 living in St.John's, the capital. Lying to the north of Antigua and covering 75 square miles is the island of Barbuda, with a population of 1,500. Main language is English. Temperature averages between 70°F and 86°F, with low humidity.

Columbus discovered Antigua in November 1493, on his second voyage to the new world, finding it inhabited by Carib Indians. For 135 years following Columbus' sighting of Antigua, neither the French, nor the major colonial powers in the region, the Dutch, made any serious attempts to colonize the island. This was primarily due to its lack of fresh water and the continual Carib raids. The island was occupied by the

French for six months in 1652, while the British settled later that year and established sugar plantations during the 17th and 18th centuries. To protect their interests they built several forts, the ruins of which are still seen today. Antigua & Barbuda were granted Associate State status in 1956 at a constitutional conference held in London. Full independence was granted on November 1, 1981.

Does Antigua have a secrecy law?

YES. Antigua's Offshore Banking Secrecy Act and the International Business Corporation Act (28/1982 sub section 244 1-5 "Confidential matters protected") prohibits the unauthorized disclosure of information pertaining to a clients affairs to a third party. The Act provides criminal penalties of up to US$50,000 or a prison term not to exceed one year for any inquiry or disclosure concerning the business affairs of a client or transaction involving an IBC bank or trust company.

Is there any situation where bank secrecy can be lifted?

YES. The Act does not prohibit the disclosure of confidential information upon court order in connection with an authorized investigation, or with the giving of evidence on an alleged criminal offense triable within Antigua or which would have been so triable if it had been committed within Antigua.

Can foreign tax authorities obtain information on Antiguan bank accounts?

NO. Foreign tax authorities can only obtain information related to a triable criminal offense. Note that tax evasion is not a criminal offense in Antigua.

Is Antigua an independent country?

YES. Antigua was a British colony from 1653 to 1967, attaining the status of a self-governing island under Associated Statehood in 1967. Antigua gained its independence on November 1, 1981 from Britain, but remains a member of the British Commonwealth of Nations.

Is the legal system based on English Common Law?

YES. Antigua enacts their own independent legislation based on British Common Law. The legal system is administered by the Eastern Caribbean States Supreme Court.

Is there an income tax in Antigua?

NO. No personal income tax. No income tax on assets held by an IBC, as a Trustee, for a minimum period of 50 years. Local businesses are required to pay a 40% income tax.

Are there any other taxes in Antigua?

NO. No personal capital gains tax. No capital gains tax on assets held by an IBC, as a Trustee, for a minimum period of 50 years. No personal inheritance tax. No inheritance tax on assets held by an IBC, as a Trustee, for a minimum period of 50 years. There is no gift tax in Antigua, except duties charged by Customs on certain gifts imported.

Are there any exchange controls in Antigua?

NO. There are currently no exchange controls in Antigua. The official currency is the East Caribbean Dollar.

Is there a tax treaty between the U.S. and Antigua?

NO. There is no double-taxation agreement between the U.S. and Antigua, although Antigua maintains double-taxation agreements with Australia, New Zealand, Singapore, and the United Kingdom.

Is there a tax treaty between Canada and Antigua?

NO. There is no double-taxation agreement between Canada and Antigua.

Does Antigua allow the formation of Limited Companies?

YES. An IBC (International Business Corporation) is a company limited by shares which is not allowed to engage in any active trade or business within Antigua, except for those activities which are solely in support of its business outside Antigua. An IBC falls under the provisions of the International Business Corporations Act of 1982.

The incorporator must either be a resident of Antigua together with a member of the Bar, or a trust company empowered by the Cabinet of Antigua to act as an incorporator. Most banking and trust companies in Antigua function as incorporators.

Every IBC must have a registered office and a resident agent in Antigua. The Company must be managed by a Board of Directors consisting of at least one director which may be corporate.

Incorporating in Antigua brings certain advantages:

- There is a guarantee that an IBC is not liable for taxation for 50 years.
- There are no requirements to have paid-up capital. There is no time limit in which the authorized capital must be fully paid (except for banks and insurance companies).
- There are no requirements to file any corporate reports with the government regarding any offshore activities.
- There are no citizenship or residence requirements for directors, officers, stockholders, or incorporators.

- Officers and directors need not be shareholders.
- Only one director is required and nationality is not an issue. The director can be a corporation.
- Meetings of directors and shareholders may be held in any country.
- The books of the corporation may be kept in any country.
- The corporation may increase or decrease its authorized capital by means of an amendment to its Articles of Incorporation.
- Share certificates can be issued in bearer form or nominee form, with or without par value.
- There are no currency restrictions of any type for Antiguan Offshore Corporations.
- Incorporation and annual government fees are a flat US$250 and not based on capital. This is very cost effective for highly capitalized corporations.

Important points to consider when forming an Antiguan Offshore Corporation include:

- The name of the corporation must end in the words Limited, Incorporated, Corporation, Société Anonyme, Sociedad Anonima, or their abbreviations. The use of the words Trust, Bank, Insurance, Fiduciary, Reinsurance, or any of their derivatives is restricted by law, unless licensed as such.
- The full names of the officers of the corporation may be the same persons that are appointed as directors. One person can hold more than one office and officers need not be shareholders.

Does Antigua allow the formation of International Trusts?

YES. No income, capital gains or inheritance tax may be levied against assets held by an IBC as a Trustee on behalf of a non-resident of Antigua for a period of 50 years from the IBC's incorporation date.

Although there is no requirement that a Trust instrument be recorded, it may be recorded in the non-public records of the Director of IBCs, who will issue a certificate of record attached to an original of the Trust instrument. There are no restrictions on accumulations by Trusts. The Rule Against Perpetuities has been abolished. The governing law of Trusts is the British common law which was adopted by Antigua as a colony and re-affirmed upon independence.

Does Antigua allow the formation of Captive Insurance Companies?

YES. Any company incorporated under the laws of Antigua may, when permitted by its Articles of Incorporation, apply for permission to register as an international insurance company. The following restrictions apply to the formation of an international insurance company:

- An international insurance company may engage in any insurance business other than domestic insurance.
- The Superintendent of International Insurance Corporations is empowered to revoke or suspend any license when he is of the opinion that the continued registration of the international insurance company is detrimental to the public interest.
- The law requires that an insurance company have a local director.
- The licensing application must include resumes for all shareholders, officers and directors of the insurance company.
- The required start-up capital is US$250,000.

- An international insurance company is required to appoint an auditor and file annual reports with the Superintendent of International Insurance Corporations.

Does Antigua allow the formation of Banking Companies?

YES. Any IBC, when permitted by its Articles of Incorporation, may apply for an international banking license. IBC Banks are exempt from the restrictions of the Exchange Control Act of 1958 and the one percent (1%) levy on foreign currency transactions imposed by the Foreign Currency Levy Act of 1976.

The following restrictions apply to the formation of an international banking company:

- The minimum capital required for a banking license is US$1,000,000.
- Biographical information for each director, officer and subscriber of 5% or more of the IBC's stock must be submitted. This information must show that the directors and officers have banking experience and have the ability to operate the bank.
- Audited corporate and personal financial statements of the organizer must be submitted before final approval.
- The granting of an international banking license is solely within the discretion of the Supervisor of Banks and Trust Corporations, who may revoke the license at any time if in his opinion the revocation is in the public interest.
- IBC banks are required to appoint an auditor and file audited quarterly returns with the Supervisor of Banks and Trust Corporations.

Does Antigua allow the formation of Shipping Companies?

YES. The Department of Marine Services and Merchant Shipping can advise on specific inquiries. Offshore shipping companies use the provisions of the International Business Corporations Act of 1982. Following are several important points:

- Antigua provides full convention registration and has entered bilateral trading agreements with major sea trade countries.
- No age restrictions are in force, providing the vessels class status is current. Exemptions from the class requirements can be made under certain conditions for cargo vessels under 500GRT, yachts, fishing vessels, and vessels in coastal trade only. Vessels of over 14 years old will be inspected by an appointed surveyor prior to acceptance.
- Statutory safety certificates are to be issued by a recognized Classification Society. The Antigua Administration provides safe manning certificates, radio licenses and certificate of competency. Certificates of other nationalities are generally recognized, providing they are obtained from an approved Nautical Institute.
- Antigua registered vessels can be owned by non-citizens, but a nationality waiver must be obtained. Incorporations of offshore companies are invited at very competitive costs (offshore companies in Antigua are not liable for taxation for 50 years).
- Bare boat registration is permitted.
- Vessels under the flag of Antigua will be liable to an annual safety inspection, prior to re-registration.
- Full-term registration will be issued after receiving a certificate of deletion from the previous register.

IMO Conventions ratified by the government of Antigua include the 1966 International Convention on Loadlines, the 1969 International Convention on Tonnage Measurement, the 1972 International Convention on Regulations for Preventing of Collisions at Sea, the 1973 International Convention for the Preventing of

Pollution from Ships, and the 1974 International Convention for the Safety of Life at Sea.

Financial Institutions:

Antigua and Barbuda Department of Tourism

Box 363	809-462-0029	dial
St.John's, Antigua, West Indies	809-462-2483	fax

- Primary business activity: government services.

Antigua Commercial Bank

St.John's, Antigua, West Indies

- Primary business activity: banking services.

Antigua Overseas Bank Ltd.

Antigua Barbuda Investment Bank Ltd. / ABI Trust Ltd.

Mr. McAlister Abbott	809-462-0067	dial
General Manager / Director	809-462-0804	fax
High Street, PO.Box 1679	2039 ABIBANK AK	telex
St.John's, Antigua, West Indies		

- Primary business activity: bank and trust services.
- Offers Private Credit Card (Visa/American Express) backed by deposit.
- Private banking services and/or savings accounts.
- Consumer loans and credit facilities.
- Company formation services are offered. Minimum formation fee US$975 plus US$250 license fee. Minimum annual fee US$475 plus US$250 license fee.
- Trust formation services are offered.
- Captive insurance company formation. Minimum formation fee US$5,000 including license fee. Minimum annual fee US$4,000.
- Banking company formation. Minimum formation fee US$6,500 plus US$5,000 license fee. Minimum annual fee US$2,500 plus US$5,000 license fee.

Bank of Antigua

Mr. K.J.E. Byron	809-462-4282	dial
Manager	809-462-4718	fax
PO.Box 315	2180 REGAL AK	telex

High Street, St.John's, Antigua, West Indies

- Primary business activity: banking services.
- Offers Private Credit Card (Visa Gold) backed by deposit.
- Private banking services and/or savings accounts.

Bank of Nova Scotia

PO.Box 342	809-462-1104	dial

High Street, St.John's, Antigua, West Indies

- Primary business activity: banking services.
- Private banking services and/or savings accounts.
- Consumer loans and credit facilities.
- Safekeeping and custodian services.

CIBC (Canadian Imperial Bank Commerce)

High Street and Corn Alley	809-462-0998	dial

St.John's, Antigua, West Indies

- Primary business activity: banking services.

Hill & Hill Chambers

Mr. Hill
Partner
PO.Box 909, Long Street, St.John's, Antigua, West Indies

- Primary business activity: law office.

Kendall & Forde Chambers

Mr. Kendall
Partner
Long Street, St.John's, Antigua, West Indies

- Primary business activity: law office.

Phillips, Phillips & Archibald Chambers
Mr. Phillips
Partner
PO.Box 546, St.John's, Antigua, West Indies

- Primary business activity: law office.

Royal Bank of Canada (Antigua)

Mrs. E. Maundy	809-462-0325	dial
Assistant Manager Lending	809-462-1304	fax
High and Market Streets	2120	telex

PO.Box 252, St.John's, Antigua, West Indies

- Primary business activity: banking services.
- Private banking services and/or savings accounts.
- Consumer loans and credit facilities.
- Safekeeping and custodian services.

Swiss American Bank Ltd.

Mr. Ken Fisher	809-462-4460	dial
Manager Loans	809-462-0274	fax
High Street	2181 AIT-SAB AK	telex

PO.Box 1302, St.John's, Antigua, West Indies

- Primary business activity: banking services.
- Offers Private Credit Card (Visa/MasterCard) backed by deposit.
- Private banking services and/or savings accounts.
- Consumer loans and credit facilities.
- Executor and administrator of wills and estates.
- Safekeeping and custodian services.
- Portfolio management of securities and mutual funds.
- Company formation services are offered. Minimum formation fee US$725 plus US$250 license fee. Minimum annual fee US$475 plus US$250 license fee.
- Trust formation services are offered. Minimum formation fee US$1,000. Minimum annual fee US$500 plus transaction fee.
- Captive insurance company formation. Minimum formation fee US$5,000 plus US$2,500 license fee. Minimum annual fee US$5,000.
- Banking company formation. Minimum formation fee US$10,000 plus US$5,000 license fee. Minimum annual fee US$7,500.

AUSTRIA

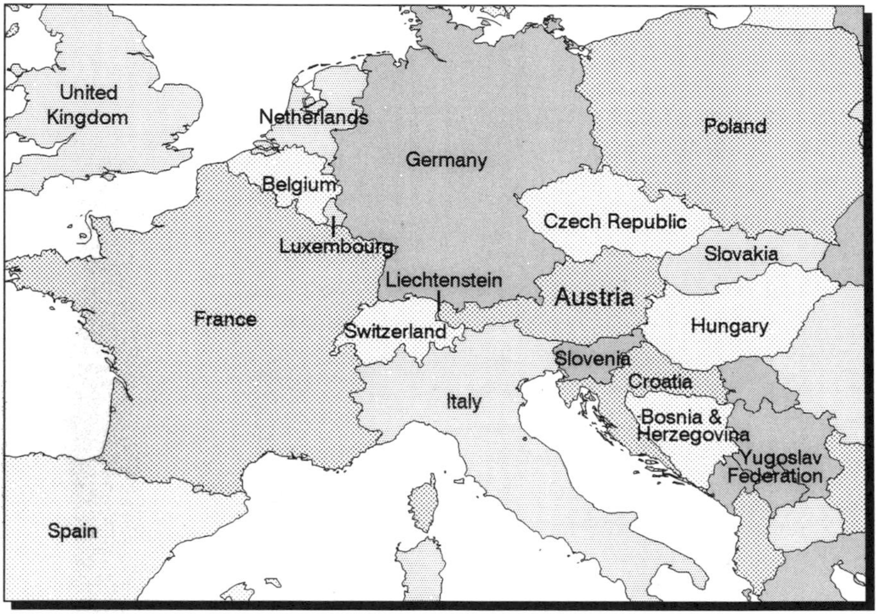

In Western Europe. Borders with Germany to the north, Italy to the south, Switzerland to the west, and Hungary to the east. Population is approximately 8 million. Main language is German, although English is spoken.

Until 1918 Austria was the heart of the vast Hapsburg Empire, encompassing the Danube Basin and much of the Balkans. Austria is now a democratic republic based upon the German speaking parts of the former empire.

Some banks allow you to take advantage of low interest and high leverage (up to 5 times original investment amount) to multiply investment power.

Does Austria have a secrecy law?

YES. Bank secrecy is certified by the Austrian Banking Act, Section 23, which states:

"*The banks, their shareholders, their partners, members of their various bodies, employees as well as all other persons in any way acting for the banks may not disclose or make use of secrets which have been entrusted or made accessible to them solely due to the business relationships with customers. The obligation to maintain secrecy shall apply without time restriction. Whoever discloses or makes use of facts which are subject to bank secrecy in order to obtain financial benefit for himself or a third party, or to cause disadvantages to another, shall be sentenced by the court to imprisonment of up to one year or a penalty of up to 360 days court rates.*"

Instead of using numbered accounts, Austrian banks offer password accounts, providing an added level of secrecy protection.

Is there any situation where bank secrecy can be lifted?

YES. Bank secrecy may be lifted under certain extreme conditions relating to national security. The obligation to maintain bank secrecy does not exist:

- In context with commenced criminal court proceedings for fiscal violations, not including fiscal petty offenses.
- In case of probate procedures as against the probate court and the notary public acting as court commissioner.
- In case the client is of minor age or is otherwise granted curatorship.
- If the client explicitly and in writing authorizes the disclosure of the secret.

- To the extent the disclosure is necessary for clarification of legal matters originating from the relationship between the credit institution and the client.
- With regard to the reporting obligation pursuant to the Inheritance and Gift Tax Law (applying to residents of Austria).

Can foreign tax authorities obtain information on Austrian bank accounts?

NO. Bank secrecy is protected by the Austrian Banking Act, and prohibits the release of financial information for foreign tax investigations.

Is Austria an independent country?

YES. Austria is a neutral, democratic federal republic, with the United States, Russia, France and Britain as signatory powers to its neutrality. Government is a parliamentary democracy divided into three branches; the executive branch (including federal president, chancellor, and cabinet), the legislative branch (federal assembly), and judicial branch (constitutional, administrative, and supreme court).

Is the legal system based on English Common Law?

NO. The legal system based on civil law and is governed by the Federal Constitutional Act of 1920.

Is there an income tax in Austria?

YES. Austrian tax laws focus primarily on Austrian residents. Non-resident banking income is free of Austrian income, inheritance or capital gains taxes. No Austrian taxes are levied on the interest from either Austrian or foreign bonds or mutual funds held by non-residents. International Certificates of Deposit (ICDs) are also tax free. Precious metals can be bought tax-free if stored outside Austria.

Are there any other taxes in Austria?

YES. There is a 20% withholding tax on share dividends and participation capital dividends.

Are there any exchange controls in Austria?

NO. Non-residents can freely transfer funds or exchange currencies in Austria. Currency is the Austrian Schilling.

Is there a tax treaty between the U.S. and Austria?

YES. The tax treaty between the U.S. and Austria is modeled after the standard Organization for Economic Cooperation and Development (OECD) model treaty. Austria also maintains tax treaties with Argentina, Australia, Belgium, Brazil, Bulgaria, Canada, Denmark, Egypt, Finland, France, Germany, Greece, Hungary, India, Indonesia, Ireland, Israel, Italy, Japan, Korea, Liechtenstein, Luxembourg, Malta, the Netherlands, Norway, Pakistan, the Philippines, Poland, Portugal, Spain, Sweden, Switzerland, Thailand, Tunisia, Turkey, and the United Kingdom.

Is there a tax treaty between Canada and Austria?

YES. The tax treaty between Canada and Austria is modeled after the standard OECD model treaty.

Does Austria allow the formation of Limited Companies?

YES. Both a limited company (Gesellschaft mit beschrankter Hftung - GesmbH), and a stock corporation (Aktiengesellschaft - AG) are subject to certain taxes.

Does Austria allow the formation of International Trusts?

NO. Civil law does not readily support the formation of International Trusts.

Does Austria allow the formation of Captive Insurance Companies?

YES. Although Captive Insurance Companies can be formed in Austria, there are other jurisdictions with lower costs and friendlier legislation.

Does Austria allow the formation of Banking Companies?

YES. Although Banking Companies can be formed in Austria, there are other jurisdictions with lower costs and friendlier legislation.

Financial Institutions:

Anglo Irish Bank

Mr. Peter Zipper	43-1-43-6161	dial
Vice President	43-1-42-8142	fax
Rathausstrasse 20	114911 RTB A	telex

PO.Box 306, Vienna, Austria A-1011

- Primary business activity: bank and trust services.
- Offers Private Credit Card (VISA/MasterCard) backed by deposit.
- Private banking services and/or savings accounts.
- Consumer loans and credit facilities.
- Safekeeping and custodian services.
- Portfolio management of securities and mutual funds. Minimum annual fee 0.25% of assets plus US$30 per transaction.

Bankhaus Daghofer & Co.

Postfach 16, A-5010 Salzburg, Salzburg, Austria 662-80-48-333 fax

- Primary business activity: banking services.

Centro Internationale Handelsbank AG

PO.Box 272, A-1015 Vienna, Vienna, Austria

- Primary business activity: banking services.

Citibank (Austria) AG

Ms. Maria Rind	43-1-717-170	dial
Customer Service Officer	43-1-713-9206	fax

Lothringerstrasse 7, Vienna, Austria A-1015

- Primary business activity: banking services.

Creditanstalt Die Bank zum Erfolg

Mr. Herbert Hofbauer	53-1-31-4612	dial

Investment Manager

Schottengasse 6-8, Vienna, Austria A-1011

- Primary business activity: banking services.
- Private banking services and/or savings accounts.
- Consumer loans and credit facilities.

BAHAMAS

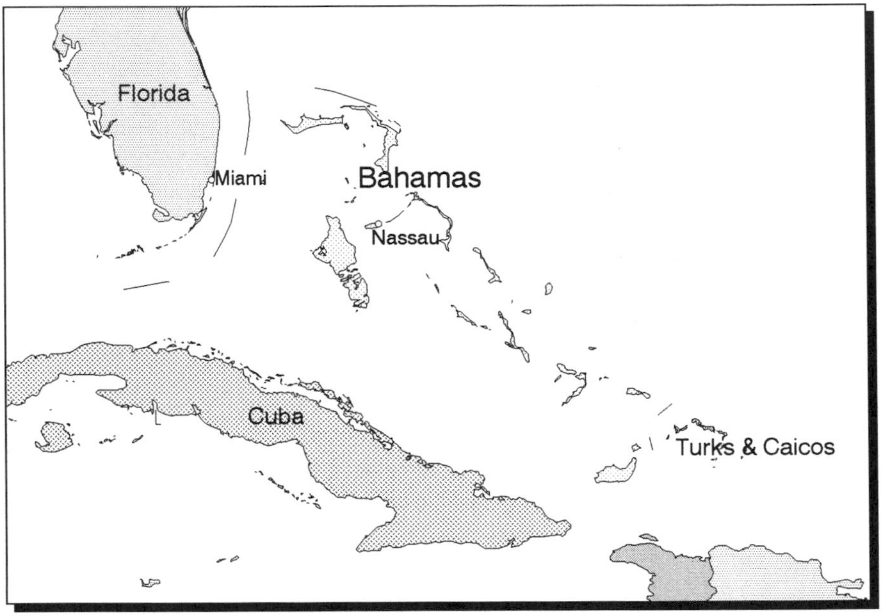

In the Caribbean, 60 miles southeast of Florida, north of Haiti. An archipelago of approximately 700 islands and 2,500 cays stretching from 60 miles east of Palm Beach Florida nearly to the Turks & Caicos Islands, over 500 miles away. Population is approximately 350,000. Main language is English. Climate is semi-tropical, with temperatures averaging 85°F in summer and 73°F in winter.

The Bahamas was initially settled in 1640 by the Eleutheran Adventurers, a group of Englishmen who sailed from Bermuda. The Bahamas has had a Parliamentary government since 1729, and became an independent nation in July, 1973.

Bahamian bank employees are said to have sold information about clients and their accounts to private investigators. Scandals throughout the 1980's involving drugs and underworld crime have been largely subdued. The Bahamas Investment Authority, operating out of the office of the Prime Minister, was created to stimulate growth in the financial sector and promote foreign direct investment.

Does the Bahamas have a secrecy law?

YES. The Bahamas Bank and Trust Company Regulatory Act prohibit the unauthorized disclosure of information pertaining to a clients affairs to a third party, without the customer's written permission. The secrecy laws are imposed on all Bank and Trust companies, their directors, officers, employees, attorneys, auditors, and outside agents. Only by Supreme Court Order can information be supplied about any account. A fine of US$5,000 applies to any person disclosing details of accounts contrary to the Bank and Trust Company Regulatory Act.

The commitment to bank secrecy was reaffirmed by Mr. Orville A. Turnquest, Minister of Justice and Foreign Affairs, on June 10, 1993, who stated that "*Bahamas is not only committed to the bank secrecy laws, but to the prevention of intrusion by foreign governments.*"

Is there any situation where bank secrecy can be lifted?

YES. There is a requirement to report bank deposits of more than US$100,000 to the Bahamas government, although this information is protected by the Bahamas Bank and Trust Company Regulatory Act. It is possible for foreign law enforcement agencies to obtain a court order demanding production of documents in criminal matters, although a very high standard of proof is required. An example of bank secrecy being lifted is the case of

Dennis Levine, an American who was suspected of insider trading. Under pressure from U.S. authorities, Bahamian banks violated secrecy laws and released information, even though no crime had been committed in the Bahamas. This example casts a negative view of Bahamian bank secrecy, indicating that if you absolutely require secrecy, look elsewhere. Political pressure seems to weigh heavily on the validity of bank secrecy laws.

Can foreign tax authorities obtain information on Bahamian bank accounts?

NO. Tax evasion in the Bahamas or in any other jurisdiction is not a criminal matter in the Bahamas, therefore any bank account or financial record is protected by the Bahamas Bank and Trust Company Regulatory Act.

The following quote is from a Government of Bahamas publication covering the banking industry: "*Tax evasion is not illegal in the Bahamas, since we do not have income, capital gains or inheritance taxes. Tax evasion is not considered suitable grounds for ordering access to information about an account.*"

Is the Bahamas an independent country?

YES. The Bahamas became an independent nation in 1973, although it remains a member of the British Commonwealth of Nations. A Governor General appointed by the British Government is responsible for defense, external affairs and internal security. An elected Prime Minister consults with a Cabinet of nine ministers chosen from the Legislature.

Is the legal system based on English Common Law?

YES. The Bahamas enacts their own Independent Legislation based on British Common Law, supplemented by local statutes. The Supreme Court is responsible for major criminal and civil cases.

The Court of Appeals handles appeals, while the Magistrate's Court is responsible for civil and criminal cases. The ultimate Court of Appeal is the Privy Council of the United Kingdom.

Is there an income tax in the Bahamas?

NO. No personal income tax. No tax on personal, business or company profits. No income tax on assets held by an IBC for a minimum period of 20 years. No taxes payable on the holding, income from, or transfer of IBC shares.

Are there any other taxes in the Bahamas?

NO. No personal capital gains tax. No capital gains tax on assets held by an IBC for a minimum period of 20 years. No gift or distribution tax. No personal estate, probate, or inheritance tax.

The government derives its income from tourism, import and stamp duties, and license fees on companies.

Are there any exchange controls in the Bahamas?

YES. An exchange control is exercised over citizens of the Bahamas to keep their funds in the local currency. Offshore entities use other currencies and are exempted from exchange controls. The official currency is the Bahamian Dollar. The Bahamian Dollar is at par with the U.S. dollar.

Is there a tax treaty between the U.S. and the Bahamas?

NO. There is no tax treaty between the U.S. and the Bahamas, although there is an exchange of information agreement applied if drug trafficking is suspected.

Is there a tax treaty between Canada and the Bahamas?

NO. There is no double-taxation agreement between Canada and the Bahamas.

Does the Bahamas allow the formation of Limited Companies?

YES. Offshore companies are known as International Business Companies. An IBC (International Business Corporation) falls under the provisions of the International Business Companies Act of 1989, which came into force on January 15, 1990. Internal Companies are governed by the Companies Act of 1992, which came into force on August 1, 1992. An IBC is a company limited by shares which is not allowed to engage in any active trade or business within the Bahamas except for those activities which are solely in furtherance of its business outside Bahamas. IBCs are governed by the following:

- The Company must be managed by a Board of Directors consisting of at least one director which need not be a natural person.
- The name of the company must include either Limited, Corporation, Incorporated, GmbH, Société Anonyme, Sociedad Anonima or their abbreviations.
- The name of the company may not include the words Bank, Building Society, Chamber of Commerce or any word that may indicate a connection with the Government or the Royal family.
- The Memorandum of Association may include the standard objects clause "*the company is allowed to engage in any act or activity which is not prohibited under any law for the time being in the Bahamas.*"
- An IBC must always have a registered office and a registered agent in the Bahamas.
- An IBC requires a minimum of two shareholders, although this may be reduced to one shareholder after incorporation.

- There must be at least one director who may be an individual or a corporation. A director may appoint an alternate. Other officers may be appointed.
- Subject to the Memorandum and Articles, the directors may call meetings inside or outside the Bahamas.

IBCs incorporated in the Bahamas offer the following advantages:

- To reduce annual tax (which is based on authorized capital), an authorized capital of US$5,000 is often used. This results in an annual fee payable to the Registrar of Companies of only US$100.
- An IBC is guaranteed to be exempt from any taxes for 20 years.
- The shares may be with or without par value, in bearer or registered form, and issued in any currency.
- There is no requirement to file annual returns or accounts.
- No public record is maintained of the identities of the shareholders or directors.
- There is no requirement for an annual general meeting.
- Company names can be set out in script applicable to Japanese, Chinese, Thai, Arabic, and other languages.

Any Bahamian company can empower any person as its attorney to execute deeds on its behalf in any place not situated in the Bahamas. Every deed signed by the attorney on behalf of the company and under his seal shall be binding on the company, and have the same effect as if it were under the common seal of the company.

Does the Bahamas allow the formation of International Trusts?

YES. International Trusts have had a long and stable record in the Bahamas, being governed by the Trustee Act of 1893 and amendments. Trusts formed in the Bahamas offer the following benefits:

- There is no requirement to register the Trust.
- A stamp duty payable upon declaration of Trust. This establishes the existence of the Trust and Trust deed for legal purposes.
- Assets held by an IBC as a Trustee on behalf of a non-resident of the Bahamas is guaranteed to be exempt from income, capital gains and inheritance tax at least until the year 2035.

The Trust (Choice of Governing Law) Act of 1989 protects Trusts established in the Bahamas from attack from other jurisdictions.

Does the Bahamas allow the formation of Captive Insurance Companies?

YES. Any IBC, when permitted by its Articles of Incorporation, may apply for a re-insurance license, and may engage in any insurance business other than domestic insurance.

Does the Bahamas allow the formation of Banking Companies?

YES. Any IBC, when permitted by its Articles of Incorporation, may apply for an international banking license.

Financial institutions and contacts:

Ansbacher International Trust Group Ltd
Bahamas International Trust Company Ltd
Mr. Alan E. Cole 809-322-1161 dial
Director 809-326-5020 fax
PO.Box N-7768, Bank Lane, Nassau, Bahamas

- Primary business activity: bank and trust services.
- Safekeeping and custodian services.
- Portfolio management of securities and mutual funds.
- Company formation services are offered.
- Trust formation services are offered.

Arthur Young & Co.
PO.Box N-3231 809-322-3805 dial
Nassau, Bahamas

- Primary business activity: accounting services.

Bahamas Investment Authority
West Bay Street 809-327-5970 dial
PO.Box CB-10980 809-327-5907 fax
Nassau, Bahamas

- Primary business activity: government services.

Bank of Montreal
Arcade Building, PO.Box F 2608, Freeport, Bahamas

- Primary business activity: bank and trust services.

Bank of New Providence
PO.Box N-4723, Nassau, Bahamas 809-322-1291 dial

- Primary business activity: banking services.

Bank of Nova Scotia Trust Company (Bahamas) Limited

Mr. H.H. Holst	809-356-1500	dial
Deputy Managing Director	809-326-0991	fax
PO.Box N-3016	2-0247	telex

Scotiabank Building, Nassau, Bahamas

- Primary business activity: bank and trust services.
- Private banking services and/or savings accounts.
- Consumer loans and credit facilities.
- Corporate services such as registered agent services.
- Executor and administrator of wills and estates.
- Safekeeping and custodian services.
- Company formation services are offered. Minimum formation fee US$2,500. Minimum annual fee 3/5% of assets or US$2,500.
- Trust formation services are offered. Minimum formation fee US$3,000. Minimum annual fee 3/5% of assets or US$3,500.
- Captive insurance company formation services are offered.
- Banking company formation services are offered.

Bank of Nova Scotia

Miss N.E. Vincent	809-322-4630	dial
Senior Operations Officer	809-328-8473	fax

PO.Box N-7518, Bay Street, 3rd Floor
Scotiabank Building, Nassau, Bahamas

- Primary business activity: banking services.

Bank of The Bahamas Limited

Mrs. S. Seymour
Acting Assistant Manager
Bank Lane & Woodstock Street, PO.Box F-42608, Freeport, Bahamas

- Primary business activity: bank and trust services.
- Private banking services and/or savings accounts.
- Consumer loans and credit facilities.

Bank of The Bahamas Limited

PO.Box N-7118	809-322-2690	dial
Euro Canadian Centre	809-325-2762	fax

Nassau, Bahamas

- Primary business activity: banking services.

BankAmerica Trust & Banking Corporation

PO.Box N-9100	809-393-7411	dial
BankAmerica House, East Bay Street	809-393-3030	fax
Nassau, Bahamas	2-0159	telex

- Primary business activity: banking services.

Barclays Bank PLC

PO.Box N-8350	809-322-4921	dial
Shirley & Charlotte Streets	809-328-7979	fax
Nassau, Bahamas		

- Primary business activity: banking services.
- Private banking services and/or savings accounts.
- Consumer loans and credit facilities.
- Safekeeping and custodian services.

British American Bank

PO.Box N-3744	809-325-3273	dial
Nassau, Bahamas	809-325-6912	fax

- Primary business activity: banking services.

Callender, Sawyer, Klonaris & Smith

PO.Box 7117	809-322-2511	dial
Nassau, Bahamas		

- Primary business activity: law office.

Central Bank of The Bahamas

PO.Box N-4868	809-322-2193	dial
Frederick St.	809-322-4321	fax
Nassau, Bahamas		

- Primary business activity: banking services.

Chase Manhattan Bank, N.A.

PO.Box N-4921	809-322-8721	dial
Nassau, Bahamas		

- Primary business activity: banking services.
- Private banking services and/or savings accounts.
- Consumer loans and credit facilities.
- Safekeeping and custodian services.
- Portfolio management of securities and mutual funds.
- Company formation services are offered.
- Trust formation services are offered.

Chase Manhattan Trust Corporation Ltd.

Charlotte House	809-323-6811	dial
Shirley & Charlotte Streets, Nassau, Bahamas		

- Primary business activity: banking services.
- Private banking services and/or savings accounts.
- Consumer loans and credit facilities.
- Safekeeping and custodian services.
- Portfolio management of securities and mutual funds.
- Company formation services are offered.
- Trust formation services are offered.

Chemical Bank & Trust (Bahamas) Limited

Shirley Street	809-322-1290	dial
Nassau, Bahamas	809-326-7339	fax

- Primary business activity: banking services.
- Private banking services and/or savings accounts.
- Safekeeping and custodian services.
- Company formation services are offered.
- Trust formation services are offered.

CIBC Trust Company (Bahamas) Limited

Mr. Hywel Jones	809-323-3314	dial
Manager, Business Development	809-328-2102	fax
PO.Box N-3933	20343 CANBANKTRUST	telex
Nassau, Bahamas		

- Primary business activity: bank and trust services.

Citibank NA

PO.Box N-8158	809-322-4240	dial
Nassau, Bahamas	809-323-3088	fax

- Primary business activity: banking services.

Commonwealth Bank

Mrs. J. Wilson-Fraser	809-322-1154	dial

Senior Branch Accountant
Bay Street, PO.Box SS 6263, Nassau, Bahamas

- Primary business activity: banking services.
- Private banking services and/or savings accounts.
- Consumer loans and credit facilities.

Coutts & Co. (Bahamas) Limited

Mr. Hermann-Josef Hermanns	809-326-0404	dial
Private Banking	809-326-6709	fax
PO.Box N4889	2-0111	telex

West Bay Street, Nassau, Bahamas

- Primary business activity: bank and trust services.
- Private banking services and/or savings accounts.
- Corporate services such as registered agent services.
- Safekeeping and custodian services.
- Portfolio management of securities and mutual funds. Minimum annual fee 0.6% of assets or US$3,600 plus 0.25% per transaction.
- Company formation services are offered.
- Trust formation services are offered.
- Captive insurance company formation services are offered.
- Banking company formation services are offered.

Credit Suisse (Bahamas) Limited

Mr. Max Lutz	809-322-8345	dial
Private Banking Department	809-326-6589	fax
Scotiabank Building, Rawson Square	20 166	telex
PO.Box N-4928, Nassau, Bahamas		

- Primary business activity: banking services.
- Private banking services and/or savings accounts.
- Executor and administrator of wills and estates.
- Safekeeping and custodian services.
- Portfolio management of securities and mutual funds. Minimum annual fee 0.5% of assets or US$5,000 plus US$100 per transaction. Minimum deposit US$100,000.
- Company formation services are offered.
- Trust formation services are offered. Minimum formation fee US$1,000. Minimum annual fee 0.2% of assets or US$1,000.

Darier Hentsch Private Bank & Trust Ltd

PO.Box N-4938	809-322-2721	dial
Charlotte Street	809-326-6983	fax
Nassau, Bahamas		

- Primary business activity: bank and trust services.

Deltec Panamerica Trust Company Ltd.

PO.Box N-3229	809-362-4549	dial
Nassau, Bahamas	809-362-4623	fax

- Primary business activity: banking services.

ENI International Bank Ltd.

PO.Box SS-6377	809-322-1928	dial
Nassau, Bahamas		

- Primary business activity: banking services.

Finance Corporation of The Bahamas

PO.Box N-3038	809-322-4823	dial
Shirley & Charlotte Streets	809-328-8848	fax
Nassau, Bahamas		

- Primary business activity: banking services.
- Private banking services and/or savings accounts.
- Consumer loans and credit facilities.

First Trust Bank

PO.Box N-7776	809-326-4308	dial
Nassau, Bahamas		

- Primary business activity: banking services.

Gotthard Bank Nassau

Mr. Beat Wernli	809-325-1531	dial
Senior Vice President	809-323-8561	fax
IBM House, PO.Box 6312, Nassau, Bahamas	20 151	telex

- Primary business activity: banking services.
- Private banking services and/or savings accounts.
- Safekeeping and custodian services.
- Portfolio management of securities and mutual funds. Minimum deposit US$250,000.
- Company formation services are offered.
- Trust formation services are offered.

Graham Thompson & Co.

PO.Box N-272	809-322-4130	dial
Nassau, Bahamas		

- Primary business activity: law office.

Handels Bank NatWest (Overseas) Ltd.

Beaumont House	809-325-5534	dial
PO.Box N-4214	809-326-8807	fax
Nassau, Bahamas		

- Primary business activity: banking services.

Handelsfinanz-CCF Bank International

PO.Box N-10441	809-328-8644	dial
Frederick St.	809-328-8600	fax
Nassau, Bahamas		

- Primary business activity: banking services.

Hang Seng Bank (Bahamas) Limited

Ms. Jackie Wu	809-322-2173	dial
Assistant Manager	809-328-1057	fax

PO.Box N-3019, Euro Canadian Centre, 2nd floor, Nassau, Bahamas

- Primary business activity: banking services.

Harry B. Sands and Company

Mr. Harry B. Sands	809-322-2670	dial
Barrister-at-Law	809-323-8914	fax

PO.Box N-624, 50 Shirley Street, Nassau, Bahamas

- Primary business activity: law office.
- Company formation services are offered.
- Trust formation services are offered.

Hentsch Private Bank & Trust Ltd.

PO.Box N-4232	809-325-4485	dial
Nassau, Bahamas		

- Primary business activity: banking services.

Higgs & Johnson

PO.Box N-3247	809-322-8571	dial
Nassau, Bahamas		

- Primary business activity: law office.

Higgs & Kelly

PO.Box N-1113	809-322-7511	dial
Nassau, Bahamas		

- Primary business activity: law office.

HSBC HongkongBank

PO.Box N-4917	809-322-3895	dial
Claughton House, Shirley Street	809-322-5622	fax
Nassau, Bahamas	20-288	telex

- Primary business activity: banking services.

Laurentian Bank & Trust Company Limited

Euro Canadian Centre	809-326-5935	dial
Nassau, Bahamas	809-326-5871	fax

- Primary business activity: banking services.

Leu Trust & Banking (Bahamas) Limited

PO.Box N-3926	809-326-5054	dial
Norfolk House	809-323-5825	fax
Nassau, Bahamas		

- Primary business activity: banking services.

Lloyds Bank International (Bahamas)

PO.Box N-1262	809-322-8711	dial
George and King Streets	809-322-8719	fax
Nassau, Bahamas		

- Primary business activity: banking services.

Maynard & Co.

PO.Box N-7525	809-322-8956	dial
Nassau, Bahamas		

- Primary business activity: law office.

McKinney, Turner & Co.

PO.Box N-8195	809-322-8914	dial
Nassau, Bahamas		

- Primary business activity: law office.

Mossack Fonseca & Co.

Attorneys at Law	809-322-7601	dial
PO.Box N-8188	809-322-5807	fax
Bitco Building, 3rd floor, Nassau, Bahamas		

- Primary business activity: law office.

National Bank of Canada (International)

PO.Box N-3015	809-322-4024	dial
Charlotte House, Charlotte Street	809-323-8088	fax
Nassau, Bahamas		

- Primary business activity: banking services.

Overseas Company Registration Agents

UCBM Ltd.

Ms. Rachel Miller	809-356-2903	dial
Company Formation Agent	809-326-8434	fax

43 Elizabeth Avenue, PO.Box N-8680, Nassau, Bahamas

- Primary business activity: company and trust formation services.
- Corporate services such as registered agent services.
- Company formation services are offered. Minimum formation fee US$500 plus US$100 license fee. Minimum annual fee US$100.

Overseas Union Bank & Trust

PO.Box N-8184	809-322-2476	dial

Nassau, Bahamas

- Primary business activity: banking services.

Paribas Suisse (Bahamas) Ltd.

PO.Box N-8323	809-393-3460	dial
East Bay Street	809-393-8424	fax

Nassau, Bahamas

- Primary business activity: banking services.

People's Penny Savings Bank Ltd.

PO.Box N-1481	809-322-4140	dial

Nassau, Bahamas

- Primary business activity: banking services.

Pictet Bank & Trust Ltd.

PO.Box N-4837	809-322-3938	dial
Charlotte House, Charlotte Street	809-323-7988	fax

Nassau, Bahamas

- Primary business activity: banking services.

Royal Bank of Canada

Mrs. B.M. Clarke	809-322-8700	dial
D.D.A. Supervisor	809-322-6381	fax

323 Bay Street, PO.Box N-7537, Nassau, Bahamas

- Primary business activity: bank and trust services.
- Private banking services and/or savings accounts.
- Consumer loans and credit facilities.
- Safekeeping and custodian services.

Royal Bank of Canada Trust Company (Bahamas) Ltd.

Royal Bank House	809-322-1365	dial

101 East Hill Street, Nassau, Bahamas

- Primary business activity: bank and trust services.
- Private banking services and/or savings accounts.
- Consumer loans and credit facilities.
- Safekeeping and custodian services.
- Portfolio management of securities and mutual funds.
- Company formation services are offered.
- Trust formation services are offered.

Royal Bank of Scotland (Nassau) Limited

PO.Box N-3045	809-322-4643	dial
50 Shirley Street	809-326-7559	fax

Nassau, Bahamas

- Primary business activity: banking services.

Swiss Bank Corporation (Overseas) Ltd.

Mr. Philip J. White	809-322-7570	dial
Executive Director & President	809-323-8953	fax
PO.Box N-7757, Claughton House	20 181	telex

Corner Shirley and Charlotte Streets
Nassau, Bahamas

- Primary business activity: banking services.

Toothe, Unwala & Leonard

PO.Box N-9360	809-328-7404	dial

Nassau, Bahamas

- Primary business activity: law office.

Transcontinental Management Services

PO.Box N-4826	809-322-8549	dial
Nassau, Bahamas	809-322-3919	fax

- Primary business activity: company and trust formation services.
- Offers private credit card backed by deposit.
- Company formation services are offered.
- Trust formation services are offered.
- Captive insurance company formation services are offered.

Westpac Bank and Trust (Bahamas) Ltd.

Mr. Peter Yeomanson	809-328-8064	dial
General Manager	809-326-0067	fax
PO.Box N-8332	20621 WBTL BS	telex

Charlotte House, Suite 301, Nassau, Bahamas

- Primary business activity: bank and trust services.

BARBADOS

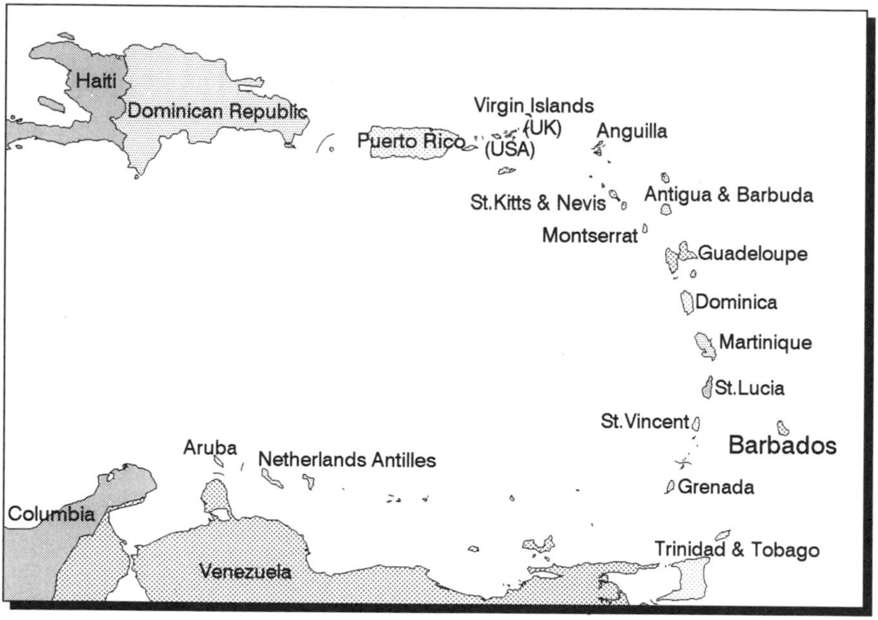

In the Caribbean (Windward Islands). A 166 square mile island that is the most easterly of the Caribbean Islands, and the most easterly part of the West Indies. Population is approximately 260,000. Main language is English and Bajan Creole. Average temperature is between 20°C and 31°C.

The first inhabitants of the island were Arawak and Carib Indians. Portuguese sailors stopped in 1536 on the way to Brazil, calling the island Los Barbados, after the ficus trees whose aerial roots look like beards. The English arrived in 1625, found the island uninhabited and claimed it for King James I of England. Settlers arrived in 1627 at the site which is now known as Holetown. During the next two decades the population grew dramatically due to political unrest in England between

Oliver Cromwell and Charles I, causing the arrival of many English subjects. The introduction of sugar cane as the island's main crop brought slaves from Africa. English law and tradition took hold so fast that soon the island was called "Little England." The first Parliament was held in 1639 making it the third oldest in the Commonwealth, after the British House of Commons and the Bermuda House of Assembly. Barbados moved toward the formation of an independent society with the freeing of slaves on 1834, enfranchisement of women in 1944, and the universal adult suffrage in 1951. With the emergence of a two-party system and a cabinet government during the 1950's, Barbados was well prepared for independence which was granted on November 30, 1966.

Does Barbados have a secrecy law?

NO. Although Barbados does not have a secrecy law, confidentiality can be maintained through the use of an IBC, which is exempted from filing financial statements in the public registry.

Is there any situation where bank secrecy can be lifted?

YES. As Barbados does not have a secrecy law, therefore bank accounts are open to government inspection.

Can foreign tax authorities obtain information on Barbados bank accounts?

YES. Barbados has signed exchange of information agreements with several countries. Banking information is not subject to any secrecy laws.

Is Barbados an independent country?

YES. Barbados gained its independence in November, 1966. Barbados is now a self-governing state within the British Commonwealth.

Is the legal system based on English Common Law?

YES. The legal system is based on the Westminster parliamentary system of government. Judicial, political, and administrative institutions are closely modeled on the British system.

Is there an income tax in Barbados?

YES. Maximum rate of 2.5% of net income for International Business Companies, Investment Companies, and Offshore Banks.

Full tax exemption from all dividends, royalties, interest, fees and management fees paid to a non-resident person or to another IBC. Full tax exemption for Foreign Sales Corporations doing business outside of Barbados and for Captive Insurance Companies.

Shipping Corporations receive a 10-year tax holiday.

No withholding taxes on dividends, interest and management fees and royalties paid to non-residents.

Are there any other taxes in Barbados?

NO. There is no capital gains tax in Barbados. Exempt Insurance Companies pay no capital gains tax.

There are no estate taxes or death duties payable in Barbados.

Are there any exchange controls in Barbados?

NO. There are currently no exchange controls in Barbados. The official currency is the Barbados Dollar.

Is there a tax treaty between the U.S. and Barbados?

YES. There is a double-taxation agreement between the U.S. and Barbados. There was also a double-taxation agreement signed in

1985. Barbados maintains double-taxation agreements with Denmark, Norway, Switzerland, and the United Kingdom.

Is there a tax treaty between Canada and Barbados?

YES. There is a double-taxation agreement between Canada and Barbados.

Does Barbados allow the formation of Limited Companies?

YES. Legislation to provide for the creation of International Business Companies was enacted in 1965, but saw little activity until 1986. In March 1992 Barbados enacted a new International Business Companies Act and brought into force supporting regulations.

New features of the International Business Companies Act include:

- Maintenance of confidentiality by the exemption from filing of financial statements in the public registry.
- Option of ministerial guarantee that the benefits and exemptions granted will apply for 15 years from the IBC becoming a licensee.
- Simplification of the rules so that an IBC will be deemed to be resident in Barbados if it is incorporated or registered in Barbados.
- Option to offset foreign taxes against taxes due, provided that the net tax payable in Barbados is not less than 1% of taxable profits.
- Ability to negotiate special tax rates, provided that the net tax payable in Barbados is not less than 1% of taxable profits.
- Facility for companies engaged in manufacturing products for export outside of the Caribbean, to be licensed as IBCs.

- Complete exemption from taxation for IBCs owned by a resident Trust managed by an offshore bank, provided that the IBC is engaged only in the holding or dealing in securities.

Incorporation requires the filing of the following with the Registrar of Companies:

- Articles of incorporation in duplicate.
- Declaration that no incorporator is less than 18 years of age or of unsound mind or bankrupt.
- A notice of directors.
- A notice of registered office and place of business.

The new legislation allows IBCs the option to carry on the business of international manufacturing under the IBC regime for the life of the company or under the Fiscal Incentives regime which offers tax holidays for a specific period. There are no restrictions on foreign ownership of business enterprises. Barbados offers tax holidays, concessions, and other incentives for manufacturing and information service companies.

Foreign Sales Corporation (FSC) - A Foreign Sales Corporation is a corporation specifically developed to assist U.S. exporters. FSC legislation emerged as part of the 1984 Tax Reform Act. In order to qualify for the partial U.S. tax exemption, the FSC is required to maintain a foreign presence and to earn export income outside of U.S. customs territories. In response to the 1984 Tax Reform Act, the Barbados Parliament passed the Barbados Foreign Sales Corporation Act of 1984. The Act contains the following restrictions:

- No person may engage in foreign trade transactions from within Barbados without license under the Act.

- No license may be issued other than to a company that is incorporated under the Companies Act, whose principal object and activity is designated as a foreign sales corporation under the laws of the US, including the Commonwealth of Puerto Rico.

Does Barbados allow the formation of International Trusts?

YES. The Barbados Offshore Bank Act allows for the establishment of common Trust funds by Barbados offshore banks, provided the instrument creating the Trust gives express permission for investment of the assets it holds in Trust. The Act provides further protection to Beneficiaries by requiring the licensee company to keep all assets held in Trust separated from its other assets.

Barbados International Business Companies legislation takes into special account the ability to form an IBC, all of whose shares are part of a common Trust fund within the terms of the Offshore Bank Act. This special provision allows for the formation of tax free Trusts which meet the shareholder and location of business activity restrictions of the International Business Companies Act.

Since the Domestic Trustee Act limits Trustees' investing powers to Barbados related investments (whether in Barbados or elsewhere), then the ability to merge the Offshore Banking Act and the International Business Companies Act facilitates the easier establishment of Trusts.

Barbados observes all of the protections afforded under the solicitor client privilege relationships, as they apply to a particular Trust. While there may be disclosure requirements under the Offshore Banking Act, confidentiality of Trustees names and interests can be safely and legally protected by involving the use of an IBC.

The available High Court powers of examination only come into effect in very exceptional circumstances where the licensee company is insolvent, and where a very well supported application is made to the Court. Disclosure is very limited because of the court appointment of an examiner who is also restricted by very rigid disclosure requirements. These exceptional powers have never been used against any active licensee banking institutions operating as Barbados offshore banks.

Trusts set up under the Barbados Offshore Bank Act attract no taxation to the Trust or Beneficiaries. No tax is payable by an IBC which is owned as part of the Trust's assets, however the IBC must be engaged only in the holding or dealing in securities.

Does Barbados allow the formation of Captive Insurance Companies?

YES. International insurance companies are governed by the Exempt Insurance Act of 1983. The advantages of establishing a captive insurance company in Barbados include:

- Dividends paid to a Canadian company out of income earned from a captive insurance business in Barbados are considered exempt earnings and are not subject to Canadian taxes, providing the risks insured are non-Canadian or third party risks.
- Exemption from all corporate taxes on income or capital gains or any tax on the transfer of assets or securities to any person.
- Exemption from withholding tax on any dividends, interest or other returns to shareholders.
- Business convention expenses incurred by U.S. corporations and organizations are deductible in the U.S. against U.S. taxes.
- Simple statutory filing requirements.

- Minimum capitalization of US$125,000. Annual license fee of US$2,500.
- 35% of earnings tax free by resident expatriate employees.
- Exemption from exchange control regulations.

Does Barbados allow the formation of Banking Companies?

YES. International banking companies are governed by the Offshore Banking Act of 1979.

Financial institutions and contacts:

Bank of Nova Scotia
Miss E.M. Williams 809-431-3000 dial
Customer Service Supervisor
PO.Box 202, Bridgetown, Barbados, West Indies

- Primary business activity: banking services.
- Consumer loans and credit facilities.
- Safekeeping and custodian services.

Barbados International Bank & Trust Co.
Bridgetown, Barbados, West Indies

- Primary business activity: banking services.

Barbados Investment & Development Corp.
Mr. Errol L. Humphrey 809-427-5350 dial
Director, International Business 809-426-7802 fax
Pelican House
Princess Alice Highway
Bridgetown, Barbados, West Indies

- Primary business activity: government services.

Barbados National Bank

Mrs. A.E. Als	809-431-5800	dial
Senior Operations Officer	809-426-5037	fax
No.1 Broad Street	2271 WB	telex

PO.Box 1009, Bridgetown, Barbados, West Indies

- Primary business activity: banking services.
- Private banking services and/or savings accounts.
- Consumer loans and credit facilities.

Barbados Savings Bank

Bridgetown, Barbados, West Indies

- Primary business activity: banking services.

Barbados Supervisor of Insurance

Ministry of Finance & Economic Affairs	809-426-3815	dial
Treasury Building, 6th floor	809-436-2699	fax

Bridgetown, Barbados, West Indies

- Primary business activity: government services.
- Specific product: booklet: "Barbados - A Guide For Investors in the Exempt Insurance Industry."

Barclays Bank PLC Offshore Banking Unit

Mrs. M.Y. Odle	809-431-5151	dial
Manager's Assistant	809-429-4785	fax

PO.Box 301, Broad Street, Bridgetown, Barbados, West Indies

- Primary business activity: banking services.
- Private banking services and/or savings accounts.
- Consumer loans and credit facilities.
- Safekeeping and custodian services.
- Portfolio management of securities and mutual funds.

Central Bank of Barbados

Legal Counsel	809-436-6870	dial
Bridgetown, Barbados, West Indies	809-427-9559	fax

- Primary business activity: government services.

Chancery Chambers
Dr. Trevor A. Carmichael
Attorney at Law
Barbados, West Indies

- Primary business activity: law office.

CIBC (Canadian Imperial Bank Commerce)
Bridgetown, Barbados, West Indies

- Primary business activity: banking services.

Price Waterhouse

Collymore Rock	809-436-7000	dial
PO.Box 634C, Bridgetown	809-436-7057	fax
St.Michael, Barbados, West Indies	2456	telex

- Primary business activity: accounting services.
- Specific product: booklet: "Doing Business in Barbados."

Ross Williams Management Services Ltd.

Mr. Clyde Williams	809-424-3461	dial

PO.Box 839E, St.Michael, Bridgetown, Barbados, West Indies

- Primary business activity: company and trust formation services.

Rothscarmon Corporation

Newstead Chambers	809-426-3406	dial
Pinfold Street	809-436-2947	fax

Bridgetown, Barbados, West Indies

- Primary business activity: company and trust formation services.

Royal Bank of Canada

Mrs. A.P. King	809-426-5200	dial
Assistant Manager - Deposits	809-427-8393	fax
PO.Box 68	2242 WB	telex

Bridgetown, Barbados, West Indies

- Primary business activity: banking services.
- Private banking services and/or savings accounts.
- Consumer loans and credit facilities.
- Safekeeping and custodian services.

Royal Bank of Canada Financial Corporation

Miss G.Y. Corbin	809-431-6580	dial
Securities & Trust Officer	809-426-4139	fax
Royal Bank House	2242 WB	telex

PO.Box 48B, Garrison, St.Michael, Barbados, West Indies

- Primary business activity: banking services.
- Private banking services and/or savings accounts.
- Consumer loans and credit facilities.
- Executor and administrator of wills and estates.
- Safekeeping and custodian services.
- Portfolio management of securities and mutual funds.
- Company formation services are offered.
- Trust formation services are offered.

BELIZE

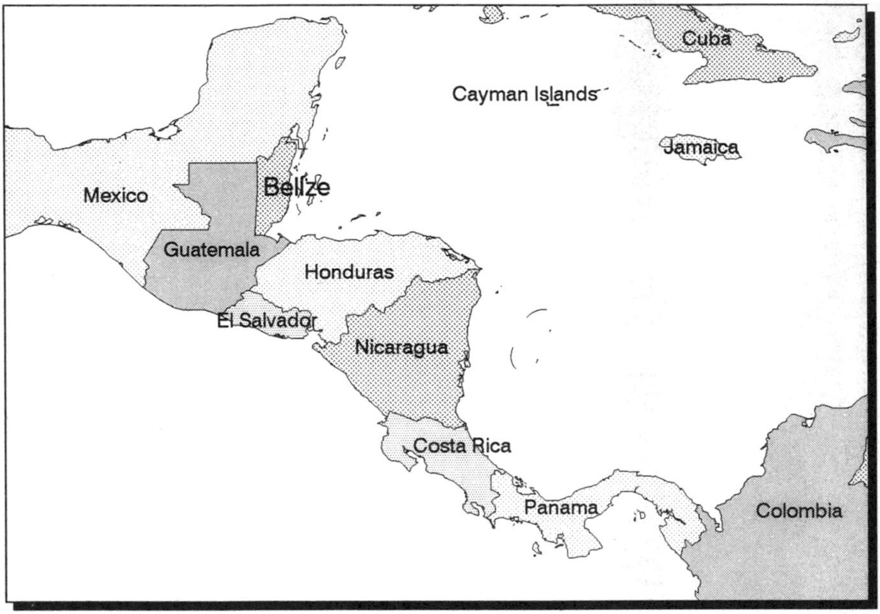

In Central America. On the east coast of Central America bordering Mexico to the north and Guatemala to the west and south. Belize is 174 miles long and 68 miles wide, covering an area of 8,865 square miles. Population is approximately 240,000 with approximately 60,000 living in Belize City, the capital. Main language is English and Spanish. Climate is sub-tropical.

Formerly known as the British Honduras, Belize became a British Crown Colony in 1862. The name was changed from British Honduras to Belize in 1973. Belize became an independent self ruling republic on September 21, 1981. A British military garrison remains, however, to protect against Guatemala which has claimed Belize.

You must live in Belize one year to be granted permanent residency. Upon entering Belize, apply for residency, and then renew your tourist visa every 30 or 90 days until residency is granted.

Does Belize have a secrecy law?

YES. Belize's secrecy laws prohibit the unauthorized disclosure of information, providing for criminal penalties of up to US$50,000 and a prison term of up to one year for any disclosure concerning the business affairs of a client. A bank would receive the maximum penalty.

Is there any situation where bank secrecy can be lifted?

YES. Although Belize has imposed strict bank secrecy laws, the law does not apply to activities that are considered crimes in Belize, such as illegal drug activities, theft, or fraud.

Can foreign tax authorities obtain information on Belize bank accounts?

NO. Although the secrecy laws protect against unauthorized disclosure to foreign tax authorities, confidential information has been released in the past through an exchange of information agreement between the U.S. and Belize. The new Trust Act, enacted in May 1992, has further enhanced secrecy, hopefully preventing any further compromising of bank secrecy.

Is Belize an independent country?

YES. Formerly under British rule as the British Honduras, the republic of Belize became an independent country with its own constitution in 1981. Government is a parliamentary democracy based on the Westminster model. The cabinet, under the leadership of the Prime Minister, directs the policy of the government which consists of the Prime Minister and ministers chosen by him from an elected house of representatives. Belize is a member of the British Commonwealth and the United Nations.

Is the legal system based on English Common Law?

YES. The legal system is based on the Westminster model and is supplemented by local statutes. The court system is also similar to that in England. Contract and commercial law is based on the English model.

Is there an income tax in Belize?

NO. Both a Belize Trust and an IBC are exempt from any form of income tax in the country if they do not produce income in Belize. IBC's are exempt from capital gains tax, inheritance tax, and stamp duties.

For residents of Belize, pension and social security income received in Belize is tax free. Other income from outside Belize is taxed at 5% on the first Bz$1,000, graduated up to 50% on income over Bz$60,000.

Are there any other taxes in Belize?

NO. There is no capital gains taxes, gift taxes, or estate taxes in Belize for an IBC or Trust.

Are there any exchange controls in Belize?

NO. There are currently no exchange controls in Belize. The official currency is the Belize dollar which is tied to the U.S. dollar with a fixed exchange rate of Bz$2.00 = US$1.00.

Is there a tax treaty between the U.S. and Belize?

NO. There is no double-taxation agreement between the U.S. and Belize, although there is an exchange of information agreement in certain tax cases.

Is there a tax treaty between Canada and Belize?

NO. There is no double-taxation agreement between Canada and Belize.

Does Belize allow the formation of Limited Companies?

YES. The International Business Companies Act 1990, based on the British Virgin Islands Act, created a special class of company called an IBC. The law was enacted to permit asset protection and tax minimization at competitive rates. Some advantages of Belize IBCs are as follows:

- Total exemption from all forms of local taxation including stamp duty.
- Only one shareholder (who could be corporate) is required.
- An IBC may have bearer shares or registered shares.
- The person creating the corporation can remain secret by appointing nominee shareholders and directors.
- IBCs require only one director. Directors can be corporate and need not be resident in the country.
- Meetings of shareholders and directors can be held in any country, at any time and they may attend meetings by proxy.
- No accounts or information pertaining to the identity of shareholders or directors need be filed on public record. An IBC's Register of Shareholders is available for inspection only by shareholders or by order of the Belize Courts at the request of a shareholder.
- Limited filing requirements, mainly certificate of incorporation, memorandum and articles of association, registered office and name and address of registered agent.

- The process of incorporation is simple, requiring the filing of a memorandum and articles of association, and the fee paid to the relevant registrar.
- The annual filing fee may be as low as US$100.

You are restricted from forming an IBC only under two conditions: if that IBC would be doing business with residents of Belize or if it would own real estate in the country. Company names must end with the following words or their abbreviations: Limited, Corporation, Incorporated, Société Anonyme, or Sociedad Anonima.

Public Investment Company - Belize also offers a Public Investment Company (PIC) that grants additional benefits, such as the right to manage funds belonging to Belize residents. A PIC is guaranteed exemption from all forms of taxes and duties for up to 30 years. Dividends paid to shareholders are not subject to withholding tax. PIC shares must be listed on an approved international stock exchange.

Does Belize allow the formation of International Trusts?

YES. The Belize Trusts Act of 1992 was enacted in May 1992 to offer innovative programs in the areas of Trusts and taxation. The new Belize trust and incorporation legislation is perhaps the cleanest and most user-friendly in the world. The Belize Trusts Act allows you to achieve a high level of asset protection, protecting from both Belize taxation and your local taxation. The Trust Act avoids any restrictions placed on what the Trustee can do with the money. Belize Trusts offer the following advantages:

- The maximum life for a Belize Trust is 120 years.
- Trusts of a finite duration can convert to charitable Trusts of indefinite duration.

- Trust can be registered, which may appeal to residents of civil law countries.

The cost of registering a Trust is US$100 and the process takes one to two weeks.

Does Belize allow the formation of Captive Insurance Companies?

YES. A Belize IBC may apply for an insurance license.

Does Belize allow the formation of Banking Companies?

YES. A Belize IBC may apply for a banking license.

Financial institutions and contacts:

Belize Bank (Corporate Services)

Mr. Philip Osborne	501-2-72390	dial
Corporate Services Division	501-2-77018	fax
60 Market Square	158 BZE BANK BZ	telex

PO.Box 364, Belize City, Belize

- Primary business activity: banking services.
- Private banking services and/or savings accounts.
- Consumer loans and credit facilities.
- Company formation services are offered. Minimum formation fee US$700 plus US$300 register agent fee. Minimum annual fee US$400.
- Trust formation services are offered.

Belize Trust Company Limited

Mrs. Monica Musa	501-2-72660	dial
Assistant Manager	501-2-70983	fax

60 Market Square, PO.Box 1764, Belize City, Belize

- Primary business activity: bank and trust services.

Glenn D. Godfrey Barrister-at-Law

Mr. Glenn Godfrey	501-2-72457	dial
Barrister-at-Law	501-2-78909	fax

PO.Box 1074, 2A King St., Belize City, Belize

- Primary business activity: law office.

Government of Belize

Immigration and Nationality Service	501-8-22423	dial
Belmopan, Belize	501-8-22662	fax

- Primary business activity: government services.

Pannell Kerr Forster

Regent House, 35 Regent Street, PO.Box 280, Belize City, Belize

- Primary business activity: accounting services.

BERMUDA

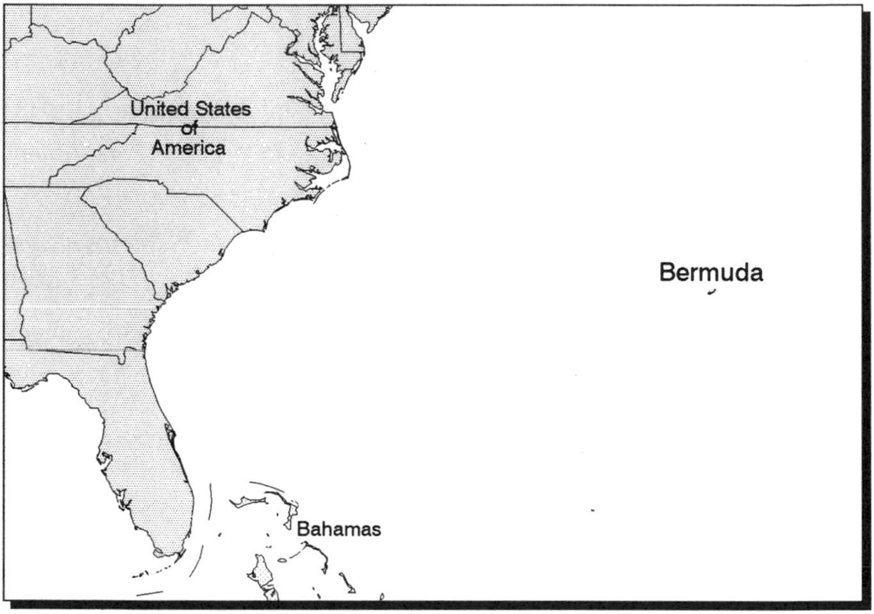

In the Western Atlantic Ocean, 570 miles off the North Carolina coast, and 774 miles southeast of New York. Over 150 small islands, the seven largest connected by bridges and causeways. Population is approximately 60,000. Main language is English. The climate is semi-tropical and frost free, and humid due to the warming effect of the Gulf Stream. Average temperatures are 89°F in summer and 47°F in winter.

In the 16th Century Spaniard Juan de Bermudez discovered the islands. He visited there in 1503 but failed to claim them for his country. It wasn't until July 28, 1609 that British Admiral Sir George Somers, leading a fleet on its way to the struggling colony of Virginia with his flag ship "Sea Venture," was shipwrecked on Bermuda's treacherous reefs. It was a mishap which led to the British colonization in 1612 what is officially known today as the Bermudas, or Somers Island. Bermuda has remained under the flag of Great Britain, and Bermudans are proud of the fact that their country is the oldest British colony with a House of Assembly elected by the people.

Bermuda has now signed a double-taxation agreement with the United States that includes exchange of information. The Florida branch of the Bank of Nova Scotia was hit with a fine of US$25,000 per day until it released information on clients of its Bermuda branch. Switzerland's Banca dela Svizzera Italiana was fined US$50,000 per day until it revealed information about Kuwaiti investors for whom it had bought stock (because the clients volunteered the information, the Swiss bank did not have to disclose any information).

Does Bermuda have a secrecy law?

NO. There are no bank secrecy laws in Bermuda, although the Bermudan government will not allow disclosure of confidential bank information in cases strictly involving tax evasion.

Is there any situation where bank secrecy can be lifted?

YES. A tax treaty ratified in July 1986 provides U.S. law enforcement agencies with financial information concerning U.S. civil and criminal tax cases.

Can foreign tax authorities obtain information on Bermudan bank accounts?

YES. See above.

Is Bermuda an independent country?

NO. Since 1684 Governors of Bermuda, acting on behalf of Her Majesty, have been appointed by the Crown. The Bermuda Constitution Order, effective June 8, 1968, provides for internal self-government. The UK, through the Governor, is responsible for external affairs, defense, internal security, and the police.

Is the legal system based on English Common Law?

YES. As the oldest British colony with a House of Assembly elected by the people, the legal system is based on English Acts of general application which were in force on July 11, 1612. These Acts have been subject to Amendments since 1612 that have repealed, modified, and amended those laws. The judicial system incorporates the Court of Appeals, Supreme Court, Magistrate's Court, and Special Court.

Is there an income tax in Bermuda?

NO. There are no income taxes, profit taxes, withholding taxes or capital gains taxes in Bermuda. Under the Exempted Tax Protection Act, Exempted Companies can obtain a guarantee of exemption from any taxes that may be imposed in the future, until March 29, 2016. It is expected that as this date approaches, the guarantee will be further extended. No income tax, gift tax, business, property, capital gains, sales, estate, or any other kind of tax, except for certain annual fees.

The government receives revenue from customs duties, an employment tax of 7%, a hotel occupancy tax of 6%, an annual land tax on properties ranging from 1.5% to 22.5% of assessed ARV (Annual Rental Value), and a $15 departure tax when departing from Bermuda. There is a tax on payrolls and a charge for estates probated in Bermuda.

Are there any other taxes in Bermuda?

YES. There is a charge for estates probated in Bermuda There are no capital gains taxes or gift taxes in Bermuda.

Are there any exchange controls in Bermuda?

YES. An exchange control is exercised over Bermuda's citizens, subject to the controls imposed by the Exchange Control Act, 1972. Legislation provides for the formation of companies which are exempted from the 60% Bermudan ownership requirement on condition that they carry on business outside Bermuda. Since February 6, 1970, the official currency has been the Bermuda dollar. The Bermuda Dollar is at par with the U.S. dollar.

Is there a tax treaty between the U.S. and Bermuda?

YES. A tax treaty ratified in July 1986 provides U.S. law enforcement agencies with financial information concerning U.S. civil and criminal tax cases.

Is there a tax treaty between Canada and Bermuda?

NO. There is no tax treaty between Canada and Bermuda.

Does Bermuda allow the formation of Limited Companies?

YES. Bermuda companies are governed by the Companies Act, 1981, and the Companies Amendment Act, 1992, stating that:

- A minimum of two directors are required who need not be shareholders.
- The issue of bearer shares is prohibited.
- A public offering requires a prospectus that complies with the terms of the Act.

Two types of companies can be incorporated in Bermuda, Local Companies and Exempted Companies.

Local Companies - Local Companies may carry on commercial activity within Bermuda, and must have at least 60% of the voting shares owned by Bermudans.

Exempted Companies - Exempted Companies are exempt from statutes applying to local companies, including exchange controls, and can trade in any currency other than Bermuda dollars. No Exempted Company can hold titles to Bermuda land, and are prohibited from trading within Bermuda. The Companies Act, 1981 and Companies Amendment Act, 1992 require that:

- Exempted Companies must have a registered office in Bermuda where corporate records (minute book, corporate seal, share certificate book, share register, and incorporation documents) are maintained.
- A minimum of one shareholder is required.
- A minimum of two directors resident in Bermuda are required. Directors need not be shareholders.
- An Exempted Company must elect a president and vice-president from among its directors.
- A secretary must be appointed who may be a director.

Advantages of a Bermuda Exempted Company include:

- A nominee or nominee company may hold shares and provide directors.
- No financial statements of a private company are open to public inspection, and there is no reporting to any authority.
- Exempted companies can obtain a guarantee of exemption from any taxes that may be imposed in the future, until March 29, 2016.
- Annual meetings need not be held in Bermuda.
- Exempted Companies may provide financial assistance for their employees to buy shares.

Does Bermuda allow the formation of International Trusts?

YES. Bermuda Trusts are governed by the Trustee Act 1975, the Trust (Special Provisions) Act 1989 and the Perpetuities and

Accumulations Act 1989, which incorporate most of the provisions of the English Trustee Act 1925.

Bermuda's modern Trust law allows for no limit on the income accumulation within the 100 year perpetuity period. Bermuda Trust law allows "Purpose Trusts" permitting the establishment of Trusts for the benefit of business, scientific, or charitable purposes. Advantages include:

- The Trust may be governed by the laws of any jurisdiction.
- The governing laws of the Trust may be changed to the laws of another jurisdiction at any time.
- No Bermuda Trust may be set aside if the laws of a foreign jurisdiction do not recognize the concept of a Trust. Forced heirship provisions are ignored.
- Accumulation of income is permitted throughout the Trust period.
- Bermuda allows the formation of Discretionary Trusts, Fixed Trusts, and combinations thereof.
- A Trust may be revocable or irrevocable.
- There are no filing requirements for Trusts.

The Stamp Duties Amendment Act 1993 abolished the maximum stamp duty (US$250 plus 0.1% of assets up to US$4,000) if the Trust is administered by a Bermudan Trustee.

Does Bermuda allow the formation of Captive Insurance Companies?

YES. Under the Insurance Act, 1978, insurance companies must have a minimum paid-up capital of US$120,000 for general business, US$250,000 for long-term business, or US$370,000 for both general and long-term business. Applications for registration are reviewed in detail by the Bermuda Monetary Authority, the Registrar of Companies and the Insurers Admissions Committee.

Insurance companies are required to prepare annual audited financial statements to be filed with the Registrar of Companies consisting of:

- An approved auditor's report.
- A certificate of solvency.
- Declaration of statutory ratios.

Long-term business includes the following additional requirements:

- Insurers must appoint an approved actuary.
- An actuarial certificate is required to be filed every year.
- Long-term business must be segregated with appropriate accounting.

The Minister of Finance has the power to investigate the affairs of an insurer. If there is a risk of insolvency, he has the power to restrict the operations of the insurer by restricting new business, restricting investments to specific classes, and requiring liquidation of certain investments.

Does Bermuda allow the formation of Banking Companies?

YES. Because the definition of "banking business" in Bermuda is narrow, it is possible to carry on many banking activities from Bermuda which in many other jurisdictions would require a banking license.

Financial institutions and contacts:

Argonaut Ltd.

Argus Insurance Building, Wesley Street PO.Box 200001, Hamilton, Bermuda

- Primary business activity: law office.

Arthur Morris & Company

Mr. Arthur Morris	809-292-7478	dial
Chartered Accountant	809-295-4164	fax

Century House, Richmond Road, PO.Box HM 1806
Hamilton, Bermuda HM HX

- Primary business activity: accounting services.
- Company formation services are offered.
- Trust formation services are offered.
- Specific product: Booklet "Doing Business in Bermuda."

Bank of Bermuda Limited

Mr. Philippe Dutranoit	809-295-4000	dial
Investment Division	809-295-7093	fax
6 Front Street	BA 3212	telex

PO.Box HM 1020, Hamilton, Bermuda HM DX

- Primary business activity: banking services.
- Private banking services and/or savings accounts.
- Safekeeping and custodian services.
- Portfolio management of securities and mutual funds.
- Company formation services are offered.
- Trust formation services are offered.

Bank of Butterfield Executor & Trustee Co. Ltd.

Mr. John P. Faiella	809-299-3805	dial
Manager - Trust	809-292-1258	fax
14 Bermudiana Road	3320 BETCO BA	telex
Pembroke, Bermuda		

- Primary business activity: bank and trust services.
- Private banking services and/or savings accounts.
- Corporate services such as registered agent services.
- Safekeeping and custodian services.
- Portfolio management of securities and mutual funds. Minimum annual fee 0.5% of assets or US$5,000.
- Company formation services are offered. Minimum formation fee US$1,500. Minimum annual fee US$2,250.
- Trust formation services are offered. Minimum formation fee US$1,500. Minimum annual fee US$2,250.

Bank of N.T. Butterfield & Son Ltd.

Mr. Charles A. Gunn	809-295-1111	dial
International & Corporate Banking	809-292-4365	fax
PO.Box HM 195	321 FIELD BA	telex
65 Front Street, Hamilton, Bermuda HM AX		

- Primary business activity: bank and trust services.
- Primary business activity: banking services.
- Private banking services and/or savings accounts.
- Safekeeping and custodian services.
- Portfolio management of securities and mutual funds.
- Company formation services are offered.
- Trust formation services are offered.

Banque SCS Alliance Ltd.

3rd Floor, Cedarpark Centre	809-296-0607	dial
48 Cedar Avenue	809-296-0608	fax
Hamilton, Bermuda HM 11		

- Primary business activity: bank and trust services.
- Safekeeping and custodian services.
- Portfolio management of securities and mutual funds.
- Company formation services are offered.
- Trust formation services are offered.

Bermuda Chamber of Commerce

PO.Box HM 655 — 809-295-4201 dial
Hamilton, Bermuda HM CX

- Primary business activity: government services.

Bermuda Commercial Bank Limited

Ms. Dominique Smith — 809-295-5678 dial
Manager, Corporate Treasury — 809-295-8091 fax
44 Church Street, PO.Box HM 1748, Hamilton, Bermuda HM GX

- Primary business activity: banking services.
- Portfolio management of securities and mutual funds. Minimum deposit US$50,000.

Bermuda Ministry of Finance

Government Administration Building
30 Parliament Street, Hamilton, Bermuda HM 12

- Primary business activity: government services.

International Trust Co. of Bermuda Ltd.

Barclays International Building
PO.Box 1255, Hamilton, Bermuda 5

- Primary business activity: banking services.

Midland Walwyn (Bermuda) Ltd.

Mr. William D. Dickson — 809-295-4791 dial
General Manager — 809-295-2718 fax
PO.Box HM951, Hemisphere House
9 Church Street, Hamilton, Bermuda HM DX

- Primary business activity: fund or portfolio manager.
- Safekeeping and custodian services.
- Portfolio management of securities and mutual funds.

Richards, Francis & Francis - Barristers and Attorneys

Mr. Arnold A. Francis	809-295-0790	dial
Barrister and Attorney	809-292-1394	fax
Cedarpark Centre	3681 RICAS BA	telex

48 Cedar Avenue, Hamilton, Bermuda HM 11

- Primary business activity: law office.
- Corporate services such as registered agent services.
- Executor and administrator of wills and estates.
- Company formation services are offered. Minimum formation fee US$1,770 plus US$1,600 license fee. Minimum annual fee US$3,100.
- Trust formation services are offered. Minimum formation fee US$900. Minimum annual fee US$1,250.
- Captive insurance company formation. Minimum formation fee US$2,895 plus US$3,600 license fee. Minimum annual fee US$5,000.

Riggs Valmet (Bermuda) Ltd.

PO.Box HM 2006	809-292-3102	dial
19 Parliament Street	809-292-5560	fax

Hamilton, Bermuda HM GX

- Primary business activity: company and trust formation services.

TISH VIRGIN ISLANDS

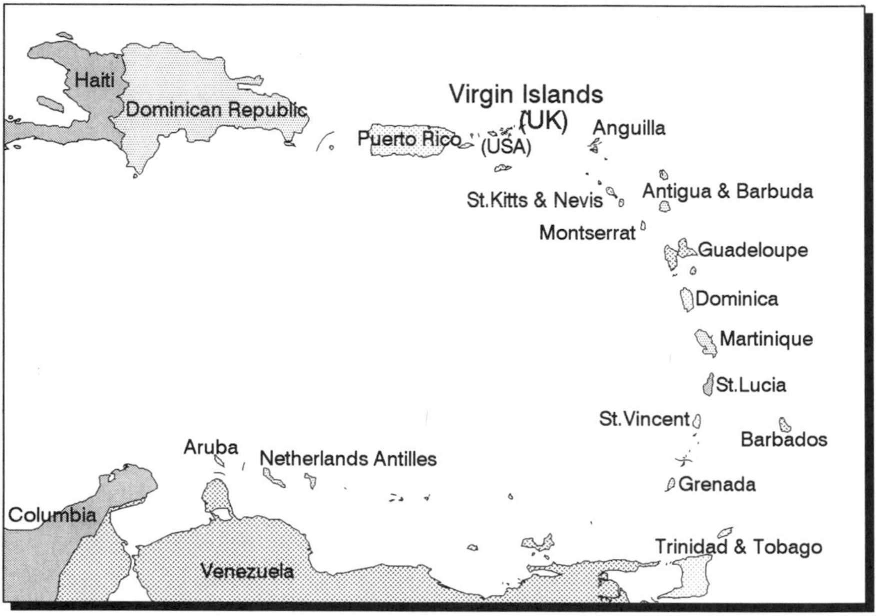

In the Caribbean. An archipelago of over 60 islands, cays and rocks spread over 58 square miles. The British Virgin Islands are 90 miles east of Puerto Rico, neighboring the U.S.Virgin Islands. Population is approximately 12,000. Main language is English.

On November 16, 1493, while en route to Puerto Rico, Christopher Columbus discovered the islands. He anchored and spent the night south-east of the island that became known as Virgin Gorda. He named the entire group of islands "Las Once Mil Virgines," after St.Ursula and her legendary 11,000 martyred companions. At that time the indigenous population consisted mainly of Carib Indians. In 1672 Britain claimed Tortola, while Denmark claimed St.Thomas and St.John in that same year. The Danish islands were then sold to the U.S. for $25 million in

1917. The British Virgin Islands became a self-governing colony with its own constitution in 1967.

Does the British Virgin Islands have a secrecy law?

YES. The British Virgin Islands' secrecy laws prohibit the unauthorized disclosure of information pertaining to a clients affairs to a third party.

Is there any situation where bank secrecy can be lifted?

YES. Although the British Virgin Island's secrecy law prohibits the unauthorized disclosure of information, the law does not apply to activities that are considered crimes in the British Virgin Islands, such as illegal drug activities, theft, or fraud.

Can foreign tax authorities obtain information on BVI bank accounts?

NO. Because tax evasion is not considered a criminal offense in the British Virgin Islands, confidential bank information can not be released.

Is the British Virgin Islands an independent country?

NO. The British Virgin Islands is a self-governing British Crown colony under the 1967 constitution. The Governor, appointed by the Crown, is responsible for external affairs, defense, and internal security. Other matters are handled by the Executive Council. Elections are normally held every five years.

Is the legal system based on English Common Law?

YES. The legal system was established by the British, and is based on English Common Law. The supreme court is the West Indies Associated States Supreme Court, with High Court of Justice and Court of Appeal branches. Lower courts are the Court of Summary Jurisdiction and the Magistrate's Court.

Is there an income tax in the British Virgin Islands?

NO. There is no income tax in the British Virgin Islands on income earned outside the islands. Personal income derived from the islands is taxed at a maximum rate of 20%. Corporate income derived from the islands is taxed at a flat rate of 15%.

Are there any other taxes in the British Virgin Islands?

NO. There is no capital gains tax, gift tax, death duty, or estate tax in the British Virgin Islands.

Are there any exchange controls in the British Virgin Islands?

NO. There are currently no exchange controls in the British Virgin Islands. The official currency is the U.S. dollar.

Is there a tax treaty between the U.S. and the British Virgin Islands?

NO. The tax treaty with the U.S. was terminated in January 1, 1983 because negotiators could not agree on a suitable arrangement, although an exchange of information agreement is a distinct possibility in the near future. An exchange of information agreement was signed with the U.S. in 1987 allowing bank accounts to be examined if there is evidence of them being used for drug trafficking or money laundering. Double taxation agreements exist with Japan and Switzerland.

Is there a tax treaty between Canada and the British Virgin Islands?

NO. The tax treaty between the UK (extended to cover the British Virgin Islands) and Canada was terminated in 1972, although an exchange of information agreement is a possibility in the near future.

Does the BVI allow the formation of Limited Companies?

YES. There are two types of companies that can be incorporated in the British Virgin Islands - Companies Act Companies and International Business Companies.

Companies Act Company - A Companies Act Company is designed to be operated within the British Virgin Islands, carrying on business with persons in the BVI.

International Business Company (IBC) - IBCs are governed by the International Business Companies Act 1984, enacted August 1, 1994. An IBC provides the following advantages and benefits:

- It is exempt from BVI taxes and stamp duty.
- There are no minimum capitalization requirements.
- Only one shareholder is required.
- The company requires only one director. No residency or nationality requirements for directors exist. Alternate directors are permitted. Directors may be corporate.
- Bearer shares, no par value shares, treasury shares, and different classes of shares are permitted.
- An IBC may purchase and own shares.
- Directors meetings may be held in any jurisdiction.
- There is no requirement to hold an annual general meeting.
- Disclosure of beneficial ownership is not required.
- The IBC laws provide for the transfer of registration of a company to another accommodating jurisdiction.
- In its title an IBC may use the word or an abbreviation of Limited, Incorporated, Corporation, Société Anonyme, or Sociedad Anonima.

- Companies incorporated in foreign jurisdictions may continue under the IBC Ordinance without the need for reciprocal arrangements with the jurisdiction of incorporation.
- Full compensation of officers or agents of an IBC from corporate funds is permitted.
- The directors are empowered to protect the assets of an IBC for the benefit of the IBC, its creditors and its members, and for any person having direct or indirect interests in the IBC by transferring the assets of the IBC in trust to Trustees or another company or legal entity, for the benefit of the IBC, its creditors or members.
- The filing of annual accounts is not required.
- The annual license fee is only US$300.

The only public record consists of the current certificate of incorporation, the Memorandum and Articles and amendments, the name and address of the registered agent, and the record of payments of the annual fees.

There is no public record identifying the shareholders or directors. However, an IBC may elect to maintain a register of directors, a share register and a register of mortgages and charges. Additionally, the International Business Companies (Amendment) Act 1990 created an optional registration facility so that shareholder and director reports can be filed with the Registrar of Companies.

IBCs may be managed and controlled from the British Virgin Islands, although they are prohibited from:

- Trading within the British Virgin Islands.
- Owning land titles in the British Virgin Islands.
- Carrying on banking, trust, insurance, or company management business without a license.

Where a foreign government expropriates or imposes confiscatory taxes upon the shares or other interests in the IBC, the IBC or any person holding shares or other interests therein, may apply to the court for an order that the IBC disregard the action of the foreign government and continue to treat as members or interest holders, those persons or shares or interests were subject to the action by the foreign government.

Does the BVI allow the formation of International Trusts?

YES. The British Virgin Islands is a suitable jurisdiction for the formation of International Trusts.

Does the BVI allow the formation of Captive Insurance Companies?

YES. An IBC may apply for an insurance license, allowing it to carry on insurance business outside the British Virgin Islands.

Does the BVI allow the formation of Banking Companies?

YES. An IBC can carry on banking or trust business if licensed under the Banks and Trust Companies Act 1990.

Financial institutions and contacts:

Ansbacher International Trust Group Ltd.
International Trust Company BVI Limited
Mr. Roger Dawes 809-494-3215 dial
Managing Director 809-494-3216 fax
PO.Box 659, Columbus Centre
Road Town, Tortola, British Virgin Islands

- Primary business activity: bank and trust services.
- Safekeeping and custodian services.
- Portfolio management of securities and mutual funds.
- Company formation services are offered.
- Trust formation services are offered.

Bank of Nova Scotia

Ms. Florence Phillips
Customer Service Dept.
PO.Box 434, Road Town, Tortola, British Virgin Islands

- Primary business activity: banking services.
- Private banking services and/or savings accounts.
- Consumer loans and credit facilities.

Barclaytrust International (BVI) Ltd.

Ms. Kay Reddy — 809-494-6976 dial
PO.Box 70 — 809-494-6320 fax
Road Town — 7928 BARDCO VB telex
Tortola, British Virgin Islands

- Primary business activity: bank and trust services.
- Offers Private Credit Card (Visa/MasterCard/Discover) backed by deposit.
- Private banking services and/or savings accounts.
- Consumer loans and credit facilities.
- Safekeeping and custodian services.
- Portfolio management of securities and mutual funds.
- Company formation services are offered. Minimum formation fee US$1,000 including US$300 license fee. Minimum annual fee US$300.
- Trust formation services are offered.

Integro Trust (BVI) Limited

Mr. Andrew Keuls — 809-494-2616 dial
PO.Box 438 — 809-494-2704 fax
Tropic Isle Building, Wickhams Cay
Road Town, Tortola, British Virgin Islands

- Primary business activity: bank and trust services.
- Portfolio management of securities and mutual funds.
- Company formation services are offered.
- Trust formation services are offered.

KPMG Peat Marwick

Mr. John J. Greenwood 809-494-5800 dial
PO.Box 650 809-494-6565 fax
Tropic Isle Building, Road Town, Tortola, British Virgin Islands

- Primary business activity: accounting services.
- Corporate services such as registered agent services.
- Specific product: "Investment in the Virgin Islands" handbook.

Mossack Fonseca & Co. (BVI) Ltd. Attorneys at Law

Skelton Building, Main Street 809-494-4840 dial
PO.Box 3136 809-494-4841 fax
Road Town, Tortola, British Virgin Islands

- Primary business activity: law office.

Overseas Company Registration Agents

PO.Box 362 800-835-2427 dial
Road Town 800-606-6622 fax
Tortola, British Virgin Islands

- Primary business activity: company and trust formation services.
- Corporate services such as registered agent services.
- Company formation services are offered. Minimum formation fee US$500 plus US$300 license fee. Minimum annual fee US$300.

Trust Co. of the Virgin Islands Ltd.

PO.Box 438, Road Town, Tortola, British Virgin Islands

- Primary business activity: bank and trust services.

CAYMAN ISLANDS

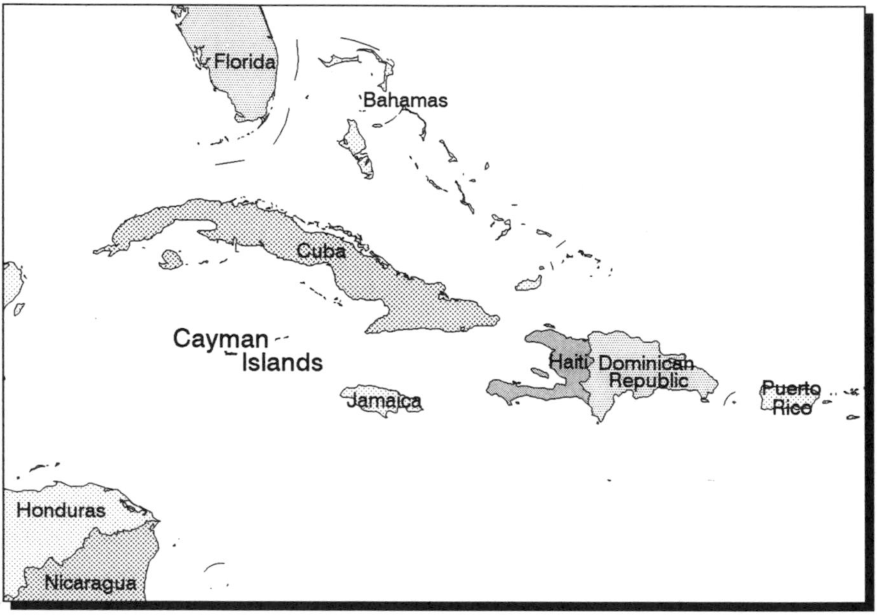

In the Caribbean. Situated in the western Caribbean, approximately 475 miles south of Miami, Florida and 180 miles northwest of Jamaica, and south of Cuba. Main language is English. They consist of three small islands with a total area of 100 square miles. Population is approximately 30,000 with the majority living on Grand Cayman. Climate is tropical with relatively low humidity, average temperature 82°F in summer and 72°F in winter.

Discovered by Columbus on May 10, 1503 during his fourth and last West Indian voyage, the trio of islands were named "Las Tortugas" after the turtles which surrounded them. By 1530 they were called "Caymanas," after the iguanas which roamed the islands. The Caymanas were ceded to Britain by Spain in 1670, and served as a favorite refuge for pirates and mariners until colonization began during the 1700's. For centuries the Caymans were associated politically with the British Colony of Jamaica. When Jamaica became independent in 1962, the Caymans chose to become a British Crown Colony. They have consistently rejected all offers of independence.

Developed as a tax haven by former Calgary, Alberta lawyer Jim MacDonald in the early 1960's, finance has become a major contributor to the island's economy. The Caymans have leaked information to some prosecutors in the U.S. In 1986, the Cayman Islands agreed to waive bank secrecy in U.S. criminal investigations. The Cayman Islands' law to stop the flow of drug money has allowed U.S. tax authorities to examine bank records.

Does the Cayman Islands have a secrecy law?

YES. Cayman Island's Confidential Relationships (Preservation) Law prohibits the unauthorized disclosure of information pertaining to a clients affairs to a third party. The Act provides criminal penalties of fines or prison terms for any disclosure of information concerning the business affairs of a client. This law extends to government officials. It is also an offense to attempt to obtain confidential information.

Is there any situation where bank secrecy can be lifted?

YES. The Mutual Legal Assistance Treaty was signed in July 1986 between the Cayman Islands (in association with the UK as appropriate sovereign power) and the US, and ratified by the U.S. Senate on October 24, 1989. This treaty states that either party can request information from the other in a criminal matter and that the requested party will furnish the information if satisfied that the request is genuine, and conforms to the parameters of the treaty. Information is subject to disclosure under compulsion of law or in satisfaction of an order of the Grand Court. The crimes included are all mutually recognized crimes drawing a sentence of one year or more, together with certain American offenses, such as insider trading and securities fraud. Tax matters are specifically excluded.

A typical Bank or Trust Company "Information Waiver" reads as follows:

> The Confidential Relationships (Preservation) Law of the Cayman Islands subjects (This Bank) to strict regulations concerning the confidentiality of client affairs. However, if and to the extent that (This Bank) shall consider that non-disclosure would result in the assets, operations, or personnel of (This Bank) becoming liable to seizure, interference or prejudice in the United States of America, (This Bank) reserves the right to make disclosures. In all other respects the rule of confidentiality remains applicable and unaffected.

This "Information Waiver" is required by many of the Cayman banks. Although the Cayman Island's Confidential Relationships (Preservation) Law prohibits the unauthorized disclosure of information, the law does not apply to activities that are considered crimes in the Cayman Islands, such as illegal drug activities, theft, or fraud.

Can foreign tax authorities obtain information on Cayman bank accounts?

NO. Confidential information can only be released if there is suspected criminal activity such as illegal drug activities, theft, or fraud. Tax matters are specifically excluded under the Mutual Legal Assistance Treaty with the U.S.

Is the Cayman Islands an independent country?

NO. The present constitution was adopted August 22, 1972. The Government is headed by a resident British Governor, appointed by and responsible to the Crown. Through him, the British Government retains direct responsibility for internal and external security, the judiciary, and external relations. The Cayman Islands internal government is provided by a Legislative Assembly, responsible for enacting the local laws.

There are no political parties and no trade unions. There is no desire for independence and the Islands are considered politically, economically, and racially stable.

Is the legal system based on English Common Law?

YES. The legal system is based on English Common Law and is supplemented by local statutes. Modern company and trust statutes have been enacted together with legislation to control the activities of banks, trust companies and insurance businesses. Modern legislation, including the preservation of secrecy, has been specifically tailored to meet the needs of an offshore financial centre on a foundation of no direct taxation. The Financial Secretary maintains a standing Advisory Committee of members from all of the sectors of the financial industry to advise on any amendments which may be desirable to keep legislation current and competitive.

Is there an income tax in the Cayman Islands?

NO. There are no direct taxes on individuals or corporations. An exempted company is guaranteed to not be taxed for a period of 30 years. An ordinary company is guaranteed to not be taxed for a period of 20 years (even though there are currently no Cayman Island taxes).

Customs duties are levied on certain goods imported into the Islands, and stamp duty is charged on documents such as transfers of land, mortgages, debentures, leases, and promissory notes.

Are there any other taxes in the Cayman Islands?

NO. There are no direct taxes on individuals or corporations. There is no income tax, corporate tax, capital gains tax, capital or wealth tax, gift tax, inheritance tax or estate duty, property or estate tax, sales tax, payroll tax, business tax, withholding or dividend tax, or profits tax.

Are there any exchange controls in the Cayman Islands?

NO. All forms of exchange control in the Cayman Islands were abolished in 1980. The local currency is the Cayman Islands Dollar, which is tied to the U.S. Dollar at a rate of CI$1.00 = US$1.20.

Is there a tax treaty between the U.S. and the Cayman Islands?

NO. No tax treaty has been signed between the U.S. and the Cayman Islands, although the Cayman Islands has signed the Mutual Legal Assistance Treaty with the U.S. The Mutual Legal Assistance Treaty covers narcotics trafficking and other specified crimes. Information may only be requested for use in the Cayman Islands or the US, and taxation is specifically excluded.

Is there a tax treaty between Canada and the Cayman Islands?

NO. No tax treaty has been signed between Canada and the Cayman Islands. There are no exchange of information agreements with any other jurisdiction.

Does the Cayman Islands allow the formation of Limited Companies?

YES. The Cayman Islands Companies Law provides for the incorporation of two types of company - the Ordinary Company and the

Exempted Company. Companies may be limited by guarantee or unlimited. Companies may also be established by a private act of the Legislative Assembly, but this is a rare occurrence. There is no legal distinction between private and public companies.

Ordinary Limited Company - An ordinary company limited by shares may be incorporated for any legal purpose by any person of legal age subscribing his name to a Memorandum of Association and agreeing to take up at least one share in the company. The Memorandum must contain:

- The name of the company.
- The address of its registered office.
- Objects of the company.
- A statement that the liability of the members is limited.
- Authorized capital, number of shares, and par value.

It is usual for companies to file articles of association prescribing regulations for the company, but it is not a legal requirement. Articles may be filed at any time. In the absence of articles of association, Table A in the schedule to the Companies Law will apply. There are no nationality or residence requirements for shareholders nor are there restrictions on where meetings of shareholders may be held. An annual general meeting of shareholders is required. The shareholders may attend in person or be represented by a proxy. Bearer shares may be issued by an exempted company but not by an ordinary company.

Every company is required to maintain a registered office in the Cayman Islands at which there must be located:

- The register of members, directors and officers, together with a register of mortgages and charges.

- The name of the company is required to be displayed outside the registered office and any change of location, authorized by resolution of the directors, must be advised to the Registrar of Companies.

In January each year, a company must file a return with the Registrar of Companies giving details of its capital structure, its shareholders, directors and officers. This return is accompanied by a registration fee based on authorized capital. There are no statutory audit requirements other than for banks, trust companies, and insurance companies.

Exempted Company - The Companies Law provides for the incorporation of exempted companies. These are incorporated in a similar manner to ordinary companies. A meeting of the board of directors must be called in the Cayman Islands at least once each year, but the meeting may be conducted by alternate directors or by properly authorized proxies. Certain exemptions and privileges apply to exempted companies:

- The words Limited, Incorporated, Société Anonyme, or their abbreviations need not appear in the name.
- The name of an Exempted Company may be in a foreign language.
- Annual general meetings of shareholders are not required.
- Bearer shares and shares of no par value may be issued.
- Annual returns to the Registrar of Companies, accompanied by appropriate fees, take the form of a declaration by a director or the secretary that the company has complied with provisions of the Companies Law. The return does not identify shareholders, directors, or officers and these names are not a matter of public record.
- Names of shareholders of an Exempted Company are not required to be filed with the Registrar of Companies.

- An Exempted Company must hold a directors meeting at least once every year in the Cayman Islands.
- A guarantee may be obtained from the Government that no income or capital taxes will be imposed on a company for a period of up to thirty years (in practice guarantees are issued for twenty years in the first instance).
- Shares and debentures issued by a company are similarly exempted from the future imposition of estate or inheritance taxes.

An Exempted Company may not carry on business in the Cayman Islands, and is prohibited from public offering in the Cayman Islands to subscribe for any of its shares or debentures.

Foreign Company - A company incorporated outside the Cayman Islands that establishes a place of business, or carries on business, in the Cayman Islands must register in compliance with the Companies Law. Registration is accomplished by filing a certified copy of the Memorandum and articles of association (or equivalent incorporation documents) with the Registrar of Companies, together with a certified list of the directors and officers giving their names, addresses and occupations. A foreign company must have an agent in the Cayman Islands authorized to accept notices or service of process.

Partnerships - The Partnership Law 1983, as amended, is virtually identical to the English Partnership Act 1890 and permits the formation of Limited Partnerships.

Does the Cayman Islands allow the formation of International Trusts?

YES. Trusts in the Cayman Islands are governed by the Trusts Law of 1967, which is similar to the English Law of Trusts. Trusts are generally created by deed, and impose upon a Trustee a duty to hold and administer assets for a Beneficiary named in the deed. Unlike a corporation, a Trust is not a separate legal entity. The law relating to Trusts has developed over centuries and serves to enforce the duties of Trustees and the rights of Beneficiaries.

A Trust may be created in the Cayman Islands by a resident of any country. The relevant deed may be signed by the Settlor in a location of his choice. The deed will normally specify:

- The powers and duties of the Trustees.
- The perpetuity period (or period of existence) of the Trust.
- The name of (or otherwise identify) the Beneficiaries.
- Direct the Trustees in relation to the distribution of the income and capital of the Trust.

There are no statutory restrictions on income accumulations. Trustees of Cayman Islands Trusts will normally be resident in the islands.

Trusts may be revocable or irrevocable. The most common form of Trust is the Discretionary Trust, where the assets are administered by the Trustees for the benefit of the Beneficiaries, as the Trustees in their absolute discretion may decide. Assets of Trusts may be located anywhere in the world but will remain under the control of the Trustees. It is usual, however, for the Trust deed to include a clause to facilitate a change in the jurisdiction if at any time this should prove to be necessary or desirable.

The Trusts (Foreign Element) Law of 1987 permits the creation of a Cayman Island Trust by a foreign Settlor of full age and capacity (as defined in Cayman Law) so that moveable property settled in the Trust governed by Cayman Law is protected against any forced heirship rules which may exist in the Settlor's domicile.

Trusts may not continue indefinitely. Trust assets must be distributed within 21 years following the death of a person living at the Trust formation date.

Exempted Trusts - The Trusts Law provides for a form of Trust known as an Exempted Trust. Similar in form to the ordinary Trust, it may continue in existence for up to 100 years. An Exempted Trust must be registered with the Registrar of Trusts who retains the original deed and issues a certificate of registration. The Trustees of an Exempted Trust may obtain a guarantee from the government against the imposition of income or capital taxes for a period of up to 50 years. Fees are payable upon registration and annually thereafter.

Mutual Funds and Unit Trusts - Investment funds may be established by Trust deed or by a limited liability company. If a fund is established by Trust deed the creator of the Trust will usually be a management company. The management company empowers Trustees to safeguard the investments purchased, and to receive the proceeds of Trust units sold.

The purchasers of units are the Beneficiaries of the fund. Each unit represents an individual interest in the net assets. The value of each unit is established by dividing the current net asset value of the fund by the number of units in issue. The powers and duties of the Trustees are set forth in the Trust deed, which also details:

- The manner in which units may be issued or redeemed.
- The investment powers, including the nature of the investments which may be acquired.
- The remuneration of the Trustee and manager.
- Units may be issued to a bearer.

If a fund is created by the incorporation of a limited liability company, the name and objects of the fund, together with details of its capital structure, will be detailed in the Memorandum of Association. Regulations governing the issue, redemption and valuation of shares and the operations of the company must be directed in the Articles of Association.

Does the Cayman Islands allow the formation of Captive Insurance Companies?

YES. The business of insurance and reinsurance companies, insurance managers, and agents and brokers dealing in the domestic market, is regulated by the terms of the Insurance Law 1979 as amended. The law requires that no insurance, or insurance related business, as defined in the law, may be conducted in the Cayman Islands other than by the holder of a valid license issued by the Governor in Council. Three categories of license are available to insurance and reinsurance companies:

Class "A" License - permits domestic business.

Class "B" Unrestricted License - permits the holder to carry on business, other than domestic business, from within the Cayman Islands.

Class "B" Restricted License - permits the holder to carry on business outside the Cayman Islands with its shareholders or such other persons where the insurer is constituted through partnership, share holding, or other acceptable mutual association by one or more persons having a common trade, profession, affinity or other special interest.

License applications must be submitted in a statutory form. The minimum net worth requirements prescribed by the Insurance Law are:

- Companies writing short term general business (property and casualty) CI$100,000 (US$120,000).
- Companies writing long term business CI$200,000 (US$240,000).
- Companies writing both short and long term business CI$300,000 (US$360,000).

The corporate and financial records of a licensee are required to be maintained in the Cayman Islands. Audited accounts must be filed each year within six months of the end of the financial year, together with a Certificate of Compliance signed by either the Company's auditor or Insurance Manager attesting to the activities of the licensed insurer or reinsurer.

Does the Cayman Islands allow the formation of Banking Companies?

YES. Bank and trust business is strictly regulated in terms of the Banks and Trust Companies Regulation Law (Revised) and the underlying Banks and Trust Companies (License Applications) Regulations (Revised). The law requires that no banking or trust business may be conducted in or from the Cayman Islands other than by a holder of a valid license granted by the Governor in Council. Applications for licenses are carefully reviewed by the Inspector of Banks and every attempt is made to preserve the high standard for which the Cayman Islands have become known in international financial circles. Types of licenses are:

Category "A" - permits unrestricted domestic and overseas business and is usually only granted to a branch or affiliate of a major international bank. The applicant must maintain a fully staffed office in the Cayman Islands.

Category "B" Unrestricted - permits the operation of banking business anywhere in the world except the Cayman Islands.

Transactions may be carried out within the Cayman Islands for clients outside the Islands.

Category "B" Restricted - This further restricts the business permitted under the Category B license and limits the holder to a small number of named clients.

Although the law stipulates a minimum capital requirement of CI$200,000, the Governor in Council currently requires a minimum paid up capital of US$500,000. For a restricted License the minimum capital requirements are CI$20,000 (US$24,000).

Does the Cayman Islands allow the formation of Shipping Companies?

YES. George Town, Grand Cayman is a British port of registry. Registration is regulated by the British Merchant Shipping Act 1988. Ships registered in the Cayman Islands are required to have certification under the major maritime conventions, including the 1966 International Convention on Loadlines, the 1969 International Convention on Tonnage Measurement, the 1972 International Convention on Regulations for Preventing Collisions at Sea, the 1973 International Convention for the Preventing of Pollution from Ships, and the 1974 International Convention for the Safety of Life at Sea.

To be registered on the Cayman Register, majority ownership of the ship must be by British citizens or a company incorporated in the Cayman Islands, UK, or any other British dependency. Benefits include exemption from U.S. Federal Income Tax for vessels trading there, Royal Navy protection, no national crewing requirements, and assistance of British Consular service world-wide.

Financial institutions and contacts:

Ansbacher Limited

Cayman International Trust Co. Limited
Mr. Michael Day — 809-949-8655 dial
Private Banking Department — 809-949-7946 fax
PO.Box 887 — CP 4305 telex
Ansbacher House, Grand Cayman, Cayman Islands, British West Indies

- Primary business activity: bank and trust services.
- Safekeeping and custodian services.
- Portfolio management of securities and mutual funds.
- Company formation services are offered. Minimum formation fee US$2,000. Minimum annual fee US$2,000 plus 4/10% of assets plus US$50 per transaction.
- Trust formation services are offered. Minimum formation fee US$3,200. Minimum annual fee US$2,000 plus 4/10% of assets plus US$50 per transaction.
- Captive insurance company formation. Minimum annual fee US$7,500.
- Banking company formation. Minimum annual fee US$10,000.

Bank of Butterfield (Cayman) Ltd. Trust and Corporate Management Division

Mr. Fred Stevenson — 809-949-7055 dial
Manager - Investment Services — 809-949-7004 fax
Butterfield House, Fort Street — 4263 BFIELD CP telex
PO.Box 705, Grand Cayman, Cayman Islands, British West Indies

- Primary business activity: bank and trust services.
- Executor and administrator of wills and estates.
- Safekeeping and custodian services.
- Portfolio management of securities and mutual funds. Minimum annual fee 1/2% of assets or US$1,000 plus US$50 per transaction.
- Company formation services are offered. Minimum formation fee US$2,500 including license fee. Minimum annual fee US$1,750.
- Trust formation services are offered. Minimum formation fee US$500. Minimum annual fee 2/5% of assets or US$2,500 plus 3/8% per transaction.
- Captive insurance company formation services are offered.
- Banking company formation services are offered.

Bank of Butterfield (Cayman) Ltd. Retail Banking Division

Ms. H.Camille Wight	809-949-7055	dial
Manager	809-949-7004	fax

Butterfield Bank Building, Edward Street, PO.Box 705
Grand Cayman, Cayman Islands, British West Indies

- Primary business activity: banking services.
- Private banking services and/or savings accounts.
- Consumer loans and credit facilities.

Bank of Nova Scotia Trust Company (Cayman) Limited

PO.Box 501	809-949-2001	dial
Cardinal Avenue	809-949-7097	fax
Grand Cayman, Cayman Islands, British West Indies	CP-4213	telex

- Primary business activity: banking services.
- Private banking services and/or savings accounts.
- Consumer loans and credit facilities.
- Corporate services such as registered agent services.
- Executor and administrator of wills and estates.
- Safekeeping and custodian services.
- Portfolio management of securities and mutual funds.
- Company formation services are offered. Minimum formation fee US$2,500. Minimum annual fee 3/5% of assets or US$2,500
- Trust formation services are offered. Minimum formation fee US$3,000. Minimum annual fee 3/5% of assets or US$3,500.
- Captive insurance company formation services are offered.
- Banking company formation services are offered.

Barclays Bank PLC

Mr. Ramesh Gopal	809-949-7300	dial
Senior Supervisor	809-949-7179	fax
PO.Box 68	CP 4219	telex

Grand Cayman, Cayman Islands, British West Indies

- Primary business activity: bank and trust services.
- Offers private credit card backed by deposit.
- Private banking services and/or savings accounts.
- Consumer loans and credit facilities.
- Executor and administrator of wills and estates.
- Safekeeping and custodian services.
- Portfolio management of securities and mutual funds.
- Company formation services are offered.
- Trust formation services are offered.

Barclays Private Bank & Trust Limited

Mr. John Fleming	809-949-7128	dial
Managing Director	809-949-7657	fax

PO.Box 487, Harbour Centre, North Church Street
Grand Cayman, Cayman Islands, British West Indies

- Primary business activity: bank and trust services.
- Offers private credit card backed by deposit.
- Private banking services and/or savings accounts.
- Consumer loans and credit facilities.
- Safekeeping and custodian services.
- Portfolio management of securities and mutual funds.
- Company formation services are offered.
- Trust formation services are offered.

Bruce Campbell & Co.

Mr. James J. Wauchope	809-949-2648	dial
Attorney-at-Law	809-949-8613	fax
PO.Box 884	CP 0293 4302	telex

Bank of Nova Scotia Building
Grand Cayman, Cayman Islands, British West Indies

- Primary business activity: law office.
- Corporate services such as registered agent services.
- Company formation services are offered. Minimum formation fee US$1,875 including license fee. Minimum annual fee US$1,000.
- Trust formation services are offered.
- Banking company formation. Minimum formation fee US$10,013 including license fee. Minimum annual fee US$6,168.

Cayman National Bank Ltd.

Ms. Janice Scott-Hummel	809-949-4655	dial
Vice President, Marketing	809-949-7506	fax
West Wind Building	4313 CNBBANK CP	telex

PO.Box 1097, Grand Cayman, Cayman Islands, British West Indies

- Primary business activity: bank and trust services.
- Offers Private Credit Card (MasterCard) backed by deposit.
- Private banking services and/or savings accounts.
- Consumer loans and credit facilities.
- Safekeeping and custodian services.
- Portfolio management of securities and mutual funds.
- Company formation services are offered. Minimum formation fee US$1,500 plus US$610 license fee. Minimum annual fee US$427.
- Trust formation services are offered. Minimum formation fee US$1,000.

Cayman National Securities Ltd.

Mr. Dan Martiuk	809-949-7722	dial
President	809-949-8203	fax
West Wind Building	4313 CNBBANK CP	telex

PO.Box 275GT, Grand Cayman, Cayman Islands, British West Indies

- Primary business activity: bank and trust services.
- Safekeeping and custodian services.
- Portfolio management of securities and mutual funds. Minimum account size US$200,000. Minimum quarterly fee 0.75% of assets plus US$100 per transaction.

Chase Manhattan Trust Ltd.

PO.Box 190 809-949-2081 dial

Grand Cayman, Cayman Islands, British West Indies

- Primary business activity: bank and trust services.

CIBC Bank and Trust Company Limited

Mrs. Edna Carter 809-949-8666 dial

Manager, Private Banking 809-949-7904 fax

PO.Box 694 4222 CP telex

Grand Cayman, Cayman Islands, British West Indies

- Primary business activity: bank and trust services.
- Private banking services and/or savings accounts.
- Consumer loans and credit facilities.
- Executor and administrator of wills and estates.
- Safekeeping and custodian services.
- Portfolio management of securities and mutual funds.
- Company formation services are offered. Minimum formation fee US$150 plus US$610 license fee. Minimum annual fee US$150.
- Trust formation services are offered.
- Captive insurance company formation services are offered.
- Banking company formation services are offered.

Cititrust (Cayman) Ltd.

PO.Box 309 809-949-5405 dial

George Town, Cayman Islands, British West Indies

- Primary business activity: bank and trust services.

Coopers & Lybrand Chartered Accountants

Mr. William Walmsley	809-949-9700	dial
Manager, Corporate Services	809-949-8154	fax
PO.Box 219	4220 COLYBRA CP	telex

Butterfield House, Grand Cayman, Cayman Islands, British West Indies

- Primary business activity: accounting services.
- Executor and administrator of wills and estates.
- Safekeeping and custodian services.
- Company formation services are offered. Minimum formation fee US$2,550 including license fee. Minimum annual fee US$1,500.
- Trust formation services are offered.
- Captive insurance company formation services are offered.
- Banking company formation services are offered.

Coutts & Co. (Cayman) Ltd.

West Bay Road	809-947-4777	dial
PO.Box 707	809-947-4799	fax

Grand Cayman, Cayman Islands, British West Indies

- Primary business activity: bank and trust services.
- Private banking services and/or savings accounts.
- Safekeeping and custodian services.
- Portfolio management of securities and mutual funds.
- Company formation services are offered.
- Trust formation services are offered.

Deloitte & Touche (RHB Trust Co.)

Mr. Christopher J. Bowring	809-949-7500	dial
Senior Manager	809-949-8238	fax
One Regis Place	4333 RHBCO CP	telex

PO.Box 1787, Grand Cayman, Cayman Islands, British West Indies

- Primary business activity: accounting services.
- Executor and administrator of wills and estates.
- Safekeeping and custodian services.
- Company formation services are offered. Minimum formation fee US$2,000 plus US$427 license fee. Minimum annual fee US$1,427.
- Trust formation services are offered.
- Captive insurance company formation services are offered.
- Banking company formation services are offered.

Euro Bank Corporation

Mr. Ivan Burges	809-949-8721	dial
Senior Assistant Manager	809-949-6232	fax
PO.Box 1792	4300 EUROBNK CP	telex

Grand Cayman, Cayman Islands, British West Indies

- Primary business activity: bank and trust services.
- Offers Private Credit Card (MasterCard) backed by deposit.
- Private banking services and/or savings accounts.
- Consumer loans and credit facilities.
- Corporate services such as registered agent services.
- Executor and administrator of wills and estates.
- Safekeeping and custodian services.
- Portfolio management of securities and mutual funds. Minimum annual fee 1/2% of assets or US$1,000 plus US$25 per transaction.
- Company formation services are offered. Minimum formation fee US$1,600. Minimum annual fee US$950.
- Trust formation services are offered. Minimum formation fee US$1,000. Minimum annual fee 1/2% of assets or US$2,500.

Finsbury Bank and Trust Company

PO.Box 1592	809-947-4011	dial

Transnational House, West Bay Road
Grand Cayman, Cayman Islands, British West Indies

- Primary business activity: bank and trust services.

IMS Ltd.

Mr. Clive Harris	809-949-4244	dial

Genesis Building, Dr.Roy's Drive
Grand Cayman, Cayman Islands, British West Indies

- Primary business activity: law office.

IncoBank and Trust Company

PO.Box 970	809-949-7807	dial

Grand Cayman, Cayman Islands, British West Indies

- Primary business activity: bank and trust services.

International Management Services, Ltd.

PO.Box 61, Grand Cayman, Cayman Islands, British West Indies

- Primary business activity: company and trust formation services.

International Trust Protector Limited

Mr. Antony Duckworth	809-949-8464	dial
Director	809-949-8460	fax
PO.Box 1310	CP 0293 4275	telex

Grand Cayman, Cayman Islands, British West Indies

- Primary business activity: law office.
- Executor and administrator of wills and estates.
- Company formation services are offered.
- Trust formation services are offered.

Maples & Calder

PO.Box 309	809-949-2081	dial
Grand Cayman	4212	telex

Cayman Islands, British West Indies

- Primary business activity: law office.

Midland Bank Trust Corporation

Mr. Kevin Sedgwick	809-949-7755	dial
Assistant Director	809-949-7634	fax
PO.Box 1109	CP 4490 MIMIC	telex

Mary Street, Grand Cayman, Cayman Islands, British West Indies

- Primary business activity: bank and trust services.
- Private banking services and/or savings accounts.
- Consumer loans and credit facilities.
- Executor and administrator of wills and estates.
- Safekeeping and custodian services.
- Portfolio management of securities and mutual funds. Minimum annual fee 3/4% of assets or US$2,000 plus US$50 per transaction.
- Company formation services are offered. Minimum formation fee US$250 plus US$702 license fee. Minimum annual fee US$1,000.
- Trust formation services are offered. Minimum formation fee US$1,000. Minimum annual fee 3/4% of assets or US$3,250 plus US$50 per transaction.
- Captive insurance company formation. Minimum formation fee US$1,450 plus license fee. Minimum annual fee 1/4% of assets or US$6,000.
- Banking company formation services are offered.

Myers & Alberga Attorneys-at-Law

Mr. Michael L. Alberga — 809-949-0699 dial
Partner — 809-949-8171 fax
PO.Box 472, Grand Cayman, Cayman Islands, British West Indies

- Primary business activity: law office.
- Corporate services such as registered agent services.
- Safekeeping and custodian services.
- Company formation services are offered.
- Trust formation services are offered.

Overseas Company Registration Agents

The Genesis Building — 809-949-2711 dial
PO.Box 61 — 809-949-8635 fax
Grand Cayman, Cayman Islands, British West Indies

- Primary business activity: company and trust formation services.
- Corporate services such as registered agent services.
- Company formation services are offered. Minimum formation fee US$1,750 plus US$710 license fee. Minimum annual fee US$710.

Price Waterhouse

First Home Tower, Jennett Street — 809-949-7944 dial
British-American Centre — 809-949-7352 fax
Grand Cayman — CP 293 4 329 telex
Cayman Islands, British West Indies

- Primary business activity: accounting services.
- Safekeeping and custodian services.
- Company formation services are offered.
- Trust formation services are offered.

Royal Bank of Canada

Mr. Ritchey Ebanks	809-949-4600	dial
Private Banking Officer	809-945-1982	fax
Trust Company (Cayman) Limited	809-949-5777	fax
PO.Box 245	CP 4244	telex

Grand Cayman, Cayman Islands, British West Indies

- Primary business activity: bank and trust services.
- Private banking services and/or savings accounts.
- Consumer loans and credit facilities.
- Safekeeping and custodian services.
- Portfolio management of securities and mutual funds.
- Company formation services are offered.
- Trust formation services are offered.

Royal Trust Bank (Cayman) Ltd.

First Home Tower, 2nd Floor	809-949-7405	dial
PO.Box 1586	809-949-7173	fax
Grand Cayman	4332 CP	telex

Cayman Islands, British West Indies

- Primary business activity: bank and trust services.
- Offers private credit card backed by deposit.
- Private banking services and/or savings accounts.
- Consumer loans and credit facilities.
- Safekeeping and custodian services.
- Portfolio management of securities and mutual funds. Minimum formation fee US$1,500 plus license fee. Minimum annual fee 1/2% of assets or US$2,500.
- Company formation services are offered. Minimum formation fee US$1,500 plus license fee. Minimum annual fee 1/2% of assets or US$1,500.
- Trust formation services are offered. Minimum annual fee 1/2% of assets or US$3,000.
- Captive insurance company formation services are offered.
- Banking company formation services are offered.

Swiss Bank & Trust Corporation Limited

The Swiss Bank Building	809-949-7344	dial
Fort Street	809-949-7308	fax
Grand Cayman	4252	telex

Cayman Islands, British West Indies

- Primary business activity: bank and trust services.
- Private banking services and/or savings accounts.
- Consumer loans and credit facilities.
- Executor and administrator of wills and estates.
- Safekeeping and custodian services.
- Portfolio management of securities and mutual funds. Minimum assets US$500,000.
- Company formation services are offered.
- Trust formation services are offered.
- Banking company formation services are offered.

Truman Bodden & Company Attorneys

Mr. Chris Narborough	809-949-7555	dial
Associate	809-949-8492	fax

PO.Box 866, Anderson Square Building
Grand Cayman, Cayman Islands, British West Indies

- Primary business activity: law office.
- Company formation services are offered. Minimum formation fee US$1,248 plus US$500 license fee. Minimum annual fee US$900.
- Trust formation services are offered.
- Captive insurance company formation services are offered.
- Banking company formation services are offered.

Union Bank of Switzerland

PO.Box 1043, Grand Cayman, Cayman Islands, British West Indies

- Primary business activity: banking services.

W.S. Walker & Co. Attorneys-at-Law

Mr. William S. Walker 809-949-0100 dial
Chairman 809-949-7886 fax
Caledonian House, PO.Box 265
Grand Cayman, Cayman Islands, British West Indies

- Primary business activity: law office.
- Corporate services such as registered agent services.
- Safekeeping and custodian services.
- Portfolio management of securities and mutual funds. Minimum annual fee 1/4% of assets or US$2,500.
- Company formation services are offered. Minimum formation fee US$2,400 including license fee. Minimum annual fee US$1,200.
- Trust formation services are offered. Minimum formation fee US$500.
- Captive insurance company formation. Minimum formation fee US$5,000 plus license fee.
- Banking company formation. Minimum formation fee US$5,000 plus license fee.

CHANNEL ISLANDS - GUERNSEY AND JERSEY

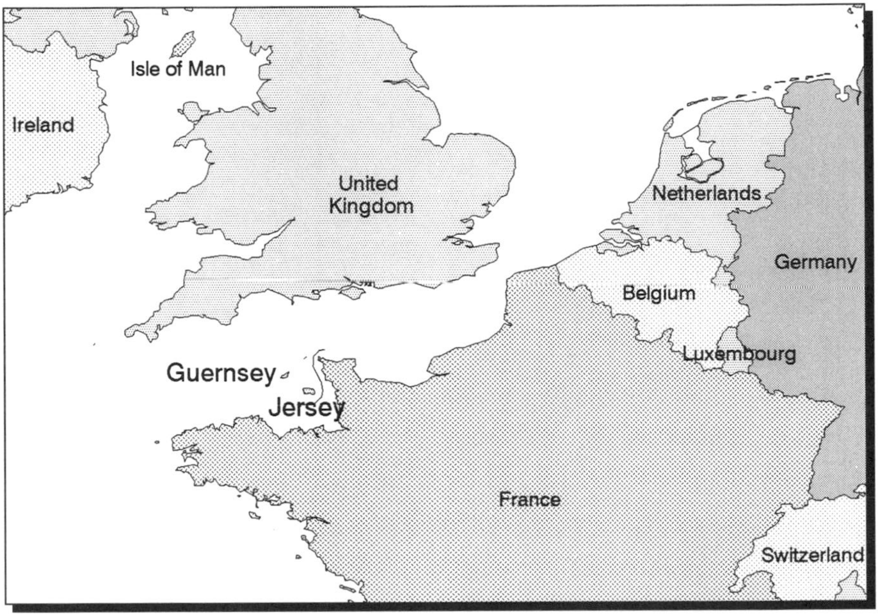

In Europe. South of Britain, North of France, in the English Channel. The two main islands Guernsey and Jersey. The smaller Channel Islands include Alderney, Herm, and Sark. Main language is English.

Guernsey

25 square miles, 30 miles west of the Cherbourg peninsula and 80 miles south of England. Population is approximately 55,000.

Jersey

The largest of the Channel Islands at 62 square miles. Jersey is 12 miles from the coast of Normandy and 90 miles south of England. Population is approximately 85,000. The official language of Jersey is French, although French is only used on ceremonial occasions.

In view of their close proximity to the French mainland it is not surprising to find that the Channel Islands originally formed a part of the Duchy of Normandy from 933. When William, Duke of Normandy, conquered England in 1066, England came under the same rule as the Channel Islands. The constitutional position then remained unaltered until 1204 when King John of England was driven out of mainland Normandy by the French, and from that time the Channel Islands have been the only part of the Duchy of Normandy to remain loyal to the Crown of England. Successive English Monarchs have given charters granting special constitutional status. As dependent territories of the English Crown they owe allegiance to the Monarch, but have no direct link with parliament.

Until World War II, Alderney was a jurisdiction of its own. During the German Occupation of the Channel Islands from 1940 to 1945 Alderney was completely evacuated, and in 1948 new constitutional and legal relationships were forged by the Government of Alderney. The Channel Islands are quite distinct from one another, having different legal systems from both one another and from the United Kingdom.

Does the Channel Islands have a secrecy law?

NO. Although English common law requires banks and their employees to maintain secrecy, no specific bank secrecy legislation has been passed, although it is technically very difficult to breach current bank secrecy. The English common law rule of confidentiality (imposed upon a bank in its relationship with its clients) applies in the Channel Islands.

Guernsey

Guernsey has no defined bank secrecy law. Secrecy is assured by the Common Law principle of confidentiality, and by the absence of any official disclosure requirements. If a Guernsey company is formed, the shareholders have their names forwarded to the Guernsey Financial Services Commission. This information is not released to the public.

Mr. Graham S. Basham, Manager, Private Banking, at CIBC Bank and Trust Company (Channel Islands) Limited provided this quote: "*Guernsey does not have any exchange of information treaties with regard to tax and therefore we certainly would not provide information concerning accounts held by ourselves.*"

Jersey

Details of a beneficial ownership of an Exempt Company must be disclosed to the appropriate local authority. This information is not available as a matter of public record, and there is no requirement for financial statements to be filed.

Is there any situation where bank secrecy can be lifted?

YES. The only way information can be obtained by a third party is for the Royal Court to issue this authority. The Royal Court would only give this authority if proof of drug trade, arms trade, or money laundering could be established. The Basle Statement of Principles on Money Laundering was circulated by the Bank of England in January 1989. The Statement does not restrict itself to drug-related money laundering, but extends to all aspects of laundering money derived from illegal activities, such as robbery, terrorism, fraud or drugs.

Can foreign tax authorities obtain information on Channel Islands bank accounts?

NO. Confidential information relating to taxation is not available to foreign authorities.

Professional advisors may only reveal confidential information by order of the Royal Court, and no order of a foreign court directing a professional advisor to disclose information can be applied locally.

Is Channel Islands an independent country?

YES. Although the Channel Islands are closely associated with the United Kingdom and part of the British Commonwealth, they are not directly a part of the UK, nor are they a colony. Alderney, Guernsey, Jersey, and Sark's constitution dates back to 1066, when Duke William of Normandy became King William I of England. In 1204 England lost the Normandy part of her Kingdom but the Channel Islands have remained loyal to the Crown of England since then. The Channel Islands have retained the right to legislate independently on domestic issues and taxation.

When the United Kingdom was admitted to the EEC, the Channel Islands were integrated with the Community, but granted a special status. This status states that they are included in the Community for the purposes of freedom of movement of goods and must apply the common external tariff, but they are not subject to the harmonization of taxes and social policies, and there is no value added tax in the Islands.

Is the legal system based on English Common Law?

NO. The legal system is based on Norman law, although the local legislature enacts laws directly influenced by English common law. In matters of real property law and inheritance the common law is the ancient customary law of Normandy, but in other areas the courts have adopted the concepts of the common laws of England. Trust law has developed very similarly to English Trust law.

Is there an income tax in the Channel Islands?

YES. All of the Channel Islands collect various forms and rates of tax.

Guernsey

The tax rates of the income and profit of an IC will be at a rate determined by the administrator of Income Tax who will review the business plan of the company in determining the appropriate tax rate. The rate of tax would be subject to review every five years. The rate of tax is subject to individual agreement and must be above 0% and no more than 30%. Dividend payments are subject to a withholding tax of 20%.

Investment income on shareholders' funds is taxable as follows:

- Up to £250,000 rate of tax 20%.
- Next £250,000 rate of tax 1%.
- Next £250,000 rate of tax 0.5%.
- Next £250,000 rate of tax 0.3%
- Excess 0.1%.

There are no capital gains, gift or estate taxes in Guernsey.

Jersey

Non-resident companies incorporated in Jersey are treated as resident for tax purposes (standard rate 20%) unless they are defined as an "exempt company," paying only a flat tax of £500 per year. The meeting place of the directors of a company does not constitute an established place of business so that the directors may meet (and conclude contracts) in the Islands without exposing profits to local tax.

Interest paid by an IBC is payable without deduction of Jersey tax, as are dividends and director's fees. There is no capital gains tax, gift tax or estate tax in Jersey.

Are there any other taxes in the Channel Islands?

NO. There are no capital gains taxes, wealth taxes, gift taxes, or estate duties charged on Company or Trust assets in the Channel Islands.

Are there any exchange controls in Jersey?

NO. As of October 23, 1979, all exchange control regulations in the Channel Islands were abolished.

Is there a tax treaty between the U.S. and the Channel Islands?

NO. There is no tax treaty between the U.S. and the Channel Islands, although there are double-taxation agreements between the UK and the Channel Islands. The Double Taxation Agreements between Guernsey & Jersey in 1956 and the UK in 1952 provide for exchange of information, but only to the revenue authorities, and not to outsiders.

Is there a tax treaty between Canada and the Channel Islands?

NO. There is no tax treaty between Canada and the Channel Islands.

Does the Channel Islands allow the formation of Limited Companies?

YES. The procedures to form either a Guernsey or Jersey Company are to:

- Obtain formal approval for the proposed name, and then for the formation of the company.
- Disclose the names of the registered shareholders, who may be nominees acting on behalf of the beneficial owners of the company.
- Disclose on a confidential basis to the island authority the names and addresses of the beneficial owners so that the island authority can satisfy itself that a company is not being formed for the benefit of undesirable persons.
- The minimum number of registered shareholders is two.
- If required a company can have only one beneficial owner with the registered shareholders acting as nominees.

In addition, Guernsey and Jersey Companies are required to:

- Maintain a register of members at its registered office, available for inspection by members of the public, together with a copy of its last annual return of shareholders.
- Make a return in January of each year stating the capital structure and the names and addresses of registered shareholders as of January 1. Guernsey companies must also supply the names of the directors.

Ad valorem stamp duty is payable on the incorporation of a company based upon the authorized share capital, subject to a minimum of £50. The company's registered office must be at an address in the island in which the company is incorporated.

Guernsey

International Company - The International Company (IC) was introduced in 1993 to include Guernsey incorporated companies, foreign incorporated companies, the Guernsey branch of a non-resident company and Limited Partnerships.

The identity of the beneficial owners must be disclosed to the Financial Services Commission to satisfy requirements that an IC is not be beneficially owned by residents of the Channel Islands. This information is not made public, and is not available to the Island's tax authorities. Information must also be provided regarding any changes in beneficial ownership.

The tax rates of the income and profit of an IC will be at a rate determined by the administrator of Income Tax who will review the business plan of the company in determining the appropriate tax rate, subject to review every five years. The tax rate will be above 0% but not more than 30%. Dividend payments are subject to a withholding tax of 20%.

Guernsey Exempt Companies - Any company incorporated in Guernsey may apply to be registered as exempt from Guernsey income tax. Details of beneficial ownership must be disclosed to the Financial Services Commission. This information is not made public, and is not available to the Island's tax authorities.

Exempt Companies are regarded as non-resident for taxation purposes. The exempt company fee is £500 per year. Exempt companies are not required to file a copy of their annual accounts with the Income Tax authorities.

Jersey

International Business Company - The International Business Company (IBC) was introduced in 1993 to provide non-residents with a company that pays tax on its income at a maximum of 2.0% (subject to a minimum of £1,200 annually). Interest paid by an IBC is payable without deduction of Jersey tax, as are dividends and director's fees. Disclosure of beneficial ownership must be made to the Financial Services Department.

Jersey Exempt Companies - A company may claim to be an Exempt Company and be treated as non-resident if it is in the beneficial ownership of non-residents. The identity of the beneficial owners must be disclosed to the Financial Services Commission to satisfy requirements that an IBC is not beneficially owned by residents of the Channel Islands. The exempt company election must be submitted by March 31 of each year, and must include a confirmation that the Registrar of Companies has been kept informed of changes in beneficial ownership. These disclosure requirements came into full force in 1991.

Exempt companies are not required to file a copy of their annual accounts with the Income Tax authorities. The exempt company fee is £500 per year.

Jersey Foreign Companies - Foreign incorporated companies managed and controlled in the Islands which are beneficially owned by non-residents may apply for exempt status. Filing requirements will then be similar to companies incorporated in the Islands.

Jersey Collective Investment Schemes - A Collective Investment Scheme may also be treated as an Exempt Company. Any Exempt Company that is a Collective Investment Scheme must deduct tax from the payment of dividends to any Jersey resident shareholders. It must also provide the name, address and share holdings of any persons resident in Jersey. A clearance procedure exists for persons having Jersey addresses, but not residence in Jersey.

The main requirements of a Jersey company are that the Memorandum of Association must specify:

- The name of the company ending with the words Limited or Avec Responsibilite Limitee.
- The amount of authorized capital (minimum £50).
- It is possible for nominee subscribers to sign blank transfers and declarations of Trust in favor of the beneficial owners for their retention. The shares may be transferred into the names of the beneficial owners or into the names of other nominees as may be required.
- The subscribers to the Memorandum of Association appoint, in writing, the first directors of the company.
- The law does not require directors of a Jersey company to be resident in Jersey, nor does it provide that they must also be shareholders.
- The minimum number of directors is one.
- A Jersey company must hold its annual general meeting in Jersey.

Does the Channel Islands allow the formation of International Trusts?

YES. There are three main types of Trust and several variations on each type may be built into the Trust document:

Discretionary Trust - The most common form of Trust used in the Channel Islands is a discretionary Trust, where the Trustee has discretion to exercise his own judgement as to the manner and amount by which Beneficiaries of the Trust might benefit from the Trust assets. The beneficiaries have no legal rights to any portion of the Trust fund. It is usual for the Settlor to indicate to the Trustee his wishes as to the disposal of the Trust fund and his expression of wishes, while not legally binding, does give the Trustee guidance on the distribution of the Trust assets.

Fixed Trust - It is possible to make a Trust in a fixed form so that the Trustee has no discretionary powers when distributing the Trust assets to Beneficiaries, as the deed will specify how the assets are to be made available to the Beneficiaries.

Protective Trust - A protective Trust may be either discretionary, or fixed, or a combination of the two. Under such a Trust the Trustee will be required to benefit an individual, or alternatively to withhold benefit on the happening of an event specified within the Trust deed. Protective Trusts are most commonly set up for children, disabled or mentally handicapped persons.

In both Guernsey and Jersey the Trust deed does not have to be registered and is not available for inspection. It remains a private document between the Settlor and the Trustee.

Guernsey

Trusts are governed by the Trusts Law 1989, which outlines the duties and obligations of the Trustees and gives the Royal Court certain powers which it can exercise on application from a Settlor, Trustee, Beneficiary or Protector. The Trusts (Amendment) Law 1990 was enacted to protect the assets of a Trust from foreign rules of forced heirship.

Jersey

Revocable Trusts can be arranged in Jersey so that upon a written instruction from the client the Trust is revoked and the assets automatically pass back to the client.

Does the Channel Islands allow the formation of Captive Insurance Companies?

YES. Captive Insurance Companies may be set up in Jersey and are generally not taxable on their underwriting profits, but are subject to tax on other income. Reinsurance Companies may also be formed.

Guernsey

Insurance companies must be licensed under the Insurance Business (Guernsey) Law, 1986. Insurance law requires certain information regarding insurers to be made available to the public, such as:

- Nominal and issued share capital.
- The location of the registered office.
- The name and address of all directors, shareholders, and secretary.

Accounts of insurance companies are not filed for public record but must be presented to the Income Tax Office to support audited tax returns.

Does the Channel Islands allow the formation of Banking Companies?

YES. Although the Channel Islands allows the formation of Banking Companies, the strict requirements make them impractical for tax planning purposes.

Financial institutions and contacts in Guernsey:

Abacus Financial Services Limited
Coopers & Lybrand Chartered Accountants
Ms. Rebecca G. Reid 441-481-726921 dial
Manager 441-481-711075 fax
PO.Box 626, Le Truchot
St.Peter Port, Guernsey, Channel Islands GY1 4PW

- Primary business activity: accounting services.
- Primary business activity: company and trust formation services.
- Private banking services and/or savings accounts.
- Executor and administrator of wills and estates.
- Safekeeping and custodian services.
- Portfolio management of securities and mutual funds.
- Company formation services are offered.
- Trust formation services are offered.

Ansbacher (CI) Limited
Mr. Robert Bannister 441-481-726421 dial
Executive Director 441-481-726526 fax
PO.Box 79, La Plaiderie House, St.Peter Port, Guernsey, Channel Islands

- Primary business activity: bank and trust services.
- Safekeeping and custodian services.
- Portfolio management of securities and mutual funds.
- Company formation services are offered.
- Trust formation services are offered.

ANZ Bank (Guernsey) Limited
Mr. Roger Knight 441-481-726771 dial
Managing Director 441-481-727851 fax
PO.Box 153, Frances House
Sir William Place, St.Peter Port, Guernsey, Channel Islands

- Primary business activity: banking services.
- Private banking services and/or savings accounts.
- Safekeeping and custodian services.
- Portfolio management of securities and mutual funds.

Bachmann Trust Company Limited

Mr. Michael Brown 441-481-723573 dial
Director 441-481-715544 fax
PO.Box 175, Frances House, Sir William Place
St.Peter Port, Guernsey, Channel Islands GY1 4HQ

- Primary business activity: bank and trust services.
- Safekeeping and custodian services.
- Portfolio management of securities and mutual funds.

Bank of Bermuda (Guernsey) Limited

Mr. Robin A. Barnes 441-481-726268 dial
Manager, Private Banking 441-481-726987 fax
Bermuda House, St.Julian's Avenue
St.Peter Port, Guernsey, Channel Islands GY1 3NF

- Primary business activity: banking services.
- Offers Private Credit Card (VISA/MasterCard) backed by deposit.
- Private banking services and/or savings accounts.
- Consumer loans and credit facilities.
- Safekeeping and custodian services.
- Portfolio management of securities and mutual funds. Minimum annual fee 0.75% of assets or £1,000.
- Company formation services are offered. Minimum formation fee £500 plus £500 license fee. Minimum annual fee £500.
- Trust formation services are offered. Minimum formation fee £500. Minimum annual fee 0.3% of assets or £1,000.
- Banking company formation services are offered.

Bank of Butterfield International (Guernsey) Limited

Mr. Neil A. Spensley	441-481-711521	dial
Private Banking Manager	441-481-714533	fax
PO.Box 25	4191362 FIELD G	telex

Roseneath, The Grange
St.Peter Port, Guernsey, Channel Islands GY1 3AP

- Primary business activity: banking services.
- Offers private credit card backed by deposit.
- Private banking services and/or savings accounts.
- Consumer loans and credit facilities.
- Safekeeping and custodian services.
- Portfolio management of securities and mutual funds.
- Company formation services are offered.
- Trust formation services are offered.
- Banking company formation services are offered.

Barclays Private Bank & Trust Limited

Mr. Stephen Oliphant	441-481-724706	dial
Chief Manager	441-481-728376	fax

PO.Box 184, Barclaytrust House
South Esplanade, St.Peter Port, Guernsey, Channel Islands

- Primary business activity: bank and trust services.
- Offers private credit card backed by deposit.
- Private banking services and/or savings accounts.
- Consumer loans and credit facilities.
- Safekeeping and custodian services.
- Portfolio management of securities and mutual funds.
- Company formation services are offered.
- Trust formation services are offered.

Castle Trust Company Limited

PO.Box 226	441-481-23372	dial
Weighbridge House, Lower Pollet	441-481-711354	fax

St.Peter Port, Guernsey, Channel Islands

- Primary business activity: bank and trust services.

Channel Islands Insurance Consultants

Mr. Tim Spafford	441-481-724212	dial
Chairman	441-481-710696	fax

PO.Box 627, 26 Cornet Street
St.Peter Port, Guernsey, Channel Islands GY1 4PP

- Primary business activity: insurance products & services.
- Corporate services such as registered agent services.
- Captive insurance company formation services are offered.

Chemical Bank (Guernsey) Limited

Albert House, South Esplanade	441-481-723961	dial
St.Peter Port, Guernsey, Channel Islands	441-481-726734	fax

- Primary business activity: banking services.
- Private banking services and/or savings accounts.
- Safekeeping and custodian services.
- Portfolio management of securities and mutual funds.
- Company formation services are offered.
- Trust formation services are offered.

CIBC Bank and Trust Company (Channel Islands) Limited

Mr. Graham S. Basham	441-481-710151	dial
Manager, Private Banking	441-481-711670	fax
CIBC House	4191594 CIBCCIG	telex

Rue du Pre, St.Peter Port, Guernsey, Channel Islands GY1 3NS

- Primary business activity: bank and trust services.
- Offers Private Credit Card (VISA) backed by deposit.
- Private banking services and/or savings accounts.
- Consumer loans and credit facilities.
- Corporate services such as registered agent services.
- Executor and administrator of wills and estates.
- Safekeeping and custodian services.
- Portfolio management of securities and mutual funds. Minimum annual fee 1/2% of assets or £1,000.
- Company formation services are offered. Minimum formation fee £1,000 plus £500 license fee. Minimum annual fee £750.
- Trust formation services are offered. Minimum formation fee £1,000. Minimum annual fee 3/4% of assets or £1,250.

Coutts & Co. (Guernsey) Ltd.

PO.Box 16, Coutts House	441-481-726101	dial
Le Truchot	441-481-728272	fax

St.Peter Port, Guernsey, Channel Islands

- Primary business activity: bank and trust services.
- Private banking services and/or savings accounts.
- Safekeeping and custodian services.
- Portfolio management of securities and mutual funds.
- Company formation services are offered.
- Trust formation services are offered.

Credit Suisse (Guernsey) Limited

Mr. Mark Trenchard	441-481-710611	dial
Associate, Private Banking	441-481-724676	fax

Helvetia Court, PO.Box 368
St.Peter Port, Guernsey, Channel Islands GY1 3YJ

- Primary business activity: bank and trust services.
- Private banking services and/or savings accounts.
- Executor and administrator of wills and estates.
- Safekeeping and custodian services.
- Portfolio management of securities and mutual funds.
- Company formation services are offered.
- Trust formation services are offered.

Deloitte, Haskins & Sells

Albert House, South Esplanade, St.Peter Port, Guernsey, Channel Islands

- Primary business activity: accounting services.

Ernst & Young

Mr. Stephen Harlow	441-534-723232	dial
Senior Partner	441-534-713901	fax

PO.Box 236, St.Peter Port, Guernsey, Channel Islands GY1 4LE

- Primary business activity: accounting services.
- Executor and administrator of wills and estates.
- Safekeeping and custodian services.
- Company formation services are offered.
- Trust formation services are offered.

Generali Worldwide Insurance Company

Mr. Mike Timmer	441-481-715400	dial
PO.Box 613	441-481-715390	fax

Sarnia House, Le Truchot
St.Peter Port, Guernsey, Channel Islands GY1 4PA

- Primary business activity: insurance products & services.
- Captive insurance company formation services are offered.

Goethe Management Ltd.

PO.Box 357	441-481-728877	dial
26 Glategny Esplanade	441-481-728712	fax

St.Peter Port, Guernsey, Channel Islands

- Primary business activity: company and trust formation services.

Guernsey Financial Services Commission

Mr. Neil Crocker	441-481-712706	dial
Chairman, Tax Sub-Committee	441-481-712010	fax

Valley House, Hirzel Street, St.Peter Port, Guernsey, Channel Islands

- Primary business activity: government services.

Guinness Flight and Calder Private Trustees

Mr. Bruce Riley	441-481-710404	dial
Director	441-481-728848	fax

Guinness Flight House, PO.Box 250
St.Peter Port, Guernsey, Channel Islands GY1 3QH

- Primary business activity: bank and trust services.
- Company formation services are offered.
- Trust formation services are offered.

Guinness Flight Fund Managers Limited

Mr. Keith Turberville	441-481-712176	dial

Managing Director
Guinness Flight House, PO.Box 250
St.Peter Port, Guernsey, Channel Islands GY1 3QH

- Primary business activity: fund or portfolio manager.
- Corporate services such as registered agent services.
- Portfolio management of securities and mutual funds.
- Company formation services are offered.
- Trust formation services are offered.

Guinness Mahon Guernsey Limited Private Bank

Mrs. A.C. Allez	441-481-723506	dial
Private Banking Officer	441-481-720884	fax
PO.Box 188	419-1482	telex

La Vieille Cour, St.Peter Port, Guernsey, Channel Islands GY1 3LP

- Primary business activity: bank and trust services.

Helveticum Management Services Limited

Mr. John G. Crowder	441-481-719196	dial
Insurance Manager	441-481-724968	fax

Helvetia Court, PO.Box 290
St.Peter Port, Guernsey, Channel Islands GY1 3RP

- Primary business activity: bank and trust services.
- Corporate services such as registered agent services.
- Captive insurance company formation services are offered.

International Risk Management Limited

Mr. John Parkinson	441-481-727220	dial
Group Vice President Europe	441-481-712443	fax

2 Grange Place, St.Peter Port, Guernsey, Channel Islands GY1 2QA

- Primary business activity: insurance products & services.
- Corporate services such as registered agent services.
- Captive insurance company formation services are offered.

Kleinwort Benson (Guernsey) Limited

Mr. Horace Camp	441-481-727111	dial
Assistant Manager Business Development	441-481-728317	fax

Westbourne, The Grange, PO.Box 44, St.Peter Port, Guernsey, Channel Islands GY1 3BG

- Primary business activity: company and trust formation services.
- Primary business activity: fund or portfolio manager.
- Safekeeping and custodian services.
- Company formation services are offered.
- Trust formation services are offered.

Legis Group

Mr. David Whitworth	441-481-726034	dial
Managing Director	441-481-726029	fax

PO.Box 186, 1 Le Marchant Street
St.Peter Port, Guernsey, Channel Islands GY1 4HP

- Primary business activity: company and trust formation services.
- Primary business activity: law office.
- Corporate services such as registered agent services.
- Executor and administrator of wills and estates.
- Safekeeping and custodian services.
- Company formation services are offered.
- Trust formation services are offered.

Lince, Salisbury, Meader & Co.

Avenue House, St.Julian's Avenue
St.Peter Port, Guernsey, Channel Islands

- Primary business activity: accounting services.

MeesPierson (CI) Limited

Mr. Jaap Van Den Ende	441-481-728921	dial
Investment Manager	441-481-710665	fax

PO.Box 253, Le Bordage, St.Peter Port, Guernsey, Channel Islands GY1 3QJ

- Primary business activity: banking services.
- Private banking services and/or savings accounts.
- Safekeeping and custodian services.
- Portfolio management of securities and mutual funds.

Mercator Trust Company Limited

Mr. Angus G. Bodman	441-481-721896	dial
Director	441-481-724500	fax

PO.Box 203, Albert House, South Esplanade
St.Peter Port, Guernsey, Channel Islands GY1 4JB

- Primary business activity: bank and trust services.

Midland Bank PLC

PO.Box 31	441-481-724201	dial

13 High Street, St.Peter Port, Guernsey, Channel Islands

- Primary business activity: bank and trust services.

Midland Bank Trustee (Guernsey) Limited

Mr. C.W. Tanner	441-481-717717	dial
Manager, Trust & Corporate Services	441-481-717850	fax
PO.Box 156	441-481-717830	dial
22 Smith Street	419-1586	telex

St.Peter Port, Guernsey, Channel Islands GY1 4EU

- Primary business activity: bank and trust services.
- Private banking services and/or savings accounts.
- Consumer loans and credit facilities.
- Executor and administrator of wills and estates.
- Safekeeping and custodian services.
- Portfolio management of securities and mutual funds. Minimum annual fee 3/4% of assets or £1,500 plus £50 per transaction.
- Company formation services are offered. Minimum formation fee £2,000 including £600 license fee. Minimum annual fee 3/4% of assets or £1,500.
- Trust formation services are offered. Minimum formation fee £1,000. Minimum annual fee 3/4% of assets or £1,500.

Midland Walwyn

Mr. Andrew P. Lampert	441-481-710405	dial
General Manager	441-481-727541	fax

10 The Grange, St.Peter Port, Guernsey, Channel Islands

- Primary business activity: fund or portfolio manager.
- Safekeeping and custodian services.
- Portfolio management of securities and mutual funds.

National Westminster Bank Finance

Mr. Colin Whalley	441-481-726486	dial
Manager	441-481-727017	fax

PO.Box 282, National Westminster House

Le Truchot, St.Peter Port, Guernsey, Channel Islands GY1 4LP

- Primary business activity: bank and trust services.
- Private banking services and/or savings accounts.
- Consumer loans and credit facilities.

Nordben Life and Pension Insurance Co.

Mr. Paul Cutter	441-481-710661	dial
General Manager	441-481-710719	fax

Harbour House, South Esplanade
St.Peter Port, Guernsey, Channel Islands GY1 1AP

- Primary business activity: insurance products & services.
- Captive insurance company formation services are offered.

Rothschild Asset Management Limited

Mr. Robin Fuller	441-481-713713	dial
Assistant Director, Marketing	441-481-711511	fax

PO.Box 242, St.Peter Port House
Sausmarez Street, St.Peter Port, Guernsey, Channel Islands

- Primary business activity: fund or portfolio manager.
- Portfolio management of securities and mutual funds.

Royal Bank of Scotland PLC

Mr. Alex Rodger	441-481-710051	dial
Regional Manager	441-481-715431	fax

St.Andrew's House, Le Bordage, 22 High Street
St.Peter Port, Guernsey, Channel Islands GY1 4BQ

- Primary business activity: banking services.
- Private banking services and/or savings accounts.
- Corporate services such as registered agent services.
- Captive insurance company formation services are offered.

Sun Alliance International Life

Mr. Edward Atter	441-481-714108	dial
General Manager	441-481-712424	fax

PO.Box 77, Les Echelons, South Esplanade
St.Peter Port, Guernsey, Channel Islands GY1 4BN

- Primary business activity: insurance products & services.
- Portfolio management of securities and mutual funds.

Financial institutions and contacts in Jersey:

Abacus Financial Services Limited
Coopers & Lybrand Chartered Accountants
Mr. John Heaps 441-534-602000 dial
Senior Manager 441-534-602002 fax
La Motte Chambers 4192231 COLY JY G telex
St.Helier, Jersey, Channel Islands JE1 1BJ

- Primary business activity: accounting services.
- Primary business activity: company and trust formation services.
- Private banking services and/or savings accounts.
- Executor and administrator of wills and estates.
- Safekeeping and custodian services.
- Company formation services are offered. Minimum formation fee £1,250 including license fee. Minimum annual fee £1,100.
- Trust formation services are offered. Minimum formation fee £1,250. Minimum annual fee £750.

Abbey National (Overseas) Limited
Mr. Peter G. Donne Davis 441-534-58815 dial
Managing Director 441-534-21615 fax
PO.Box 545 4192535 ABBNOL G telex
St.Helier, Jersey, Channel Islands JE4 8XG

- Primary business activity: banking services.
- Private banking services and/or savings accounts.

ABN-AMRO Bank, N.V.
8 Hill St. 441-534-66640 dial
PO.Box 255, St.Helier, Jersey, Channel Islands

- Primary business activity: banking services.

Advent Management Company
La Motte Chambers 441-534-602000 dial
La Motte Street 441-534-602002 fax
St.Helier, Jersey, Channel Islands

- Primary business activity: company and trust formation services.

AIB Bank (CI) Limited

AIB House, Grenville St.	441-534-36633	dial
PO.Box 468	441-534-31245	fax
St.Helier, Jersey, Channel Islands		

- Primary business activity: banking services.

ANZ Grindlays Bank (Jersey) Limited

PO.Box 80	441-534-74248	dial
West House Wests Centre	441-534-77695	fax
St.Helier, Jersey, Channel Islands		

- Primary business activity: banking services.

Bank of Nova Scotia Trust Company Channel Islands Limited

PO.Box 60, Kensington Chambers	441-534-89898	dial
46/50 Kensington Place	441-534-73327	fax
St.Helier, Jersey, Channel Islands JE2 3PA	419-2229	telex

- Primary business activity: banking services.
- Private banking services and/or savings accounts.
- Consumer loans and credit facilities.
- Corporate services such as registered agent services.
- Executor and administrator of wills and estates.
- Safekeeping and custodian services.
- Portfolio management of securities and mutual funds.
- Company formation services are offered.
- Trust formation services are offered.
- Captive insurance company formation services are offered.
- Banking company formation services are offered.

Bank of Wales (Jersey) Ltd.

31 Broad Street	441-534-73364	dial
St.Helier, Jersey, Channel Islands	419-2101	telex

- Primary business activity: banking services.

Banque Bruxelles Lambert (Jersey) Ltd.

Huguenot House	441-534-78822	dial
28 La Motte Street	441-534-73367	fax
St.Helier, Jersey, Channel Islands		

- Primary business activity: banking services.

Barclays Private Bank & Trust Limited

Mr. Howard Drake	441-534-73741	dial
Managing Director	441-534-31676	fax

PO.Box 82, Barclaytrust House
39/41 Broad Street, St.Helier, Jersey, Channel Islands

- Primary business activity: bank and trust services.
- Offers private credit card backed by deposit.
- Private banking services and/or savings accounts.
- Consumer loans and credit facilities.
- Safekeeping and custodian services.
- Portfolio management of securities and mutual funds.
- Company formation services are offered.
- Trust formation services are offered.

BDO Binder

Seaton House	441-534-21565	dial
Seaton Place	441-534-21987	fax

St.Helier, Jersey, Channel Islands

- Primary business activity: accounting services.

Beresford Group

Mr. Gary Killmister	441-534-79502	dial
White Lodge	441-534-33405	fax

Wellington Road, St.Saviour, Jersey, Channel Islands JE2 7TH

- Primary business activity: bank and trust services.
- Safekeeping and custodian services.
- Company formation services are offered.
- Trust formation services are offered.

Bilbao Vizcaya Bank (Jersey) Ltd.

2 Mulcaster St.	441-534-22600	dial
St.Helier, Jersey, Channel Islands	441-534-34649	fax

- Primary business activity: banking services.

Cantrade Private Bank Switzerland (CI)

Cantrade House, 24 Union St.	441-534-59199	dial
PO.Box 350	441-534-26340	fax

St.Helier, Jersey, Channel Islands

- Primary business activity: banking services.

Capital House Investment Management

Capital House Building	441-534-285700	dial
Bath Street	441-534-285753	fax
St.Helier, Jersey, Channel Islands		

- Primary business activity: company and trust formation services.

Cater Allen Bank (Jersey) Ltd.

Cater Allen House	441-534-77016	dial
Commercial Street	441-534-38577	fax
St.Helier, Jersey, Channel Islands		

- Primary business activity: banking services.

Centurian Management Services Ltd.

7 Library Place	441-534-70152	dial
St.Helier, Jersey, Channel Islands	441-534-20396	fax

- Primary business activity: accounting services.

Chase Manhattan Bank, N.A.

Chase House, Grenville Street	441-534-25561	dial
PO.Box 127	441-534-35301	fax
St.Helier, Jersey, Channel Islands JE4 8QH		

- Primary business activity: banking services.
- Private banking services and/or savings accounts.
- Consumer loans and credit facilities.
- Safekeeping and custodian services.
- Portfolio management of securities and mutual funds.
- Company formation services are offered.
- Trust formation services are offered.

Citibank (Channel Islands) Ltd.

38 Esplanade	441-534-608000	dial
PO.Box 104, St.Helier, Jersey, Channel Islands		

- Primary business activity: banking services.

Coutts & Co. (Jersey) Ltd.

PO.Box 6	441-534-282345	dial
23/25 Broad Street	441-534-282400	fax

St.Helier, Jersey, Channel Islands JE4 8ND

- Primary business activity: bank and trust services.
- Private banking services and/or savings accounts.
- Safekeeping and custodian services.
- Portfolio management of securities and mutual funds.
- Company formation services are offered.
- Trust formation services are offered.

Croy Trust Limited

Mrs. Marie Moss	441-534-78774	dial
Director	441-534-35401	fax

Belmont House, 1st Floor, 2-6 Belmont Road
St.Helier, Jersey, Channel Islands JE2 4SA

- Primary business activity: bank and trust services.

EBC Fund Managers (Jersey)

PO.Box 556	441-534-36331	dial
EBC House, 1/3 Seale St.	441-534-39495	fax

St.Helier, Jersey, Channel Islands

- Primary business activity: company and trust formation services.

Ermitage

PO.Box 79	441-534-76007	dial
50 Kensington Place	441-534-36095	fax

St.Helier, Jersey, Channel Islands

- Primary business activity: company and trust formation services.

Ernst & Young

PO.Box 621, Le Gallais Chambers	441-534-501000	dial
54 Bath St.	441-534-23265	fax

St.Helier, Jersey, Channel Islands

- Primary business activity: accounting services.

Europlan Financial Services Ltd.

Lister House, The Parade	441-534-38500	dial
St.Helier, Jersey, Channel Islands	441-534-38690	fax

- Primary business activity: company and trust formation services.

Fidelity International (CI) Ltd.

9 Bond St.	441-534-71696	dial
St.Helier, Jersey, Channel Islands	441-534-31344	fax

- Primary business activity: company and trust formation services.

Halifax International

PO.Box 664	441-534-59840	dial
Halifax House, 31-33 New Street	441-534-73690	fax
St.Helier, Jersey, Channel Islands		

- Primary business activity: company and trust formation services.

Hambros Bank (Jersey) Limited

PO.Box 78	441-534-78577	dial
13 Broad Street	441-534-71913	fax
St.Helier, Jersey, Channel Islands		

- Primary business activity: banking services.

Hill Samuel (C.I.) Trust Co. Limited

Ms. Kaye T. Fontaine	441-534-604604	dial
Client Services Manager	441-534-604606	fax
PO.Box 63	419-2167	telex

7 Bond Street, St.Helier, Jersey, Channel Islands JE4 8PH

- Primary business activity: bank and trust services.
- Private banking services and/or savings accounts.
- Consumer loans and credit facilities.
- Corporate services such as registered agent services.
- Safekeeping and custodian services.
- Portfolio management of securities and mutual funds. Minimum annual fee 0.25% of assets or £1,750.
- Company formation services are offered. Minimum formation fee £500 plus license fee. Minimum annual fee £1,250.
- Trust formation services are offered. Minimum formation fee £500. Minimum annual fee 0.25% of assets or £1,750.

HSBC Private Banking (C.I.) Limited

Mr. Simon Morgan	441-534-606500	dial
Business Development Manager	441-534-606504	fax
PO.Box 88, 1 Grenville Street	419-2254	telex

St.Helier, Jersey, Channel Islands JE4 9PF

- Primary business activity: banking services.
- Private banking services and/or savings accounts.
- Corporate services such as registered agent services.
- Safekeeping and custodian services.
- Portfolio management of securities and mutual funds.
- Company formation services are offered.
- Trust formation services are offered.

John Govett Management

Minden House, 6 Minden Place	441-534-26997	fax
St.Helier, Jersey, Channel Islands	441-534-38578	dial

- Primary business activity: company and trust formation services.

Jordan & Sons (Jersey) Ltd.

Mrs. Rosemary E. Marr	441-534-30579	dial
Company Formation Agent	441-534-26430	fax

PO.Box 578, 17 Bond Street, St.Helier, Jersey, Channel Islands JE4 8UT

- Primary business activity: company and trust formation services.
- Corporate services such as registered agent services.
- Company formation services are offered. Minimum formation fee £600 plus £500 license fee. Minimum annual fee £500.
- Trust formation services are offered. Minimum formation fee £500. Minimum annual fee £500.

Kleinwort Benson (Jersey) Limited

Mr. Jim Gilligan	441-534-78866	dial
Head of Business Development	441-534-78908	fax

PO.Box 76, Wests Centre, St.Helier, Jersey, Channel Islands JE4 8PQ

- Primary business activity: company and trust formation services.
- Primary business activity: fund or portfolio manager.
- Safekeeping and custodian services.
- Company formation services are offered.
- Trust formation services are offered.

KPMG Peat Marwick

PO.Box 453	441-534-888891	dial
Equity & Law House La Motte St.	441-534-888892	fax
St.Helier, Jersey, Channel Islands		

- Primary business activity: accounting services.

Lazard Brothers & Co. (Jersey) Limited

2-6 Church St.	441-534-37361	dial
PO.Box 108	441-534-70057	fax
St.Helier, Jersey, Channel Islands		

- Primary business activity: banking services.

Lloyds Bank Trust Company (CI) Limited

Waterloo House, Don Street	441-534-284200	dial
PO.Box 195	441-534-284333	fax
St.Helier, Jersey, Channel Islands		

- Primary business activity: banking services.

Lombard Banking (Jersey) Limited

Mr. Carl Lee	441-534-27511	dial
Managing Director	419-2038	telex

PO.Box 554, 39 La Motte Street, St.Helier, Jersey, Channel Islands JE4 8XH

- Primary business activity: bank and trust services.
- Private banking services and/or savings accounts.

Michael Forrest and Partners

Langtry House	441-534-73921	dial
40 La Motte St.	441-534-24668	fax
St.Helier, Jersey, Channel Islands		

- Primary business activity: accounting services.

Midland Bank Fund Managers (Jersey) Ltd

Mr. Steven Morfee	441-534-606000	dial
Manager, Customer Support Services	441-534-606356	fax
PO.Box 26	441-534-606016	fax
28/34 Hill Street	419-2026	telex

St.Helier, Jersey, Channel Islands JE4 8NR

- Primary business activity: bank and trust services.
- Private banking services and/or savings accounts.
- Portfolio management of securities and mutual funds.

Midland Bank International Finance Corporation Limited

Mr. David A. Oliver	441-534-606113	dial
Manager, Personal Offshore Services	441-534-606146	fax
PO.Box 26	419-2098	telex

28/34 Hill Street, St.Helier, Jersey, Channel Islands JE4 8NR

- Primary business activity: bank and trust services.
- Primary business activity: insurance products & services.
- Offers Private Credit Card (VISA/MasterCard) backed by deposit.
- Private banking services and/or savings accounts.
- Consumer loans and credit facilities.
- Corporate services such as registered agent services.
- Executor and administrator of wills and estates.
- Safekeeping and custodian services.
- Portfolio management of securities and mutual funds.
- Company formation services are offered. Minimum formation fee £750 plus license fee. Minimum annual fee £1,500.
- Trust formation services are offered. Minimum formation fee £750. Minimum annual fee 3/4% of assets or £1,500.

Midland Bank PLC Personal Offshore Services

Ms. Karen Lysiak	441-534-606000	dial
Customer Information Services	441-534-606145	fax
PO.Box 14	419-2098	telex

St.Helier, Jersey, Channel Islands JE4 8NJ

- Primary business activity: bank and trust services.
- Primary business activity: insurance products & services.
- Offers private credit card backed by deposit.
- Private banking services and/or savings accounts.
- Consumer loans and credit facilities.
- Corporate services such as registered agent services.
- Safekeeping and custodian services.
- Portfolio management of securities and mutual funds.
- Company formation services are offered.
- Trust formation services are offered.

Moore Stephens

PO.Box 236	441-534-80088	dial
First Island House, Peter St.	441-534-880099	fax

St.Helier, Jersey, Channel Islands

- Primary business activity: accounting services.

Morgan Grenfeld (CI) Limited

12 Dumaresq Street	441-534-66711	dial
PO.Box 727	441-534-71074	fax

St.Helier, Jersey, Channel Islands

- Primary business activity: banking services.

Mossack Fonseca & Co.

Attorneys at Law	441-534-42800	dial
PO.Box 168	441-534-42054	fax

St.Helier, Jersey, Channel Islands JE4 8RZ

- Primary business activity: law office.

Price Waterhouse

Eagle House	441-534-74222	dial
Don Road	441-534-67556	fax

St.Helier, Jersey, Channel Islands

- Primary business activity: accounting services.

Quilter Goodison Channel Islands

5 Britannia Place	441-534-506070	dial
Bath Street	441-534-68108	fax

St.Helier, Jersey, Channel Islands

- Primary business activity: company and trust formation services.

Rawlinson & Hunter

PO.Box 83	441-534-75141	dial
Ordnance House, 31 Pier Rd.	441-534-32876	fax

St.Helier, Jersey, Channel Islands

- Primary business activity: accounting services.

Royal Bank of Scotland (Jersey) Limited

22 Hill Street	441-534-26322	dial
PO.Box 542	441-534-39148	fax

St.Helier, Jersey, Channel Islands

- Primary business activity: banking services.

Royal Trust Bank (Jersey) Ltd.

PO.Box 194, Royal Trust House	441-534-27441	dial
19/21 Broad Street	441-534-32513	fax

St.Helier, Jersey, Channel Islands JE4 8RR

- Primary business activity: bank and trust services.
- Offers private credit card backed by deposit.
- Private banking services and/or savings accounts.
- Consumer loans and credit facilities.
- Safekeeping and custodian services.
- Portfolio management of securities and mutual funds.

S.G. Warburg & Co. (Jersey) Limited

Forum House	441-534-600600	dial

Grenville Street, St.Helier, Jersey, Channel Islands

- Primary business activity: banking services.

Scimitar Asset Management (CI)

Standard Chartered House	441-534-34373	dial
PO.Box 330, Conway St.	441-534-26035	fax

St.Helier, Jersey, Channel Islands

- Primary business activity: company and trust formation services.

Standard Bank Investment Corp. (Jersey)

One Waverly Place	441-534-67557	dial
PO.Box 583	441-534-70588	fax

St.Helier, Jersey, Channel Islands

- Primary business activity: banking services.

Standard Chartered Bank (CI) Limited

Mr. Steve Cartwright	441-534-507000	dial
Investment Manager	441-534-507111	fax

Standard Chartered House, Conway Street, PO.Box 830
St.Helier, Jersey, Channel Islands JE4 8PY

- Primary business activity: banking services.

States of Jersey Income Tax Department

Mr. Robert J. Gaiger	441-534-603300	dial
Comptroller of Income Tax	441-534-89142	fax

Cyril Le Marquand House, PO.Box 56
The Parade, St.Helier, Jersey, Channel Islands JE4 8PF

- Primary business activity: government services.

Strachans

Sommerville House	441-534-71505	dial
Phillips Street	441-534-23902	fax

St.Helier, Jersey, Channel Islands

- Primary business activity: accounting services.

Swiss Bank Corporation (Jersey) Ltd.

Mr. Felix Scheuber	441-534-506500	dial
Associate Director - Private Banking	441-534-506501	fax
40 Esplanade	4192288 SBCJY	telex

PO.Box 34, St.Helier, Jersey, Channel Islands JE4 8NW

- Primary business activity: banking services.
- Private banking services and/or savings accounts.
- Consumer loans and credit facilities.
- Safekeeping and custodian services.
- Portfolio management of securities and mutual funds. Minimum annual fee 0.5% of assets or £1,500.
- Company formation services are offered.
- Trust formation services are offered.

Touche Ross & Company

PO.Box 403	441-534-33944	dial
66-68 Esplanade	441-534-34037	fax

Lord Countache House, St.Helier, Jersey, Channel Islands

- Primary business activity: accounting services.

TSB Bank Channel Islands Limited Offshore Centre

Mr. John Hutchins	441-534-503939	dial
Manager, Offshore Centre	441-534-503211	fax
8 David Place	4192164 TSBCI G	telex

PO.Box 597, St.Helier, Jersey, Channel Islands JE4 8XW

- Primary business activity: banking services.
- Offers Private Credit Card (VISA) backed by deposit.
- Private banking services and/or savings accounts.
- Consumer loans and credit facilities.
- Safekeeping and custodian services.
- Portfolio management of securities and mutual funds.
- Company formation services are offered.
- Trust formation services are offered.

TSB Bank Channel Islands Limited

5 New Street, TSB House	441-534-503000	dial
PO.Box 160	441-534-503047	fax

St.Helier, Jersey, Channel Islands

- Primary business activity: banking services.

Westpac Banking Corporation (Jersey)

Mr. B.J. Ferguson	441-534-504504	dial
Manager Banking Department	441-534-504575	fax
PO.Box 393	419-2438	telex

7-11 Britannia Place, Bath Street
St.Helier, Jersey, Channel Islands JE4 8US

- Primary business activity: banking services.
- Private banking services and/or savings accounts.
- Consumer loans and credit facilities.
- Executor and administrator of wills and estates.
- Safekeeping and custodian services.
- Portfolio management of securities and mutual funds. Minimum annual fee 3/4% of assets or £1,500 plus £40 per transaction.
- Company formation services are offered. Minimum formation fee £1,000 including license fee.
- Trust formation services are offered. Minimum formation fee £500.

COOK ISLANDS

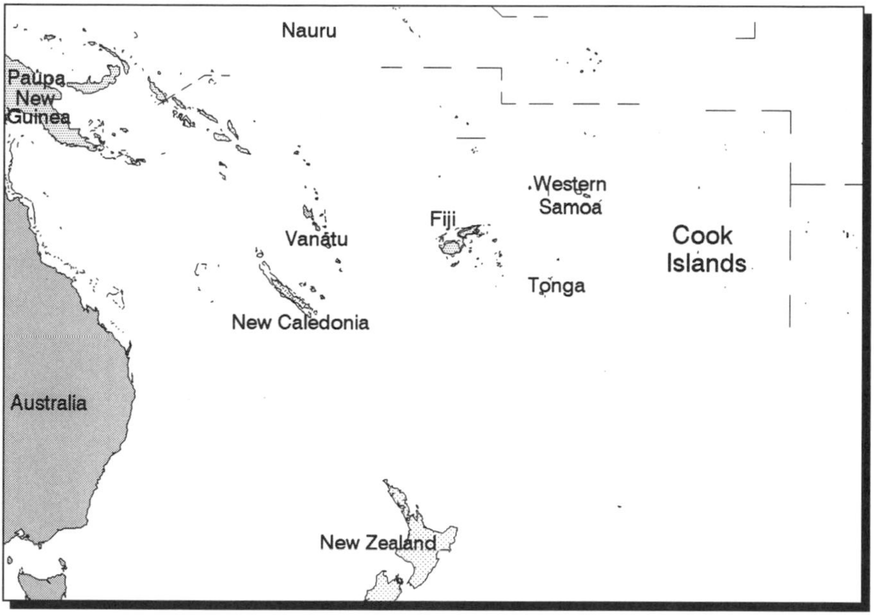

In the South Pacific. 15 islands scattered over 2 million square kilometers of the South Pacific, with a total land mass of less than 250 square kilometers. East of the Samoas, West of French Polynesia. Population is approximately 20,000, with 12,000 living in Rarotonga. Main language is English. Climate is tropical.

The Cook Islands were a protectorate of Great Britain from 1888 to 1891. In 1891 the boundaries of New Zealand were enlarged to include the Cook Islands. New Zealand's Cook Islands Act 1915 declared the common law of England as of January 14, 1840 (the year the colony of New Zealand was established) to apply to the Cook Islands. The Cook Islands became a self governing British colony in 1965. An international airport was opened in Rarotonga in 1974, and in 1977 the Development Investment Act was passed to encourage investment in the Islands.

In 1981, Australian David Lloyd identified the Cook Islands as an ideal location for the establishment of an offshore financial centre. A proposal was presented to the Cook Islands government which included legislation to provide for International Companies and Trusts. This proposed legislation was passed with full support in 1982.

Does the Cook Islands have a secrecy law?

YES. The confidentiality of all operations is protected by strict secrecy laws which apply to government officials, bank and trust company employees.

Is there any situation where bank secrecy can be lifted?

YES. The disclosure of confidential information can be obtained upon court order in connection with a criminal offense triable within the Cook Islands or which would have been so triable if it had been committed within the Cook Islands, including drug trade, fraud, and theft.

Can foreign tax authorities obtain information on Cook Islands bank accounts?

NO. Cook Island authorities only release information relating to criminal cases. Tax evasion is not a crime in the Cook Islands, as there are no taxes. Therefore, financial information relating to taxation is not available to foreign governments.

Is the Cook Islands an independent country?

NO. The Cook Islands were a British protectorate before 1891. In 1891, the Cook Islands were annexed into New Zealand territory. The islanders hold New Zealand common citizenship to this day. The Cook Islands became self governing under a Westminster model constitution in 1965.

Is the legal system based on English Common Law?

YES. The legal system is based on English common law. New Zealand's Cook Islands Act 1915 declared the common law of England as of January 14, 1840 (the year the colony of New Zealand was established) to apply to the Cook Islands. Appeals are to the Cook Islands Court of Appeal, with the supreme court being represented by the Privy Council in England.

Is there an income tax in the Cook Islands?

NO. There are no taxes in the Cook Islands. International Companies are not liable to pay income tax, capital tax, or withholding tax.

Are there any other taxes in the Cook Islands?

NO. There are no capital gains taxes, gift taxes, estate taxes, capital taxes, or stamp duties in the Cook Islands.

Are there any exchange controls in the Cook Islands?

NO. There are currently no exchange controls in the Cook Islands.

Is there a tax treaty between the U.S. and the Cook Islands?

YES. Indirectly there is a tax treaty between the U.S. and the Cook Islands, since the Cook Islands fall under the Income Tax Convention of 1948 between the U.S. and New Zealand.

Is there a tax treaty between Canada and the Cook Islands?

NO. There is no tax treaty between Canada and the Cook Islands.

Does the Cook Islands allow the formation of Limited Companies?

YES. International Companies (ICs) are governed by the International Companies Act 1981-82. The Act was amended in 1991 to allow for several different types of companies:

- No Liability Companies (shareholders have no capital liability to the company).
- Companies Limited by Guarantee (shareholders have a capital liability limited to the amount stated in their guarantee).
- Companies Limited by both Shares and Guarantee.
- Unlimited Companies (shareholders have unlimited liability for all debts of the company).
- Mutual Companies.

ICs are not liable to pay income tax, capital, estate, or gift tax. The incorporation of an IC must be handled by a licensed Trustee company, who will also provide the registered office. Advantages of Cook Islands companies include:

- Shares may be issued as bearer shares or bearer warrants.
- The holder of a bearer warrant is deemed not a shareholder of the company until the warrant is surrendered.
- Shareholders are not required to have accounts audited, and are not required to hold annual general meetings.
- Shareholders and directors meetings may be held anywhere.
- Only one shareholder is required. Nominee shareholders may be used.
- There is no minimum share capital, and there is no capital duty on share capital. Shares may have no par value.
- Only one director is required. Nominee directors may be used.

It is a requirement that there is a resident secretary.

Does the Cook Islands allow the formation of International Trusts?

YES. Trusts are governed by the International Trusts Act 1984. The requirements are that at least one Settlor or donor is an IC, Trustee company, or registered foreign company, and the Beneficiaries must be non-resident. To form an International Trust, the application to the Registrar of International Trusts must include:

- the name of the Trust and the Trustee;
- the date of the formation of the Trust; and
- the registered office of the Trust.

No other information is disclosed to the Registrar. The Trustee company must certify to the Registrar that the Beneficiaries of the Trust are non-residents. The annual renewal fee is US$100. A term of up to 100 years may be specified. No taxation of any type is applied to an International Trust.

The Cook Islands have passed specific Trust legislation providing protection against matrimonial and other creditors. No foreign judgement affecting an international Trust, the parties to the Trust, nor thc Trust property shall be entertained in a court of the Cook Islands if that judgement is based on the application of any law inconsistent with the Cook Islands Trust legislation.

Where a creditor proves beyond a reasonable doubt that an International Trust was formed with the intent of defrauding a creditor, the company or Trust is required to satisfy the claim out of the assets held. The statute of limitations on this type of action is 2 years.

Does the Cook Islands allow the formation of Captive Insurance Companies?

YES. A Mutual Company may be licensed under the Offshore Insurance Act to issue insurance to both shareholders and outsiders.

Does the Cook Islands allow the formation of Banking Companies?

YES. The Cook Islands allows the formation and management of Banking Companies.

Financial institutions and contacts:

ANZ Banking Group Limited
1st Floor, Development Bank Building
PO.Box 907, Avarua, Rarotonga, Cook Islands, South Pacific

- Primary business activity: bank and trust services.

Asiaciti Trust Pacific, Ltd.

Mr. Michael Innes-Jones	682-23387	dial
CIDB Building, 3rd Floor	682-23385	fax

PO.Box 822, Avarua, Rarotonga, Cook Islands, South Pacific 13

- Primary business activity: bank and trust services.
- Corporate services such as registered agent services.
- Safekeeping and custodian services.
- Company formation services are offered.
- Trust formation services are offered.
- Banking company formation services are offered.

Cook Islands Trust Corporation Limited
PO.Box 666, Mercury House, Rarotonga, Cook Islands, South Pacific

- Primary business activity: bank and trust services.

European Pacific Trust Company Limited

PO.Box 25, European Pacific Centre	682-22680	dial
Tutakimoa Road	682-20566	fax

Rarotonga, Cook Islands, South Pacific

- Primary business activity: bank and trust services.

International Trust Corporation Limited

PO.Box 208	682-21080	dial
CIDB Building	682-21087	fax

Avarua, Rarotonga, Cook Islands, South Pacific

- Primary business activity: bank and trust services.
- Corporate services such as registered agent services.
- Safekeeping and custodian services.
- Company formation services are offered.
- Trust formation services are offered.
- Captive insurance company formation services are offered.
- Banking company formation services are offered.

Overseas Company Registration Agents

Level 3, CIDB Building	682-23448	dial
PO.Box 822	682-23449	fax

Rarotonga, Cook Islands, South Pacific

- Primary business activity: company and trust formation services.
- Corporate services such as registered agent services.
- Company formation services are offered. Minimum formation fee US$2,250 plus US$500 license fee. Minimum annual fee US$500.

Southpac Trust Ltd.

Mr. David R. McNair	682-20514	dial
2nd Floor, Centrepoint	682-20667	fax

PO.Box 11, Rarotonga, Cook Islands, South Pacific

- Primary business activity: bank and trust services.
- Private banking services and/or savings accounts.
- Consumer loans and credit facilities.
- Company formation services are offered.
- Trust formation services are offered.

Westpac Banking Corporation Limited

Mr. Greg P. Holt	682-20802	dial
Manager, International Business	682-22014	fax
PO.Box 42	(772) 62014 RG	telex

Main Road, Avarua, Avarua, Rarotonga, Cook Islands, South Pacific

- Primary business activity: bank and trust services.
- Private banking services and/or savings accounts.
- Consumer loans and credit facilities.

GIBRALTAR

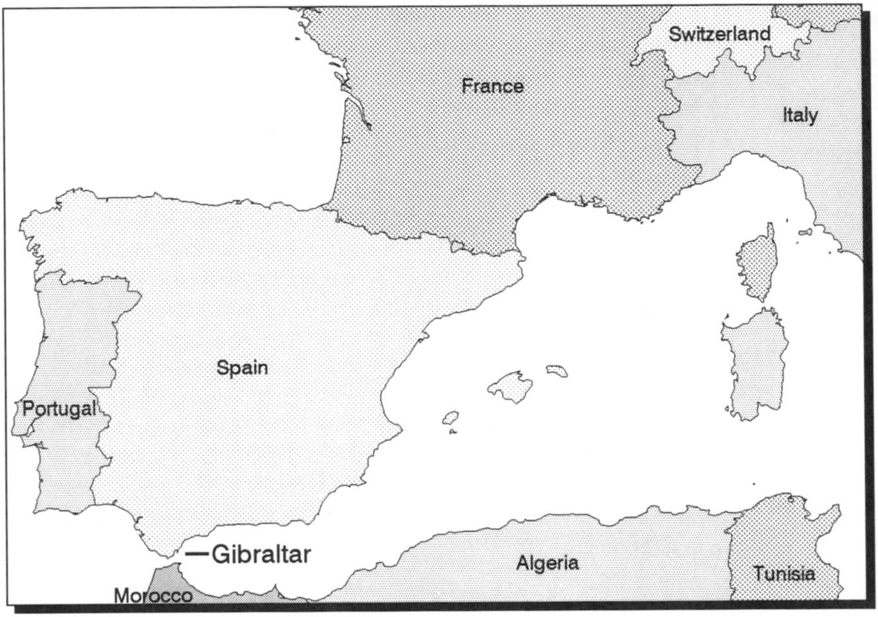

In Europe. "The Rock" is at the opening of the Mediterranean, at the extreme west end of the Mediterranean Sea, covering an area of just over 2.3 square miles. Gibraltar is connected to Spain by an isthmus, and faces North Africa 20 miles across the straits. Population approximately 35,000. Main language is English and Spanish.

The name "Gibraltar" came from the Moorish leader Tariq who used "Gibel Tariq" (Mountain of Tariq) as a base during the 8th century. Gibraltar has been a British Crown Colony since 1704, formally ceded by Spain in the 1713 Treaty of Utrecht. Gibraltar's 1965 constitution granted extensive self governing powers. Gibraltar began its development as a financial centre in 1967 through the Companies (Taxation & Concessions) Ordinance that granted income and estate duty concessions to Gibraltar companies registered as Exempt. Gibraltar was isolated by the Spanish blockade from 1969 to 1985. Stability depends on the Spanish, who would like to again have control of Gibraltar. The Rock itself is made of limestone and is over 1,300 feet high.

Does Gibraltar have a secrecy law?

YES. Banks are supervised by the Gibraltarian Banking Authority and subject to restrictive legislation that guarantees anonymity. All clients are guaranteed complete anonymity, therefore ensuring that any transaction will be a matter between the customer and the bank only. The identity of beneficial owners of Exempt companies is protected by law.

Is there any situation where bank secrecy can be lifted?

YES. The Drug Trafficking Ordinance 1989 allows the release of confidential banking information in matters of drug trafficking and money laundering.

Can foreign tax authorities obtain information on Gibraltar bank accounts?

NO. Confidential financial information is not available to foreign governments or tax investigators. Gibraltar tax authorities do not exchange or disclose information with or to any other tax authorities.

Is Gibraltar an independent country?

NO. Gibraltar is a self governing British Crown colony, in British possession since 1704. Gibraltar is self governing as a result of the 1965 constitution, and has an autonomous locally elected government which is responsible for local laws. Britain retains control over foreign policy and defense. Spain has made several unsuccessful attempts to claim sovereignty.

Is the legal system based on English Common Law?

YES. The legal system is based on English common law and acts of parliament, and is supplemented by local statutes. There is an independent judiciary with a Supreme Court, Court of First Instance, and lower Courts. The ultimate court of appeal is the Privy Council of England.

Is there an income tax in Gibraltar?

YES. There is an income tax in Gibraltar, although non-residents (other than British nationals) are tax exempt. Qualifying companies are charged a tax rate of 2% to 18%. Resident companies pay income tax at a rate of 35%, and income tax for individuals is 30% to 50%.

Exempt corporations pay no taxes. An Exemption Certificate, once granted, is valid for 25 years, and grants full exemption from income tax, estate duty and stamp duty.

There is no income tax on interest from deposits, no Value Added Tax, and no tax on trade in precious metals.

Are there any other taxes in Gibraltar?

NO. There is no capital gains tax, no tax on gifts or capital movements, and no inheritance tax, although estate duty is levied in Gibraltar.

Ad valorem taxes of 10% were introduced in 1970, applying to most merchandise imported into Gibraltar, with the exception of food, drugs, and building materials.

Are there any exchange controls in Gibraltar?

NO. There are currently no exchange controls in Gibraltar. The currency is the Gibraltar pound, at par with the pound sterling.

Is there a tax treaty between the U.S. and Gibraltar?

NO. There is no exchange of information treaty between the U.S. and Gibraltar, although there is a tax treaty between the United Kingdom and Gibraltar.

Is there a tax treaty between Canada and Gibraltar?

NO. There is no exchange of information treaty between Canada and Gibraltar.

Does Gibraltar allow the formation of Limited Companies?

YES. Gibraltar offers the Non-resident Company, the Exempt Company and the Qualifying Company, all with special tax advantages. Any Gibraltar company, or a Gibraltar registered branch of a non-Gibraltar company, may apply for registration as an Exempt company under the Gibraltar (Taxation and Concessions) Ordinance.

Non-resident Company - Non-resident Companies are incorporated in Gibraltar but managed and controlled by directors outside Gibraltar's jurisdiction. Gibraltar does not levy flat rate fees such as annual company registration tax or non-resident company duty against a Non-resident Company. Non-resident companies may not derive income from within Gibraltar and should therefore maintain bank accounts outside Gibraltar.

Exempt Company - Exempt companies are entirely exempted from Income Tax, Estate and Stamp Duties and are instead liable for a fixed annual tax of £225 (or £200 if a non-resident Exempt company, £300 if a Gibraltar registered branch of a non-Gibraltar company). The advantage of an Exempt Company over a Non-resident Company is that the Exempt Company is not presumed to be resident elsewhere.

The principal requirements for the granting of Exempt status are that:

- No Gibraltar resident has a beneficial interest in the Exempt company.
- The company does not trade or carry on business in Gibraltar.
- Professional references must be received by the Gibraltar Financial and Development Secretary from a lawyer, banker, or registered accountant.
- An outline of the company's proposed activities must be provided to the Financial and Development secretary.
- Minimum share capital is £100, issued and fully paid.
- The name of the company must end with the word Limited.

As with all Gibraltar companies, the identities of directors and shareholders are a matter of public record, although nominee shareholders may be appointed to protect the identity of beneficial owners. The statutory registers must be held in Gibraltar (usually at the registered office). The identity of beneficial owners of Exempt companies is protected by law. There are no requirements to publish accounts.

A minimum of two shareholders is required. There are no restrictions on the appointment of officers of Exempt companies, although either a director or the secretary must be a Gibraltar resident. There are no restrictions on the location of directors meetings.

When applying for Exempt status it is necessary to provide brief details of the company's proposed activities to the Financial and Development Secretary.

Gibraltar Qualifying Company - A Gibraltar company, or the Gibraltar registered branch of a non-Gibraltar company, may apply for registration as a Qualifying company under the Income Tax (Qualifying Companies) Rules 1983. Qualifying companies are charged a tax rate of 2% to 18%. Qualifying companies require a minimum issued share capital of £1,000, and must deposit £1,000 with the Gibraltar government on account of future income tax liabilities. A one-time fee of £250 is payable on the issue of a Qualifying certificate.

Does Gibraltar allow the formation of International Trusts?

YES. Based on English Common Law, there are two types of Trusts available, the Fixed Trust and the Discretionary Trust. Benefits of a Gibraltar Trust are:

- The assets of a Trust set up by a non-resident of Gibraltar are exempt from Gibraltar tax, provided that any income is derived from outside of Gibraltar (with the exception of bank interest).
- The Trust may remain in force for up to 100 years.
- The Trust is a private arrangement between the Settlor and the Trustee, providing complete anonymity for the Settlor.
- No official register is kept of Trusts, and no requirement exists for the settlement deeds to be made public.
- There are no annual filing fees or audit requirements.

Gibraltar law also allows the formation of an Asset Protection Trust, where if a Settlor (who is solvent at the time and not planning to become insolvent) transfers assets to the Trust and subsequently becomes insolvent, the Trust would not be declared void upon application by a creditor. Under the Bankruptcy (Register of Dispositions) Regulations 1990 an Asset Protection Trust must pay an initial registration fee of £300 and an annual fee of £100.

Fixed Trust - With a Fixed Trust, the Trustee holds assets exclusively for a clearly limited and well-defined group of people. The Trustee cannot change their rights under the Trust.

Discretionary Trust - The standard type of Discretionary Trust is set up for a group of Beneficiaries described in the Trust deed. The Trustee is empowered to distribute Trust funds between all Trust Beneficiaries, or restrict funds to one or several Beneficiaries at his discretion.

Does Gibraltar allow the formation of Captive Insurance Companies?

YES. Gibraltar is a suitable jurisdiction for the formation of Captive Insurance Companies.

Does Gibraltar allow the formation of Banking Companies?

YES. Gibraltar is a suitable jurisdiction for the formation of Banking Companies.

Financial institutions and contacts:

A.L.Galliano Bankers Limited

76 Main Street, PO.Box 143, Gibraltar

- Primary business activity: banking services.

Allias & Levy

3 Irish Place, Suite 3, PO.Box 466, Gibraltar

- Primary business activity: law office.

Attias & Levy Barristers-at-Law
Mr. Abraham J. Levy 350-72150 dial
Partner 350-74986 fax
Suites 1 & 3, 3 Irish Place, PO.Box 466, Gibraltar

- Primary business activity: law office.

Banesto (Gibraltar) Ltd.
Mr. Serg Gilbert Garcia 350-77775 dial
Director 350-76333 fax
114-116 Main Street, PO.Box 630, Gibraltar

- Primary business activity: banking services.
- Private banking services and/or savings accounts.
- Corporate services such as registered agent services.
- Safekeeping and custodian services.
- Portfolio management of securities and mutual funds.
- Company formation services are offered. Minimum formation fee £1,050 plus £200 exempt company tax. Minimum annual fee £1,250.
- Trust formation services are offered. Minimum annual fee 0.10% of assets on Trusts over £5,000,000.

Banque Indosuez
206/210 Main Street 350-75090 dial
PO.Box 26, Gibraltar 350-79618 fax

- Primary business activity: banking services.

Barclaytrust International Limited
Mr. Ray Tarry 350-78565 dial
Managing Director 350-79987 fax
1st Floor, Regal House, 3 Queensway, Gibraltar

- Primary business activity: bank and trust services.
- Offers private credit card backed by deposit.
- Private banking services and/or savings accounts.
- Consumer loans and credit facilities.
- Safekeeping and custodian services.
- Portfolio management of securities and mutual funds.
- Company formation services are offered.
- Trust formation services are offered.

Coutts & Co. (Gibraltar) Ltd.

National Westminster House — 350-72676 dial
57-63 Line Wall Road, PO.Box 709 — 350-78874 fax
Gibraltar

- Primary business activity: bank and trust services.
- Private banking services and/or savings accounts.
- Safekeeping and custodian services.
- Portfolio management of securities and mutual funds.
- Company formation services are offered.
- Trust formation services are offered.

CV Management Services Ltd.

Mr. Joseph Vaughan — 350-76933 dial
Company Formation Agent — 350-76718 fax
PO.Box 453, 3/1a Parliament Lane, Gibraltar

- Primary business activity: company and trust formation services.

Europa Trust Company Limited

Ms. Diana Soussi — 350-79013 dial
Client Liaison — 350-70101 fax
Suite 743, Europort, PO.Box 629, Gibraltar

- Primary business activity: bank and trust services.

Gibraltar Financial Services Handbook

Ms. Diane Sloma — 350-79385 dial
General Manager
PO.Box 555, Gibraltar

- Primary business activity: newsletters, books, or information.

Gibraltar Private Bank

Mr. Serge Mettraux — 350-73350 dial
10th Floor, ICC Building — 350-73475 fax
Main Street, Gibraltar

- Primary business activity: banking services.

Hambros Bank (Gibraltar) Limited

Hambros House, Line Wall Road	350-79037	fax
PO.Box 375	350-74850	dial
Gibraltar		

- Primary business activity: banking services.

International Company Services Limited

Mr. Simon Denton	350-76173	dial
Company Consultant	350-70158	fax

Suite 2B, 2nd Floor, Mansion House, 143 Main Street, Gibraltar

- Primary business activity: company and trust formation services.
- Corporate services such as registered agent services.
- Safekeeping and custodian services.
- Company formation services are offered. Minimum formation fee £250 plus £225 license fee. Minimum annual fee £400.
- Trust formation services are offered. Minimum formation fee £500. Minimum annual fee £500.

J.A. Hassan & Partners

Mr. J.A. Hassan	350-79000	dial
Partner	350-71966	fax

57-63 Line Wall Road, PO.Box 199, Gibraltar

- Primary business activity: law office.

Jordan & Sons (Gibraltar) Ltd.

Mr. John Swann	350-75446	dial
Manager	350-42701	fax

Suite 2A, Eurolife Building, 1 Corrall Road, PO.Box 569, Gibraltar

- Primary business activity: company and trust formation services.
- Corporate services such as registered agent services.
- Company formation services are offered. Minimum formation fee £895 plus £225 license fee. Minimum annual fee £575.
- Trust formation services are offered. Minimum formation fee £750. Minimum annual fee £250.

Jyske Bank (Gibraltar) Limited

Mr. Jens Skov	350-72782	dial
Retail Manager, Private Banking Dept.	350-76782	fax
76 Main Street	2215 JYSBK GK	telex

PO.Box 143, Gibraltar

- Primary business activity: banking services.
- Offers Private Credit Card (VISA) backed by deposit.
- Private banking services and/or savings accounts.
- Consumer loans and credit facilities.
- Safekeeping and custodian services.
- Portfolio management of securities and mutual funds. Minimum semi-annual fee 0.2% of assets plus 1.0% per transaction.
- Company formation services are offered. Minimum formation fee £1625. Minimum annual fee £1025.
- Trust formation services are offered. Minimum formation fee £170.

KPMG Peat Marwick

Mr. F.A. Isola	350-74015	dial
Partner	350-74016	fax
Regal House, Queensway	2248 KPMGIB GK	telex

PO.Box 191, Gibraltar

- Primary business activity: accounting services.
- Corporate services such as registered agent services.
- Safekeeping and custodian services.
- Company formation services are offered. Minimum formation fee £700 plus £250 license fee. Minimum annual fee £250.
- Trust formation services are offered. Minimum formation fee £1,000. Minimum annual fee £300.

Louis W. Triay & Partners

Mr. Louis W. Triay	350-72712	dial
Barrister-at-Law	350-71405	fax
Barristers At Law and Acting Solicitors	2243 TRILEX GK	telex

Suite C, 2nd Floor, Regal House, PO.Box 147, Queensway, Gibraltar

- Primary business activity: law office.

Midland Bank Trust (Gibraltar)

PO.Box 19	350-79500	dial
3 Library Street	350-72090	fax
Gibraltar	2363	telex

- Primary business activity: bank and trust services.

Riggs Valmet Finsbury

Riggs Valmet Corporate Services Limited		
Mr. William Cid de la Paz	350-40000	dial
Senior Trust Administrator	350-40404	fax
PO.Box 472	2103 RV GK	telex
50 Town Range, Gibraltar		

- Primary business activity: company and trust formation services.

HONG KONG

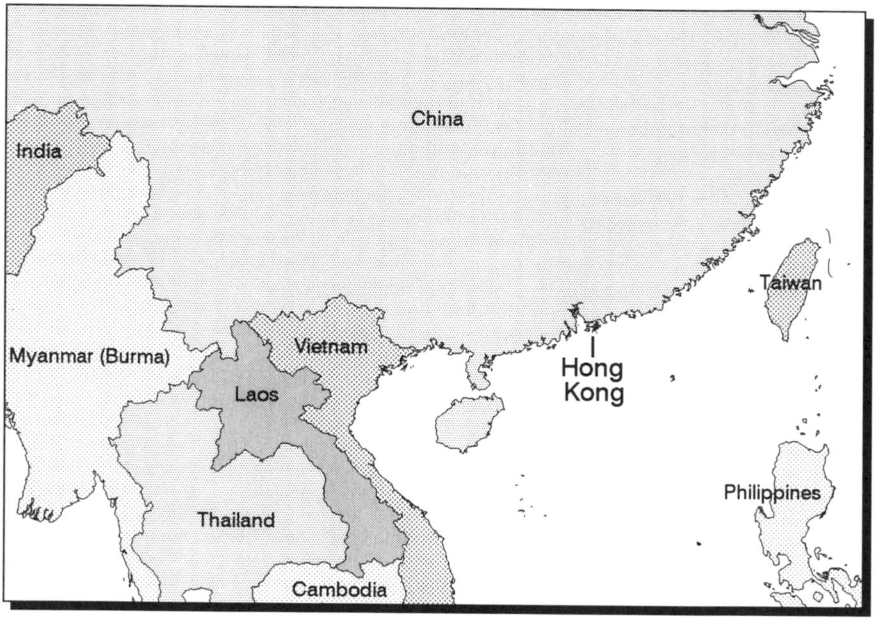

In southeast Asia. It has only 1,071 square kilometers of land, including 235 islands, and a population of approximately 6 million. Main language is Cantonese and English. Climate is moderate sub-tropical with a long, humid summer and a mild winter. Average temperatures are 31°C in summer and 15°C in winter.

The British officially arrived in Hong Kong early in 1841. Possession of the island of Hong Kong was taken on January 26, 1841 and it was proclaimed a Crown Colony by Royal Letters Patent dated April 25, 1843. The island had been ceded to Britain by the Ching government of China as a result of the Convention of Chuenpi, signed January 20,1841 and ratified by the Treaty of Nanking on August 29, 1842. Twenty years later, a small area on the Kowloon peninsula was also ceded to Britain.

In 1898 the New Territories were leased for a 99-year term. Hong Kong continued under British rule from 1841 to 1941 when it was occupied by the Japanese. The British returned in 1945 at the end of World War II. In 1949 a Communist government came to power, following the nationalist republican government which had over-thrown the Ching dynasty in 1912. The colonial status of Hong Kong was not disturbed.

Negotiations on the future of Hong Kong, after the expiry of the 1898 lease on July 1, 1997, were finalized in December 1984. Under an agreement between China and the UK, Hong Kong will revert to China in 1997. The agreement includes many detailed conditions, where the economy, life-style and freedoms will continue largely unchanged for 50 years.

Does Hong Kong have a secrecy law?

NO. Although Hong Kong does not have a secrecy law, there is an implied common law duty of advisors to keep clients relationships confidential.

Is there any situation where bank secrecy can be lifted?

YES. Confidential relationships can be lifted in cases of drug trafficking, money laundering, fraud, and theft. There is also the possibility of financial advisors accepting bribes in return for confidential information.

Can foreign tax authorities obtain information on Hong Kong bank accounts?

YES. Foreign tax authorities have obtained confidential information from Hong Kong banks.

Is Hong Kong an independent country?

NO. The British signed a 99 year lease with China in 1898 on an area called the New Territories, which was to become Hong Kong. The impending expiry of the New Territories lease prompted negotiations that led in 1984 to the signing of the Sino-British Joint Declaration, which decrees that all of Hong Kong will revert to Chinese sovereignty in 1997. Hong Kong will then become a Special Administrative Region within the People's Republic of China, with a high degree of autonomy, its own Basic Law, and a promise that its way of life will be maintained for 50 years. In the interim, Hong Kong remains a British Dependent Territory.

Is the legal system based on English Common Law?

YES. The "territory" of Hong Kong's administrative head is the Governor, formally appointed by the Queen of England, who is advised and assisted by two constitutional bodies, the Executive Council and the Legislative Council. An extensive localization policy has ensured that the Hong Kong Government is now administered largely by Hong Kong Chinese.

Is there an income tax in Hong Kong?

YES. Income is taxed at a rate of 17.5% for corporations and 15% for individuals, partnerships, and sole proprietorships. Certain income is not taxable, including:

- Dividend income.
- Profits or income from the sale of capital assets.
- Interest and profits from certain Hong Kong dollar denominated debt instruments.

Stamp duty is levied on the sale or purchase of any Hong Kong stock at a rate of 0.3% of share value.

Capital duty is levied on the authorized share capital of a company at a rate of 0.6% of share value. Any subsequent increase in share capital is subject to this Capital duty tax.

Are there any other taxes in Hong Kong?

YES. Estate taxes range from 6% where the total Hong Kong assets exceed HK$5 million to 18% where those assets exceed HK$7 million. Estate taxes do not apply to assets outside Hong Kong, even if the deceased was resident in Hong Kong.

There is no capital gains tax or gift tax in Hong Kong.

Are there any exchange controls in Hong Kong?

NO. There are currently no exchange controls in Hong Kong. The currency is the Hong Kong dollar which is freely exchangeable.

Is there a tax treaty between the U.S. and Hong Kong?

YES. Hong Kong and the U.S. signed a treaty in 1989 that provides a mutual tax exemption applicable only to shipping profits. Hong Kong maintains no other tax treaties with any other countries.

Is there a tax treaty between Canada and Hong Kong?

NO. There is no tax treaty between Canada and Hong Kong

Does Hong Kong allow the formation of Limited Companies?

YES. There are three types of Limited Companies in Hong Kong, a Private Limited Company, a Public Limited Company, and a branch office of a foreign company incorporated outside Hong Kong. Requirements are:

- At least two shareholders, who need not be residents of Hong Kong and can be corporate entities.
- At least two directors who have attained the age 18.

- A secretary who must be a resident of Hong Kong if an individual, or have its registered office in Hong Kong if the secretary is corporate.

Additionally, every business established in Hong Kong is required to obtain a Business Registration Certificate, currently HK$160 annually.

Private Limited Company - Most businesses in Hong Kong are private limited companies whose articles of association:

- Restrict the right to transfer the company's shares.
- Limit the number of members to 50.
- Prohibit the offering of shares to the public.

There are no restrictions on foreign ownership of companies in Hong Kong and no residency requirements for directors or shareholders.

Public Limited Company - Companies intending to issue shares to the general public must provide a prospectus giving full details of the proposed share value, capitalization, and details of current and future business prospects. Corporations are not permitted to act as a director or secretary of a Public Limited Company.

Branch Office - Companies operating in Hong Kong and incorporated elsewhere must register with the Registrar of Companies under Part XI of the Hong Kong Companies Ordinance. This requires:

- Certified copy of the companies documents of incorporation.
- Background information on the Directors.
- Background information on the company secretary.

- Power of Attorney or other document appointing a person to accept notices in Hong Kong.
- Details of the address of the registered office in Hong Kong.
- Details of the principal place of business in the companies country of incorporation.

Does Hong Kong allow the formation of International Trusts?

YES. Although Hong Kong is a suitable jurisdiction for forming Trusts (low tax, English common law, excellent infrastructure), questions raised by the transfer of power to China in 1997 makes Hong Kong a poor choice compared to other excellent offshore centres.

Does Hong Kong allow the formation of Captive Insurance Companies?

YES. Although Hong Kong allows the formation of Captive Insurance Companies, questions raised by the transfer of power to China in 1997 makes Hong Kong a poor choice compared to other excellent offshore centres.

Does Hong Kong allow the formation of Banking Companies?

YES. Although Hong Kong allows the formation of Banking Companies, the strict requirements make them impractical for tax planning purposes. Questions raised by the transfer of power to China in 1997 makes Hong Kong a poor choice compared to other excellent offshore centres.

Financial institutions and contacts:

Aall & Zyleman Co. Ltd.

Ms. Stephanie March	852-861-2222	dial
General Manager	852-861-2266	fax
8th Floor, Heng Shan Centre	71641 AACL HX	telex

145 Queen's Road East, Wanchai, Hong Kong

- Primary business activity: bank and trust services.

Bank Julius Baer

2101 Jardine House	852-877-3328	dial
1 Connaught Place	852-845-9272	fax
Hong Kong	8-9439	telex

- Primary business activity: banking services.
- Private banking services and/or savings accounts.
- Safekeeping and custodian services.
- Portfolio management of securities and mutual funds.

Bank of N.T. Butterfield & Son Ltd.

Mr. Hamish B. MacPherson	852-868-1010	dial
Senior Manager	852-845-0336	fax
26/F Bank of China Tower	82370 BNTB HX	telex

1 Garden Road, Central, Hong Kong

- Primary business activity: banking services.
- Safekeeping and custodian services.
- Portfolio management of securities and mutual funds.
- Company formation services are offered.
- Trust formation services are offered.

Bank of Nova Scotia

Scotiatrust (Asia) Limited 852-861-0881 dial
6th Floor, Tower 1 852-861-2740 fax
Admiralty Centre, 18 Harcourt Road, Hong Kong

- Primary business activity: banking services.
- Private banking services and/or savings accounts.
- Consumer loans and credit facilities.
- Corporate services such as registered agent services.
- Executor and administrator of wills and estates.
- Safekeeping and custodian services.
- Portfolio management of securities and mutual funds.
- Company formation services are offered.
- Trust formation services are offered.
- Captive insurance company formation services are offered.
- Banking company formation services are offered.

Barclays Private Banking

Mr. Paul Brown 852-826-1888 dial
Director, Asia 852-845-2733 fax
1801 Two Pacific Place, 88 Queensway, Hong Kong

- Primary business activity: banking services.
- Offers private credit card backed by deposit.
- Private banking services and/or savings accounts.
- Consumer loans and credit facilities.
- Safekeeping and custodian services.
- Portfolio management of securities and mutual funds.
- Company formation services are offered.
- Trust formation services are offered.

Chase Manhattan Private Bank
Ms. Rebecca Lam 852-5-841-4770 dial
Vice President, Asia Pacific Area 852-5-845-5900 fax
1 Exchange Square, 41st Floor, Central, Hong Kong

- Primary business activity: banking services.
- Private banking services and/or savings accounts.
- Consumer loans and credit facilities.
- Safekeeping and custodian services.
- Portfolio management of securities and mutual funds.
- Company formation services are offered.
- Trust formation services are offered.

Chemical Bank (Hong Kong) Limited
Edinburgh Tower, 43rd Floor 852-841-6890 dial
15 Queen's Road 852-845-0314 fax
Central, Hong Kong

- Primary business activity: banking services.
- Private banking services and/or savings accounts.
- Safekeeping and custodian services.
- Company formation services are offered.
- Trust formation services are offered.

Coutts & Co. (Asia) Ltd.
23rd Floor, One Exchange Square 852-525-6898 dial
8 Connaught Place 852-877-2183 fax
Central, Hong Kong

- Primary business activity: bank and trust services.
- Private banking services and/or savings accounts.
- Safekeeping and custodian services.
- Portfolio management of securities and mutual funds.
- Company formation services are offered.
- Trust formation services are offered.

Deloitte Touche Tohmatsu
Mr. Peter Tosi 852-545-0303 dial
Tax Services 852-541-1911 fax
26th Floor, Wing On Centre, 111 Connaught Road, Central, Hong Kong

- Primary business activity: accounting services.
- Corporate services such as registered agent services.
- Company formation services are offered.

Hill Samuel Investment Services (Asia)
35th Floor, Bank of America Tower 852-847-3000 dial
12 Harcourt Road 852-868-4733 fax
Hong Kong

- Primary business activity: bank and trust services.
- Private banking services and/or savings accounts.
- Consumer loans and credit facilities.
- Safekeeping and custodian services.
- Portfolio management of securities and mutual funds.
- Company formation services are offered.
- Trust formation services are offered.

Hong Kong Customs and Excise
8th Floor, Harbour Building 852-852-1411 dial
38 Pier Road 852-542-3334 fax
Central, Hong Kong

- Primary business activity: government services.

Hong Kong Federation of Industries
Hankow Centre, 4th Floor 852-723-0818 dial
5-15 Hankow Road, Tsimshatsui 852-721-3797 fax
Kowloon, Hong Kong

- Primary business activity: government services.

Hong Kong General Chamber of Commerce
22nd Floor, United Centre 852-525-6385 dial
95 Queensway 852-845-2610 fax
Hong Kong

- Primary business activity: government services.

Hong Kong Industries Department

14th Floor, Ocean Centre	852-737-2573	dial
5 Canton Road, Tsimshatsui	852-730-4633	fax
Kowloon, Hong Kong		

- Primary business activity: government services.

Hong Kong Inland Revenue Department

Mr. Anthony Au-Yeung	852-594-5005	dial
Commissioner of Inland Revenue	852-877-1131	fax

Revenue Tower, 5 Gloucester Road, Wan Chai, Hong Kong

- Primary business activity: government services.

Hong Kong Trade Department

Mr. Tony Miller	852-722-2333	dial
Director-General of Trade	852-789-2491	fax

Trade Department Tower, 700 Nathan Road, Kowloon, Hong Kong

- Primary business activity: government services.

Hong Kong Trade Development Council

Ms. Jenny Ip	852-584-4333	dial
Assistant Manager	852-824-0249	fax
38th Floor, Office tower	73595 CONHK HX	telex

Convention Plaza, 1 Harbour Road, Wanchai, Hong Kong

- Primary business activity: government services.

HSBC HongkongBank

Mrs. Brigitta Pedro	852-748-3322	dial
Assistant Manager Customer Services	852-729-8398	fax

PO.Box 80208, Cheung Sha Wan, Kowloon, Hong Kong

- Primary business activity: banking services.
- Private banking services and/or savings accounts.
- Consumer loans and credit facilities.

International Company Services Limited
Sovereign Trust International
Mr. Simon Hanley 852-2542-1177 dial
Consultant 852-2545-0550 fax
Suites 1-3, 16th Floor, 32 Hollywood Road, Central, Hong Kong

- Primary business activity: company and trust formation services.
- Company formation services are offered. Minimum formation fee £359 plus £293 government fee. Minimum annual fee £302.
- Trust formation services are offered.

KPMG Peat Marwick
Mr. L.S. Miller 852-522-6022 dial
Principal 852-845-2588 fax
8th Floor, Prince's Building 74391 PMMHK HX telex
Central, Hong Kong

- Primary business activity: accounting services.
- Corporate services such as registered agent services.
- Safekeeping and custodian services.
- Company formation services are offered. Minimum formation fee US$2,564 including license fee.

Manufacturers Hanover Trust Co.
Edinburgh Tower 852-5-841-6888 dial
43rd Floor, Hong Kong

- Primary business activity: bank and trust services.

Midland Bank PLC
2 Exchange Square 852-5-844-2888 dial
34th Floor 852-5-810-5266 fax
Hong Kong

- Primary business activity: bank and trust services.

Morgan Guaranty Trust Co. of NY
Edinburgh Tower 852-5-841-1311 dial
23rd Floor 852-5-868-1473 fax
Hong Kong

- Primary business activity: bank and trust services.

Mossack Fonseca & Co.

Attorneys at Law	852-376-1998	dial
Kowloon Centre, Room 903-5	852-376-0308	fax
29-43 Ashley Road, TST	33652 HX	telex

Kowloon, Hong Kong

- Primary business activity: law office.

Overseas Company Registration Agents

Mr. Anders Wadman	852-522-0172	dial
Solicitor	852-521-1190	fax

2402 Bank of America Tower, 12 Harcourt Road, Central, Hong Kong

- Primary business activity: company and trust formation services.
- Corporate services such as registered agent services.
- Company formation services are offered. Minimum formation fee £350 plus £1,550 license fee. Minimum annual fee £1,550.

Price Waterhouse

Prince's Building, 22nd Floor, Central, Hong Kong

- Primary business activity: accounting services.

Privacy Reports Inc.

Mr. Gerhard Kurtz	852-2-850-5502	fax

Publisher

26A Peel Street, Ground Floor, Central, Hong Kong

- Primary business activity: discrete camouflage passports.
- Primary business activity: newsletters, books, or information.

Royal Trust Asia Ltd.

One Exchange Square	852-847-8666	dial
32nd Floor, 8 Connaught Place	852-845-0346	fax

Hong Kong

- Primary business activity: bank and trust services.
- Offers private credit card backed by deposit.
- Private banking services and/or savings accounts.
- Consumer loans and credit facilities.
- Safekeeping and custodian services.
- Portfolio management of securities and mutual funds.

SBCI Finance Asia Limited

21st floor, One Exchange Square	852-844-6388	dial
8 Connaught Place	6-2224	telex
Central, Hong Kong		

- Primary business activity: banking services.

Secretaries Limited

Mr. Ken Deayton	852-544-2808	dial
Secretarial and Registration Services	852-541-6840	fax

5th Floor, Wing On Centre, 111 Connaught Road, Central, Hong Kong

- Primary business activity: company and trust formation services.
- Corporate services such as registered agent services.
- Safekeeping and custodian services.

Standard Chartered Bank

8/F Edinburgh Tower	852-5-842-2822	dial
The Landmark	852-5-810-0651	fax
Central, Hong Kong		

- Primary business activity: banking services.

Swiss Bank Corporation

One Exchange Square, 20th floor	852-842-1222	dial
8 Connaught Place	6-4127	telex
Central, Hong Kong		

- Primary business activity: banking services.

Wardley Investment Services Limited

Mr. Michael Sandberg	852-847-9099	dial
Chairman	852-845-2024	fax

12th Floor, BA Tower, 12 Harcourt Road, Central, Hong Kong

- Primary business activity: fund or portfolio manager.

Westpac Banking Corporation (Jersey)

Level 20, Exchange Square III	852-842-9811	dial
8 Connaught Place	852-842-9868	fax
Central, Hong Kong		

- Primary business activity: banking services.

Yorkwo Consultancy Services

Leader Industrial Centre, Room 311	852-684-1098	dial
57-59 Au Pui Wan Street, Fo Tan	852-601-6935	fax
Shatin, Hong Kong NT		

- Primary business activity: bank and trust services.

ISLE OF MAN

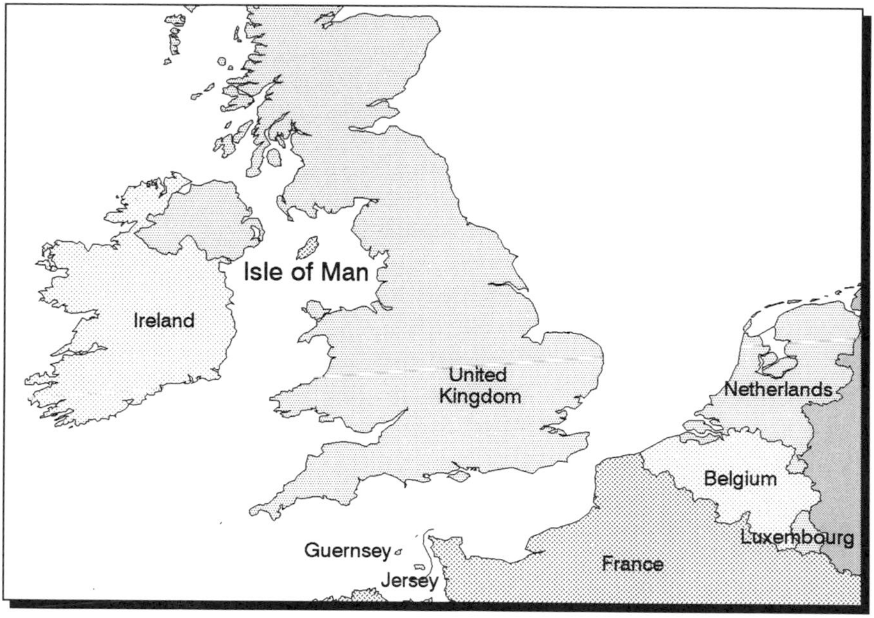

Off the British coast. A 227 square mile island in the Irish Sea, roughly equidistant from England, Wales, Scotland and Ireland. Population is approximately 70,000. Main language is English and Gaelic.

The Isle of Man is an ancient kingdom that was part of an independent Norse Kingdom which disintegrated in the 13th century, leading to a dispute between the Kingdoms of Scotland and England. The Manx parliament, called Tynwald, was founded by the early Vikings and boasts the longest continuous history of any legislature in the world (celebrating 1,000 years of continuous parliamentary rule in 1979). The ruler of the Isle of Man was known as the Lord of Man, with the Lordship being purchased by the English Crown in 1765. This led to indirect rule from England until the Island's finances were separated from England's in 1866.

Throughout this period Tynwald existed, enacting legislation on all domestic matters.

Its origin as an international finance centre can be traced back to the early 1960's with the introduction of low taxation policies. The first investments in the Island were made by British expatriates.

Does the Isle of Man have a secrecy law?

NO. Although members of the financial industry are required to sign a security pledge if they join the industry, the Isle of Man has no specific bank secrecy legislation. The Island's status with the European Community is governed by a Protocol, with no requirement to harmonize laws relating to disclosure of information or taxation.

There is an implied contractual duty for advisors to keep their client information confidential, and it should be noted that confidentiality is a bank license condition.

Is there any situation where bank secrecy can be lifted?

YES. The Isle of Man followed the UK by introducing Drug Trafficking Offenses legislation to prevent criminals from using the Island's financial industry facilities. Client confidentiality is not available where a banker has reason to suspect drug trafficking, insider trading, or the finance of terrorism. Confidential information can be released if there is a suspected criminal activity such as illegal drug activities, theft, or fraud.

Can foreign tax authorities obtain information on Isle of Man bank accounts?

NO. Confidential financial information is not released to foreign governments for tax investigations.

Is the Isle of Man an independent country?

YES. Although the British Government purchased the regalities of the Isle of Man on behalf of the crown, the Isle of Man is not, and never has been, part of the United Kingdom. The Isle of Man's parliament, Tynwald, is over 1000 years old and legislates on all domestic matters. The United Kingdom assumes responsibility for foreign affairs and external defense. The Isle of Man is not a member of the European Economic Community, although it has a special relationship with the EEC, set out under Protocol 3 of the UK's Treaty of Accession to the European Community, which guarantees free movement of goods. The UK is responsible for external affairs and defense, receiving an annual contribution for this service.

Is the legal system based on English Common Law?

NO. The Island has its own legal system, Anglo Saxon in origin. Most Manx legislation, Company and Trust law in particular, has been modeled on English law, and the rules of English Common Law and Equity are generally followed by the Manx courts. The Island has its own courts, with the heads of the judicial system known as "Deemsters." The supreme court is the English Privy Council.

Is there an Income Tax on the Isle of Man?

YES. Income derived from the Isle of Man is taxable. The standard rate of personal income tax is 15%. Non-residents are taxed only on income derived from the Isle of Man.

Resident Companies are subject to Manx Income Tax which is a flat rate of 20% on taxable profit. Exempt Companies require an annual payment (Exempt Fee) of £300 made in lieu of tax. Non-Resident Companies pay a duty of £600 annually in lieu of tax.

Interest on bank accounts maintained in the Isle of Man in the names of exempt companies is not taxed. There is no income tax for non-resident activities.

Value added tax is collected by the Isle of Man Customs & Excise at standard UK rates.

Are there any other taxes in the Isle of Man?

NO. There is no capital gains or capital transfer tax, no gift tax, and no estate or succession tax in the Isle of Man. There is no stamp duty, no capital transfer tax, no wealth tax, and no death duty.

Are there any exchange controls in the Isle of Man?

NO. There are currently no exchange controls in the Isle of Man. The Isle of Man issues its own currency, which is interchangeable with the pound sterling.

Is there a tax treaty between the U.S. and the Isle of Man?

NO. There is no double-taxation agreement between the U.S. and the Isle of Man, although there is a double-taxation agreement between the UK and the Isle of Man.

Is there a tax treaty between Canada and the Isle of Man?

NO. There is no double-taxation agreement between Canada and the Isle of Man.

Does the Isle of Man allow the formation of Limited Companies?

YES. Company law is based on The Companies Acts 1931-1992 and subsequent amendments. The three types of Isle of Man companies are Resident Company, Exempt Company, and Non-Resident Company.

All three types of companies have the same minimum statutory requirements, requiring:

- At least two shareholders (need not be residents of the Isle of Man).
- A minimum two directors and one secretary. Alternate directors are permitted, corporate directors are not permitted. Exempt companies must appoint at least one Isle of Man resident director.
- A registered office on the Isle of Man.
- Maintain a register of members, directors and secretary, register of charges, and minutes of shareholders meetings.
- At least two shares must be issued. Shares must be issued at par value.
- Bearer share warrants may be issued.
- Companies must hold an annual general meeting.
- Annual general meeting may be held in any jurisdiction.

Each year the company must prepare audited accounts to be placed before the members of the company, although these are not filed at the companies registry and not available to the public (in the Manx Budget of April 1993, the Treasury Minister stated that he was to allow Private Exempt and Non-Resident companies to dispense with the need to provide audited accounts).

Since June 1988, companies governed by the Companies Act 1986 have the capacity, rights, powers, and privileges of an individual. A Manx company can undertake different types of activity, such as holding investments, holding intellectual property rights, trade, re-invoice, and any other activity an individual can undertake. Advantages of Isle of Man companies include:

- Directors meetings may be held in any jurisdiction.
- Bearer shares are permitted.
- No minimum authorized share capital is required.

Resident Company - A resident company is required to pay a flat income tax of 20%.

Exempt Company - Any company may apply for and obtain exemption from Isle of Man corporation taxes provided that ownership of the company is non-resident and that income is earned from sources outside the Isle of Man. An Exempt Company is only required to pay an annual registration tax which is currently £300. The company must have a resident director and a resident qualified secretary. The company is required to keep proper books of account but has no filing requirements unless requested to do so.

Non-Resident Company - A non-resident company is only required to pay an annual registration tax which is currently £600. Beneficial ownership, trading, management, and control must be outside of the Isle of Man. A majority of directors must be resident outside the Isle of Man, and their meetings should not be held on the Island. Other than bank interest, there should be no Isle of Man source of income. Non-Resident companies may be administered in, but not directed from the Isle of Man.

International Company - The International Business Act 1994 was introduced following close consultation with the Isle of Man's finance community. The legislation provides for a minimum 1% rate of taxation on a sliding scale to a maximum of 35%, subject to a minimum income tax charge of £300, based upon the specific requirements of the International Company. Applications must be made to the Assessor of Income Tax who will determine the appropriate rate based on the nature of the company's application.

Does the Isle of Man allow the formation of International Trusts?

YES. Trust law is based on the Trustee Act 1961, The Perpetuities & Accumulation Act 1968, Variation of Trusts Act 1961 and Recognition of Trusts Act 1988. They are based on normal common law precedents.

A Manx resident Trust and any distributions of income are exempt from tax providing the Settlor and Beneficiaries are non-resident, the funds did not originate in the Isle of Man, and there is no local income apart from bank deposit interest.

No registration is required for Trusts. There is no restriction on the accumulation of income within the perpetuity period which is 80 years. It is possible to provide for the transfer of such Trusts to another jurisdiction if needed. Types of Trusts available in the Isle of Man include the Fixed Trust, Discretionary Trust, and Protective Trust.

Fixed Trust - The interest of the Beneficiaries are so defined as to leave the Trustee with no discretion as to how to benefit them.

Discretionary Trust - The disposal of the Trust assets is at the sole discretion of the Trustee, who may receive recommendations from the Settlor.

Protective Trust - This is a form of Trust where the object of the Trust is to provide for a Beneficiary with some form of disability.

Does the Isle of Man allow the formation of Captive Insurance Companies?

YES. The Isle of Man is a tax-free international insurance centre with high standards. Throughout the 1980's, the Isle of Man has emerged as a stable offshore financial centre with hundreds of captive insurance companies. The Parliament (Tynwald) has full autonomy on internal affairs, and is firmly committed to developing a secure, tax efficient international insurance centre, with:

- No tax on underwriting profits.
- No tax on investment income.
- No withholding tax on dividends.
- No capital gains tax.
- No currency exchange controls.

Captive Insurance Companies are governed by the Insurance Act of 1986 (and supporting regulations), defining:

- Minimum requirements for paid-up share capital.
- Minimum solvency margins to be maintained.
- The financial credentials of companies involved.
- Specific requirements enacting "fit and proper" officers of insurance companies.
- Government licensing and tax exemption fees.
- Statutory reporting requirements.

The regulatory and tax exemption legislation of the Isle of Man applies to captive insurance companies, general insurance companies, life assurance companies, and reinsurance companies. Annual fees are £2,000 payable to the Manx government.

Does the Isle of Man allow the formation of Banking Companies?

YES. Isle of Man Companies based on The Companies Act 1931-1992 may apply for a banking license governed by the Banking Acts 1975-1986. International Companies may not apply.

Financial institutions and contacts:

Aarawak Trust Co (Isle of Man) Ltd.
Barclays House, Victoria Street, PO.Box 34, Douglas, Isle of Man

- Primary business activity: company and trust formation services.

Abchurch Corporate Services Limited

Mr. Martin Neville	441-624-662262	dial
Managing Director	441-624-662272	fax

PO.Box 204, 20 North Quay, Douglas, Isle of Man IM99 1QZ

- Primary business activity: company and trust formation services.
- Corporate services such as registered agent services.
- Executor and administrator of wills and estates.
- Safekeeping and custodian services.
- Company formation services are offered. Minimum formation fee £905 plus £600 license fee. Minimum annual fee £1,215.
- Trust formation services are offered.
- Captive insurance company formation services are offered.

Anglo Manx Bank Limited

5 Anthol Street	441-624-23845	dial
Douglas, Isle of Man	441-624-76080	fax

Primary business activity: banking services.

Aston Corporate Management Limited

Mr. David Griffin	441-624-626591	dial
Director	441-624-625126	fax
19 Peel Road	627691 ASTON G	telex

Douglas, Isle of Man IM1 4LS

- Primary business activity: company and trust formation services.
- Corporate services such as registered agent services.
- Executor and administrator of wills and estates.
- Safekeeping and custodian services.
- Company formation services are offered. Minimum formation fee £450 plus £300 license fee. Minimum annual fee £450.
- Trust formation services are offered.
- Captive insurance company formation services are offered.
- Banking company formation services are offered.

Bank of Bermuda (Isle of Man) Limited

Mr. Howard R. Callow	441-624-637777	dial
Manager, Private Banking	441-624-637778	fax

PO.Box 34, 12/13 Hill Street, Douglas, Isle of Man IM99 1BW

- Primary business activity: banking services.
- Offers Private Credit Card (VISA) backed by deposit.
- Private banking services and/or savings accounts.
- Corporate services such as registered agent services.
- Safekeeping and custodian services.
- Portfolio management of securities and mutual funds. Minimum annual fee 0.75% of assets or £2,500.
- Company formation services are offered. Minimum formation fee £1,650 plus £110 license fee. Minimum annual fee £1,100.
- Trust formation services are offered. Minimum formation fee £750. Minimum annual fee 0.3% of assets or £500.

Barclays Private Bank & Trust Limited

Mr. Colin Jones	441-624-673514	dial
Managing Director	441-624-620905	fax
PO.Box 48, 4th floor	629587 BARTRTG	telex

Queen Victoria House, Victoria Street, Douglas, Isle of Man IM99 1DF

- Primary business activity: bank and trust services.
- Offers private credit card backed by deposit.
- Private banking services and/or savings accounts.
- Consumer loans and credit facilities.
- Safekeeping and custodian services.
- Portfolio management of securities and mutual funds.
- Company formation services are offered.
- Trust formation services are offered.

Bennett Roy & Co.

Viking House, Nelson Street, Douglas, Isle of Man

- Primary business activity: accounting services.

Bradford & Bingley Isle of Man Limited

Mr. Chris Lees	441-624-661868	dial
Client Relations Manager	441-624-661962	fax

30 Ridgeway Street, Douglas, Isle of Man IM1 1TA

- Primary business activity: bank and trust services.

Celtic Bank Ltd.
Barclays House, Victoria Street, Douglas, Isle of Man

- Primary business activity: banking services.

City Trust Limited
Mr. Gordon J. Mundy 441-624-661881 dial
Director 441-624-611423 fax
3rd Floor, Murdoch House, South Quay, Douglas, Isle of Man IM1 5AS

- Primary business activity: company and trust formation services.
- Corporate services such as registered agent services.
- Company formation services are offered. Minimum formation fee £500 plus £300 license fee. Minimum annual fee £1,000.
- Trust formation services are offered. Minimum formation fee £1,000. Minimum annual fee £1,000.

CWL Management Services Ltd.
Treger House, Circular Road, Douglas, Isle of Man

- Primary business activity: company and trust formation services.

IFG International Limited
Mr. Anthony R. Hulse 441-624-626931 dial
Director 441-624-624469 fax
International House, Castle Hill
Victoria Road, Douglas, Isle of Man IM2 4RB

- Primary business activity: company and trust formation services.
- Corporate services such as registered agent services.
- Executor and administrator of wills and estates.
- Safekeeping and custodian services.
- Company formation services are offered. Minimum formation fee £350 plus £300 license fee. Minimum annual fee £1,340.
- Trust formation services are offered. Minimum formation fee £1,000. Minimum annual fee £500.

International Company Services Limited

Mr. Robert G. Drysdale 441-624-801801 dial
Company Consultant 441-624-801800 fax
Sovereign House, Station Road, St.Johns, Isle of Man IM4 3AJ

- Primary business activity: company and trust formation services.
- Company formation services are offered. Minimum formation fee £290 plus £300 government fee. Minimum annual fee £340.
- Trust formation services are offered. Minimum formation fee £500. Minimum annual fee £500.

Island Resources Limited

National House 441-624-824555 dial
Stanton, Isle of Man IM4 1HA 441-624-823949 fax

- Primary business activity: company and trust formation services.
- Corporate services such as registered agent services.
- Company formation services are offered. Minimum formation fee £500. Minimum annual fee £500.
- Trust formation services are offered. Minimum formation fee £350.

Isle of Man Government Insurance Authority

Mr. W.J. Hastings 441-624-685695 dial
Chief Executive 441-624-663346 fax
S&F House, 12-14 Ridgeway Street, Douglas, Isle of Man

- Primary business activity: government services.

Isle of Man Income Tax Division

Mr. I.Q. Kelly 441-624-685350 dial
Assessor of Income Tax 441-624-685351 fax
Treasury, Government Offices, Douglas, Isle of Man

- Primary business activity: government services.

Isle of Man Financial Services Commission

Mr. J.E. Noakes 441-624-624487 dial
Chief Executive 441-624-629342 fax
PO.Box 58, 1-4 Goldie Terrace, Douglas, Isle of Man

- Primary business activity: government services.

Isle of Man Assurance Company

Mr. C.A. Bowen	441-624-624141	dial
Investment Manager	441-624-622500	fax

PO.Box 179, IOMA House, Douglas, Isle of Man

- Primary business activity: insurance products & services.

Isle of Man Bank

Ms. Jane Pickard	441-624-625533	dial
Manager, Specialist Deposit Unit	441-624-662468	fax

PO.Box 13, Douglas, Isle of Man IM99 1AN

- Primary business activity: banking services.

Isle of Man Financial Trust Limited

Isle of Man Insurance Management Limited

Mr. Nigel H. Wood	441-624-663466	dial
Managing Director	441-624-663467	fax
IOMA House, Prospect Hill	627924 IOMINS	telex

Douglas, Isle of Man IM99 1HA

- Primary business activity: company and trust formation services.
- Corporate services such as registered agent services.
- Executor and administrator of wills and estates.
- Safekeeping and custodian services.
- Portfolio management of securities and mutual funds.
- Company formation services are offered. Minimum formation fee US$1,850 including US$450 license fee. Minimum annual fee US$1,850.
- Trust formation services are offered.
- Captive insurance company formation services are offered.

J.P. Collins

14 Anthol Street, Douglas, Isle of Man

- Primary business activity: accounting services.

Jordan & Sons (Isle of Man) Ltd.

Miss Marcell Farrell	441-624-624298	dial
Assistant Company Services Manager	441-624-626719	fax

24 Ridgeway Street, Douglas, Isle of Man IM1 1QA

- Primary business activity: company and trust formation services.
- Corporate services such as registered agent services.
- Company formation services are offered. Minimum formation fee £710 plus £300 license fee. Minimum annual fee £450.
- Trust formation services are offered. Minimum formation fee £500. Minimum annual fee £500.

Jowik Corporate Trust Services Ltd.

11 Myrtle Street, Douglas, Isle of Man

- Primary business activity: company and trust formation services.

Lloyds Bank PLC

Mr. R.D. Willcox	441-624-638100	dial
Manager	441-624-638181	fax

Isle of Man Expatriate Centre, Box 12
Peveril Buildings, Peveril Square, Douglas, Isle of Man IM99 1SS

- Primary business activity: banking services.

Lorne House Trust Limited

Mr. Ronald Buchanan	441-624-823579	dial
Managing Director	441-624-822952	fax
Lorne House	629265 LORNHO G	telex

Castletown, Isle of Man IM9 1AZ

- Primary business activity: company and trust formation services.
- Corporate services such as registered agent services.
- Portfolio management of securities and mutual funds. Minimum annual fee 1% of assets or £500 plus £30 per transaction.
- Company formation services are offered. Minimum formation fee £750 plus £300 license fee. Minimum annual fee £250.
- Trust formation services are offered. Minimum formation fee £250. Minimum annual fee 0.25% of assets or £750.
- Banking company formation. Minimum formation fee £1,400 plus £6,500 license fee.

Mannin International Ltd.

Lorne House, Castletown, Isle of Man

- Primary business activity: banking services.

Manx Corporate Services Limited

Mr. F.G. Quinn 441-624-662727 dial

Director 441-624-662332 fax

Capital House, 5 Hill Street, Douglas, Isle of Man IM1 1EF

- Primary business activity: company and trust formation services.
- Corporate services such as registered agent services.
- Company formation services are offered. Minimum formation fee £250 plus license fee. Minimum annual fee £300.
- Trust formation services are offered. Minimum formation fee £400. Minimum annual fee £400.

MeesPierson (Isle of Man) Limited

Mr. Juan I. Corkish 441-624-688300 dial

Senior Investment Manager 441-624-688334 fax

Pierson House, PO.Box 156 626159 MEESPN G telex

18-20 North Quay, Douglas, Isle of Man IM99 1NR

- Primary business activity: banking services.
- Offers Private Credit Card backed by deposit.
- Private banking services and/or savings accounts.
- Corporate services such as registered agent services.
- Safekeeping and custodian services.
- Portfolio management of securities and mutual funds.
- Company formation services are offered. Minimum formation fee US$1,500.
- Trust formation services are offered.
- Banking company formation services are offered.

Midland Bank PLC

PO.Box 20 441-624-623051 dial

10 Victoria Street, Douglas, Isle of Man IM99 1AU

- Primary business activity: bank and trust services.

Midland Bank Trust (Isle of Man) Ltd.

PO.Box 39 Heritage Court	441-624-623118	dial
39 Athol Street	441-624-623202	fax
Douglas, Isle of Man	62-8037	telex

- Primary business activity: bank and trust services.

Overseas Company Registration Agents

Mr. Stephen Porter	441-624-815544	dial
Director	441-624-815558	fax
Companies House, Tower Street	800-283-4444	free

PO.Box 28, Ramsey, Isle of Man IM99 4AN

- Primary business activity: company and trust formation services.
- Corporate services such as registered agent services.
- Company formation services are offered. Minimum formation fee £250 plus £360 license fee. Minimum annual fee £360.

Riggs Valmet Isle of Man Limited

4 Finch Road	441-624-677522	dial
Douglas, Isle of Man	441-624-677523	fax

- Primary business activity: company and trust formation services.

Robert Fleming (Isle of Man) Limited Private Client Investment Management

Mr. Nicholas Owen	441-624-661880	dial
Director	441-624-627218	fax

5 Mount Pleasant, Douglas, Isle of Man IM1 2PU

- Primary business activity: fund or portfolio manager.

Royal Bank of Scotland (I.O.M.) Limited

Mr. Russ Hewlett	441-481-710051	dial
Business Development	441-481-715431	fax

PO.Box 151, Victory House
Prospect Hill, Douglas, Isle of Man IM99 INJ

- Primary business activity: banking services.
- Private banking services and/or savings accounts.
- Corporate services such as registered agent services.
- Safekeeping and custodian services.
- Portfolio management of securities and mutual funds.
- Company formation services are offered.
- Trust formation services are offered.
- Captive insurance company formation services are offered.

Royal Trust Bank (Isle of Man) Limited

Ms. Jacqui Fletcher	441-624-629521	dial
Assistant Manager Banking	441-624-661819	fax

60-62 Athol Street, Douglas, Isle of Man

- Primary business activity: banking services.
- Offers Private Credit Card (AMEX) backed by deposit.
- Private banking services and/or savings accounts.

Tyndall Bank International Limited

Mrs. F.M. Martland	441-624-29201	dial
Manager's Assistant	441-624-20200	fax
PO.Box 62	62-8732	telex

Tyndall House, Kensington Road, Douglas, Isle of Man IM99 1DZ

- Primary business activity: banking services.
- Private banking services and/or savings accounts.
- Safekeeping and custodian services.
- Portfolio management of securities and mutual funds.

William's & Glyn's Bank (Isle of Man)

Victory House, Prospect Hill, Douglas, Isle of Man

- Primary business activity: banking services.

LIECHTENSTEIN

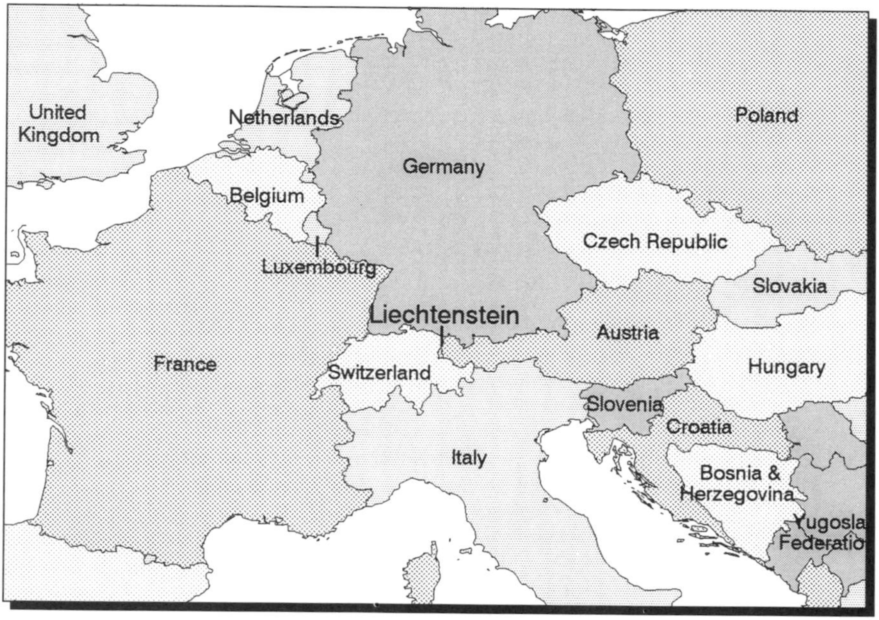

In Europe. Borders Switzerland and Austria. A sliver on the eastern border of Switzerland, only 150 square km in area, with approximately 30,000 citizens. Zurich is one hour's drive away. Main language is German and Alemanni, although English is widely spoken. Climate is cold with snow in winter and mild in summer.

The Principality of Liechtenstein includes the former territories of the County of Vaduz and the Lordship of Schellenberg. These territories were united by inheritance in 1434 with the status of fiefs of the Holy Roman Empire. In 1712 the two territories were purchased separately by Prince John Adam Andrew of Liechtenstein, whose name was taken from Liechtenstein's Castle, a family possession in Vienna. In 1719, the two territories were formally united as the Principality of Liechtenstein, becoming a sovereign state in 1806. In 1923 Liechtenstein joined Switzerland in a customs and currency union. Today Prince Franz Joseph II is the head of state. His Gutenberg castle overlooks the capital city, Vaduz. The royal family is also the majority shareholder of BIL (Bank in Liechtenstein).

Does Liechtenstein have a secrecy law?

YES. Revealing bank-account information is a criminal offense punishable by jail time. Liechtenstein's very strict secrecy laws prohibit the unauthorized disclosure of information pertaining to a clients affairs to a third party.

Some banks offer a "discreet customer" status. As a discreet customer, all contact you maintain with the bank, whether oral or in writing, are dealt with under an agreed password. Neither statements of account nor receipts mention the account holder by name. Thus, a customer's name is disclosed only to a limited group of employees. The account holder's anonymity is maintained toward other employees and unauthorized third parties.

Banking establishments domiciled in Liechtenstein and the Government of the Principality of Liechtenstein have signed an agreement on establishing business relations with the bank in the receipt of money. The banking establishments are bound to determine their customers identities and to clarify who the beneficial owner of the deposited assets is. In the case of juridical persons such determination of the beneficial owner may be replaced by a declaration submitted by a Liechtenstein official in charge of professional secrets. An appropriate form has to be signed upon establishing an account relationship.

Is there any situation where bank secrecy can be lifted?

YES. In case of criminal offenses committed by an account holder, the bank is not permitted to rely on banking secrecy. The banks have also instituted precautionary measures intended to curb money laundering and insider trading.

A typical Bank or Trust Company "Information Waiver" reads as follows:

> The undersigned (hereinafter called the "Customer") hereby confirms that he will not carry out any transaction concerning his securities account with (This Bank) which is considered as insider trading not allowed by law or other regulations in that country in which the transaction is carried out ("Insider Trading").
>
> If proceedings against the bank are by the authorities having jurisdiction for investigations in insider trading in the respective countries ("Authorities"), the Bank will inform the customer ("Information") immediately after receipt of a request for information.
>
> The Bank reserves the right to take any steps which it may deem appropriate after due consideration and the expiration of 30 days since the forwarding of the information to the Customer. In such case the Customer authorized the Bank to reveal to the Authorities his name and details of any alleged insider trading.
>
> This authorization shall be effective only if proceedings are initiated against the Bank because of insider trading.

In 1970, the Principality of Liechtenstein joined the European Agreement on Mutual Judicial Assistance in Criminal Matters. This agreement allows for bank secrecy to be lifted only if the underlying act is liable to prosecution in the State requesting judicial assistance as well as in accordance with Liechtenstein law.

Can foreign tax authorities obtain information on Liechtenstein bank accounts?

NO. Liechtenstein does not have any exchange of information agreements that would allow foreign tax authorities to obtain banking information. Liechtenstein banking and government officials consider their strict secrecy laws to be an important advantage, and the foundation of their success.

Is Liechtenstein an independent country?

YES. Liechtenstein gained independence on July 12, 1806, after being part of the Holy Roman Empire for nearly 100 years. Directed by the constitution of 1921, the Principality of Liechtenstein is a hereditary constitutional monarchy, with the last ruling Hapsburg, Prince Franz Josef III. The Customs Treaty with Switzerland, signed in 1923, is the basis of the strong economic ties between the two countries. It was followed by the Currency Treaty after the introduction in 1924 of the Swiss Franc as Liechtenstein's legal tender.

Is the legal system based on English Common Law?

NO. The legal system has Austrian influence (criminal and civil law), Swiss influence (contract and property law), and German influence (commercial law). The present constitution, formed in 1921, calls for a 15 member legislature that is elected every 4 years, with the Prince sanctioning all law passed by the legislature.

Is there an income tax in Liechtenstein?

NO. There is no income tax in Liechtenstein on income or profits derived from outside Liechtenstein. There is, however, a net worth, or capital tax of 0.1% of total capital resources, subject to a minimum tax of SFr1,000, applying to Domiciliary and Holding Companies.

Dividends are subject to a withholding tax of 4%. Interest payments on loans exceeding SFr50,000 with a term longer than two years, and interest from bank deposits having a term longer than one year are subject to a withholding tax of 4%.

There are no local income taxes on corporations. Corporations pay an annual capital tax of 0.1% of capital and reserves, with a minimum annual capital tax of SFr1,000. Non-resident corporations and individuals are liable to tax only on income derived from a permanent establishment in Liechtenstein.

Are there any other taxes in Liechtenstein?

YES. Capital gains realized from the sale of real property located in Liechtenstein are subject to a real estate profits tax ranging from 3.6% to 35.6%. There is no capital gains tax in Liechtenstein on capital gains derived from outside Liechtenstein. Please note the net worth tax of 0.01% of total capital, with a minimum tax of SFr1,000.

Estate taxes of up to 5%, gift taxes of up to 27%, and succession taxes of up to 27% apply to Liechtenstein residents only.

There is no gift tax in Liechtenstein.

Are there any exchange controls in the Liechtenstein?

NO. There are currently no exchange controls in the Liechtenstein. The official currency is the Swiss Franc.

Is there a tax treaty between the U.S. and Liechtenstein?

NO. There is no double-taxation agreement between the U.S. and Liechtenstein, although there is a double-taxation agreement between Liechtenstein and Austria and between Liechtenstein and the Swiss Cantons of Graubuenden and St.Gallen.

Is there a tax treaty between Canada and Liechtenstein?

NO. There is no double-taxation agreement between Canada and Liechtenstein.

Does Liechtenstein allow the formation of Limited Companies?

YES. Limited companies registered in Liechtenstein are governed by the regulations outlined in the Persons and Companies Act (Personen und Gesellschaftsrecht or PGR).

Forms of legal entities acknowledged by the Liechtenstein Persons and Companies Act are:

- Aktiengesellschaft (company limited by shares).
- Kommanditaktiengesellschaft (partnership limited by shares).
- Verein (association).
- Gesellschaft mit beschrankter Haftung (private company limited by shares).
- Genossenschaft (registered co-operative society).
- Versicherungsverein auf Gegenseitigkeit/Hilfskassen (registered mutual insurance association / registered relief fund).
- Anstalt (establishment).
- Stiftung (foundation).

Companies may be classified as either a Domestic Operating Company, Domiciliary Company, or Holding Company:

Domestic Operating Company - A Domestic Operating Company is allowed to trade and conduct commercial activities in Liechtenstein.

Domiciliary Company - A Domiciliary Company will have its registered office in Liechtenstein, but will now be allowed to trade or conduct commercial activities in Liechtenstein.

Holding Company - A Holding Company is a company that has been incorporated for the purpose of administering or managing assets and investments.

Companies are required to provide certain information to be entered in the Public Register. Third parties may obtain information from the Public Register without providing any evidence of direct interest. The following information is subject to registration:

- Company name, domicile, and object.
- Statutory capital.
- Date of the articles of association.
- Administration body (number, names, addresses).
- Legal representative.
- Signature rights.
- Form in which official announcements are made.

The entry of a company in the Public Register must be published in the journal provided for official announcements (Amtsblatt). In the case of Domiciliary Companies and Holding Companies, the relevant information is displayed on the court notice board. The identity of company owners can be kept discreet through bearer shares held anonymously or by nominees.

The registration documents (formation deed, articles, etc.) may be inspected by third parties with the Registrar's consent, provided that they can submit evidence of a justified interest in doing so.

At least one member of the administration authorized to manage and represent the company must fulfill the following requirements, pursuant to Article 180a of the Persons and Companies Act:

- Member must be a Liechtenstein citizen with residence in the Principality of Liechtenstein or a foreigner with permission to settle in the Principality of Liechtenstein.
- Member must posses a professional license to act as lawyer, legal agent, auditor or Trustee, or alternately a government recognized business qualification, or he must exercise the authority to manage and represent the company within the framework of a fixed, main employment with a lawyer, legal agent, fiduciary enterprise, auditor or bank.

The above requirements are not applicable to:

- Legal entities which pursuant to the trade law have a qualified manager.
- Legal entities pursuing activities in Liechtenstein which do not fall within the scope of application of the trade law.

The administration body is liable only for damages caused intentionally or by neglect.

Companies limited by shares, establishments and Trust enterprises must comply with accounting and disclosure requirements, and are under obligation to:

- Keep orderly books of account.
- Submit within six months of the close of each business year the annual balance sheet and the profit and loss account drawn up according to recognized business rules.

- Preserve the accounting books for a period of at least ten years.

The PGR Code provides for the following types of shares:

- Bearer shares and registered shares.
- Preference shares and ordinary shares.
- Quota shares.

Does Liechtenstein allow the formation of International Trusts?

YES. Forms of Trusts acknowledged by the Liechtenstein Persons and Companies Act (PGR) are:

- Treuhandschaft (Trust settlement).
- Treuunternehmen (Trust enterprise).

A Trust enterprise is set up by means of a formation deed with the attached notarized signature of the Settlor. The Trust articles must contain at least the following:

- Declaration of the settlor's intent to form a Trust enterprise.
- Trust articles.
- Amount of the Trust fund.
- Appointment of the board of trustees.
- Appointment of the legal representative.

The Trust enterprise acquires its legal personality only upon registration. Settlors of a Trust enterprise may be persons with residence in Liechtenstein or abroad. More than one Settlor is not required. The object must clearly indicate whether the Trust enterprise may engage in commercial activities. The minimum capital of the Trust enterprise is SFr30,000 which may be provided by payment in cash or contributions in kind.

Only the Trust assets are liable for the debts of the Trust enterprise. The governing bodies and the Settlor are not under obligation to make further contributions.

The legal representative is the permanent local agent appointed to represent the Trust enterprise. The legal representative is able to receive documents of all kinds from the local authorities, and may act on other matters only if the legal representative has power of attorney.

Does Liechtenstein allow the formation of Captive Insurance Companies?

YES. A form of Insurance Company acknowledged by the Liechtenstein Persons and Companies Act (PGR) is:

- Konzessionierte Versicherungsunternehmen (licensed insurance company).

It is not practical to use Liechtenstein as a base for a Captive Insurance Company, as there are other jurisdictions with lower costs and friendlier legislation.

Does Liechtenstein allow the formation of Banking Companies?

YES. A form of Banking Company acknowledged by the Liechtenstein Persons and Companies Act (PGR) is:

- Hypothekarinstitute (mortgage lending institution).

Liechtenstein banking licenses are very restricted and not practical for investment purposes.

Financial institutions and contacts:

Bank in Liechtenstein AG

Mr. W.L. Eberle	41-75-235-1122	dial
Investment Manager	41-75-235-1522	fax
Postfach 85	889 222	telex

Herrengasse 12, Furstentum, Vaduz, Liechtenstein FL-9490

- Primary business activity: banking services.
- Offers Private Credit Card (EuroCard) backed by deposit.
- Private banking services and/or savings accounts.
- Consumer loans and credit facilities.
- Safekeeping and custodian services.
- Company formation services are offered.
- Trust formation services are offered.

Bilfinanz Aktiegesellschaft

Bangarten 6, Postfach 47, Vaduz, Liechtenstein

- Primary business activity: banking services.

Liechtensteinische Landesbank AG

Stadtle 44	41-75-236-8811	dial
Postfach 384	41-75-236-8760	fax

Vaduz, Liechtenstein FL-9490

- Primary business activity: banking services.
- Private banking services and/or savings accounts.
- Consumer loans and credit facilities.
- Safekeeping and custodian services.
- Portfolio management of securities and mutual funds. Minimum annual fee 0.25% of assets or SFr750.

Verwaltungs- und Privat-Bank AG

Mr. R. Gassner	41-75-235-6655	dial
Vice President	41-75-235-6500	fax
Postfach 885	889 200	telex

Vaduz, Liechtenstein FL-9490

- Primary business activity: banking services.
- Private banking services and/or savings accounts.
- Consumer loans and credit facilities.
- Safekeeping and custodian services.
- Portfolio management of securities and mutual funds. Minimum annual fee 2% of assets. Discreet Customer status. Minimum annual fee 1% of assets.

LUXEMBOURG

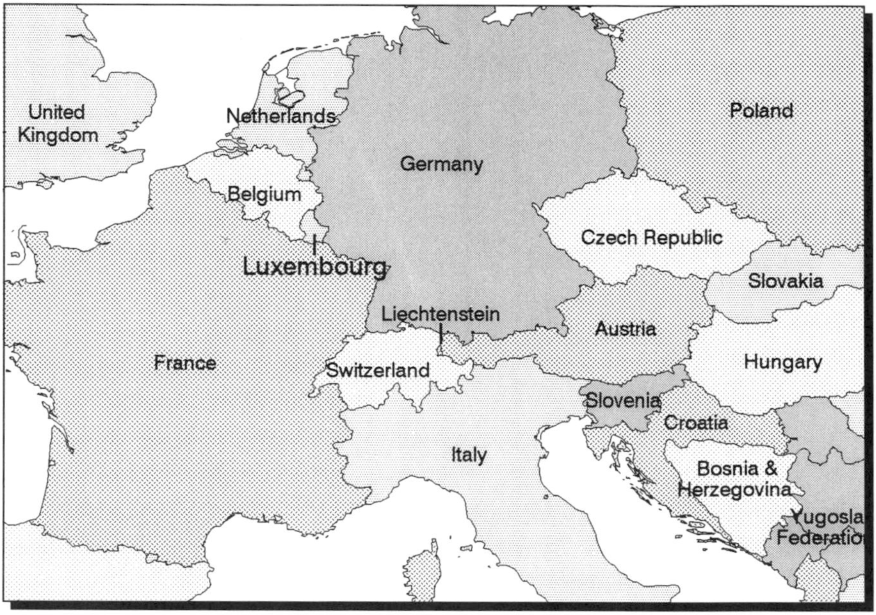

In Europe. Borders Belgium, France, and Germany. Main language is French, German, Luxembourgeois, and English.

The tiny state of Luxembourg enjoyed varying degrees of self-government until being conquered by France in 1795. In 1815 the current Grand Duchy came into being under the Dutch monarchy, and in 1890 full independence came when a junior branch of the Dutch royal family inherited Luxembourg. The Grand Duke is closely involved in administration with the democratically elected parliament. Luxembourg is considered a constitutional monarchy in the form of a Grand Duchy.

Does Luxembourg have a secrecy law?

YES. Luxembourg's secrecy laws prohibit the unauthorized disclosure of information pertaining to a clients affairs to a third party.

Revealing bank-account information is punishable by jail time, however, violation of secrecy laws is only a civil offense, not a criminal offense.

Is there any situation where bank secrecy can be lifted?

YES. Although Luxembourg's secrecy law prohibits the unauthorized disclosure of information, the law does not apply to activities that are considered crimes in Luxembourg, such as illegal drug activities, theft, or fraud. Furthermore, activities such as money laundering are criminal offenses, effectively canceling bank secrecy. Luxembourg's participation in the EC may further reduce bank secrecy. The collapse of the Bank of Credit and Commerce International (BCCI) based in Luxembourg has also further compromised bank secrecy.

Can foreign tax authorities obtain information on Luxembourg bank accounts?

NO. Confidential information can only be released if there is a suspected criminal activity such as illegal drug activities, theft, or fraud. Luxembourg banks will not release information for tax investigations.

Is Luxembourg an independent country?

YES. Luxembourg gained independence in 1839.

Is the legal system based on English Common Law?

NO. The legal system is based on a combination of Belgian, French, and German systems supplemented by local statutes. The courts in Luxembourg deal in Civil Law and Civil Code. The Supreme Court is the highest legal authority.

Is there an income tax in Luxembourg?

NO. Holding companies pay no income taxes, though there are modest levies on their capital.

Are there any other taxes in Luxembourg?

N/A.

Are there any exchange controls in Luxembourg?

NO. There are currently no exchange controls in Luxembourg. The official currency is the Luxembourg Franc.

Is there a tax treaty between the U.S. and Luxembourg?

YES. There is a double-taxation agreement between the U.S. and Luxembourg. Luxembourg also maintains double-taxation agreements with Belgium, Brazil, Denmark, Finland, France, Germany, Iceland, Ireland, Italy, Korea, Morocco, the Netherlands, Norway, Spain, Sweden, and the United Kingdom.

Is there a tax treaty between Canada and Luxembourg?

NO. There is no double-taxation agreement between Canada and Luxembourg.

Does Luxembourg allow the formation of Limited Companies?

YES. Although Limited Companies can be formed in Luxembourg, there are other jurisdictions with lower costs and friendlier legislation.

Does Luxembourg allow the formation of International Trusts?

NO. Civil law does not readily support the formation of International Trusts.

Does Luxembourg allow the formation of Captive Insurance Companies?

YES. Although Captive Insurance Companies can be formed in Luxembourg, there are other jurisdictions with lower costs and friendlier legislation.

Does Luxembourg allow the formation of Banking Companies?

YES. Although Banking Companies can be formed in Luxembourg, there are other jurisdictions with lower costs and friendlier legislation.

Financial institutions and contacts:

Banque de Luxembourg
80 Place de la Gare, Boite Postale 1123, Luxembourg L-1022
- Primary business activity: banking services.

Banque Generale du Luxembourg

14, rue Aldringen	352-4799-6501	dial
Luxembourg L-2951	352-4799-2579	fax

- Primary business activity: banking services.

Banque Internationale a Luxembourg

Mr. Frank Kayser	352-4590-1	dial
Premier Counsellor	352-4590-2010	fax
69, route d'Esch	3626 BIL LU	telex

2, boulevard Royal, Luxembourg L-2953
- Primary business activity: banking services.
- Private banking services and/or savings accounts.

BfG Luxembourg Siegesocial
17 Rue do Fosse, Boite Postale 1123, Luxembourg L-1011
- Primary business activity: banking services.

Chase Manhattan Bank Luxembourg, S.A.

5, rue Plaetis 352-462-6851 dial

Luxembourg L-2338

- Primary business activity: banking services.
- Private banking services and/or savings accounts.
- Consumer loans and credit facilities.
- Safekeeping and custodian services.
- Portfolio management of securities and mutual funds.
- Company formation services are offered.
- Trust formation services are offered.

Citibank (Luxembourg)

Mr. J. Fraas 352-477-9571 dial

16, Avenue Marie-Theresa, PO.Box 1373, Luxembourg L-1013

- Primary business activity: bank and trust services.

G.T.Management PLC

Bank in Liechtenstein Representative 352-462-844 dial

9A Boulevard Prince Henri 352-465-701 fax

Luxembourg L-1724

- Primary business activity: banking services.

Gotthard Bank

Mr. Louis Ottaviani 352-461-566 dial

Senior Vice President 352-471-272 fax

6, avenue Marie-Therese 3241 telex

Luxembourg L-2017

- Primary business activity: banking services.
- Private banking services and/or savings accounts.
- Safekeeping and custodian services.
- Portfolio management of securities and mutual funds.
- Company formation services are offered.
- Trust formation services are offered.

Hoogewerf & Co.

25 Boulevard Royal, PO.Box 878, Luxembourg L-2018

- Primary business activity: banking services.

Kredietbank S.A. Luxembourgeoise

Mr. Y. Leclerc	352-47-971	dial
Commercial Department	352-47-2667	fax
43, Boulevard Royal	3418 KBLUX LU	telex
Luxembourg L-2955		

- Primary business activity: banking services.
- Primary business activity: insurance products & services.
- Private banking services and/or savings accounts.
- Consumer loans and credit facilities.
- Safekeeping and custodian services.
- Portfolio management of securities and mutual funds. Minimum deposit LUF200,000.

Mossack Fonseca & Co.

Attorneys at Law	352-458-193	dial
43, Boulevard Joseph II	352-458-673	fax
Luxembourg L-1840		

- Primary business activity: law office.

Overseas Company Registration Agents

Ms. Eveline Karls	352-224-286	dial
Company Formation Agent	352-224-287	fax

Eurotrust International Group S.A., 19 rue Aldringen, Luxembourg L-1118

- Primary business activity: company and trust formation services.
- Corporate services such as registered agent services.
- Company formation services are offered. Minimum formation fee US$5,000 plus license fee.

VP Bank (Luxembourg) S.A.

23, avenue de la Liberte	352-404-7771	dial
B.P. 923	352-481-117	fax
Luxembourg L-2019		

- Primary business activity: banking services.

Wardley Investment Services S.A.

Mr. Michael Sandberg	352-476-8121	dial
Chairman	352-475-569	fax

Maison Gilly, 7 Rue du Marche-aux-Herbes, Luxembourg L-1728

- Primary business activity: fund or portfolio manager.

MALTA

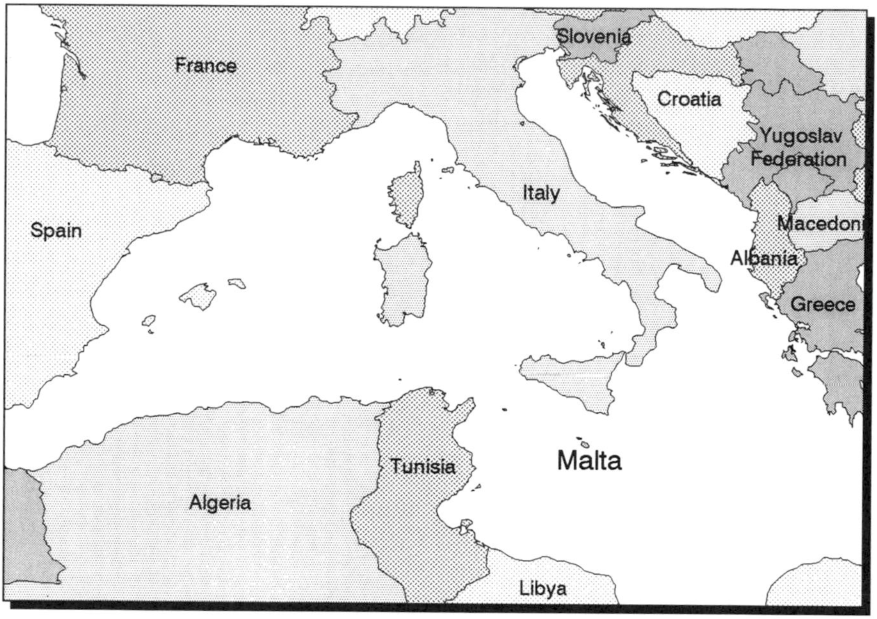

In the centre of the Mediterranean. Five islands positioned between Gibraltar and Suez. Italy is to the north, North Africa to the south. Main language is English, Italian, French, and Maltese (of Semitic origin and related to Arabic, although written in the Roman alphabet). Population is approximately 350,000. Climate is subtropical with relatively low humidity.

Malta's cultural heritage dates back to some time before 4,000 B.C. The Phoenicians, Carthaginians and the Romans; the Byzantines, Arabs and the Normans; the Knights of St.John; the French and the British; all have played a notable part in Malta's history. The arrival of the Knights of St.John marks what may be the most impressive point in the island's history. After a victory over the Turks in the Great Siege of 1565, the

Knights built on the island some of the finest examples of fortifications and architecture in Europe. The period of the Knights in Malta lasted nearly 270 years from 1530 to 1798, until the islands fell to Napoleon Bonaparte. This short period of unrest came to an end with the arrival of British rule in Malta. During World War II Malta was a vital British naval base and came under massive attack by German and Italian forces. In 1942 King George VI awarded the George Cross for Bravery to Malta, the only time a nation as a whole has received this type of award. Malta became fully independent in 1964, though economic ties to Britain remain strong.

Does Malta have a secrecy law?

YES. Malta's secrecy laws are governed by the Maltese International Business Authority (MIBA) Act, prohibiting the unauthorized disclosure of information pertaining to a clients affairs to a third party. Confidentiality is maintained even after cessation and cancellation of a company (MIBA Act section 38).

The Professional Secrecy Bill, 1994, was introduced to clarify the fact that the duty of professional secrecy extends not only to government officials and professionals, but also to their employees, agents, accountants and solicitors, with all secret information being protected by penal sanctions.

Information collected for one regulatory purpose, such as the prevention of money laundering, can not be made available for another connected purpose, such as taxation.

Is there any situation where bank secrecy can be lifted?

YES. The supervisory authorities of the financial sector are obliged to report any evidence of money laundering to the Commissioner of Police. The financial sector does not have the power to communicate directly with authorities in other countries.

The MIBA Act provides investigation regulations to safeguard against abuse of offshore status in cases of criminal activity.

Can foreign tax authorities obtain information on Maltese bank accounts?

NO. Tax evasion is not a criminal activity in Malta, with no requirement for the disclosure of financial information in tax cases.

Is Malta an independent country?

YES. Malta is a sovereign European state with a democratic parliamentary system based on the British model. It is a member of the commonwealth with its first self-governing constitution dating back to 1921. Malta became an independent sovereignty with its own constitution on September 21, 1964. In 1974 the constitution was revised and Malta became a republic within the British Commonwealth.

Is the legal system based on English Common Law?

YES. Malta's legal system is based on Roman Law and the Napoleonic Codes, while more recent fiscal, company, shipping and Trust laws are based on a model of English Common Law and statutes.

Is there an income tax in Malta?

YES. There is a domestic income tax of 15% deducted at source. An outright 10 year corporate tax holiday is guaranteed for any export-oriented project.

The following companies are exempt from income tax:

- General Trading Offshore Companies.

- Non-trading Offshore Companies.
- Banking Offshore Companies.
- Insurance Offshore Companies.
- Insurance Broking Offshore Companies.
- Shipping Companies.

Trusts pay a small fixed annual tax in lieu of a registration fee.

Are there any other taxes in Malta?

NO. No tax is chargeable on any capital-gain, dividend or interest paid by an Offshore Trading or Non-Trading company to a non-resident.

There is no gift tax or customs duty on company property or on expatriate employees' personal belongings being imported into Malta. Property held under a Trust is likewise exempt from Customs Duty if imported into Malta. There are no municipal or local taxes.

No death, donation or stamp duties are levied in relation to offshore companies or Trusts. No duty is chargeable under the Death and Donation Duty Act, 1973, in respect of any asset held under an Offshore Trust.

Are there any exchange controls in Malta?

NO. No exchange control restrictions apply to offshore companies. The same applies to Trusts.

Is there a tax treaty between the U.S. and Malta?

YES. There is a double-taxation agreement between the U.S. and Malta. There are also double-taxation treaties with all the major European countries, Australia, and others.

Is there a tax treaty between Canada and Malta?

YES. There is a double-taxation agreement between Canada and Malta.

Does Malta allow the formation of Limited Companies?

YES. The Maltese government set up a specific Ministry, in May 1987, with responsibility to develop the offshore sector, resulting in the Malta International Business Activities Act, 1988, the Offshore Trusts Act, 1988, and various amendments to revise and update the Merchant Shipping Act, 1973.

Trading Offshore Companies - Trading Offshore Companies are divided into four categories:

- Banking Offshore Companies.
- Insurance Offshore Companies.
- Insurance Broking Offshore Companies.
- General Trading Offshore Companies.

Trading offshore companies will be expected to have a physical and functional presence on the Island, following Malta's determination to establish itself as a reputable international financial and business centre. A general trading offshore company is an offshore company which has as its object any trade or business other than the business of banking, insurance and insurance broking.

Non-Trading Offshore Companies - Non-Trading offshore companies are totally exempt from tax and may opt for non-disclosure of shareholders and directors, registration being possible in the name of local nominees. The law provides for protection of this privacy in legal proceedings and includes special provisions to facilitate the transfer of shares in a non-trading company after death. Non-Trading companies do not require that their accounts be audited, nor are they required to file an annual return or copy of their accounts with the Registrar of Partnerships or with the MIBA. Non-Trading companies include:

- Corporate and personal holding companies.
- Other companies which limit their activities to the ownership, management and administration of their own property of any kind, including patents, copyrights, trademarks and similar property (fund and financial management operations are regarded as a trading activity and require classification as a Trading Company).

An offshore activity is defined as any business activity carried on from Malta:

- In a convertible foreign currency.
- By persons not resident in Malta, with persons not resident in Malta.

An offshore company may use a bank in Malta for the purposes of any transaction in foreign currency which it could lawfully carry out with any other bank.

Does Malta allow the formation of International Trusts?

YES. Offshore Trusts are regulated by the Offshore Trusts Act, 1988, and by certain provisions of the Malta International Business Activities Act, 1988. A Trust is an Offshore Trust if:

- The Settlor is not resident in Malta at the time the Trust is created.
- The Trust property does not include any immovable property situated in Malta; or shares, stock or debentures in a company whose assets include immovable property situated in Malta; or a company, other than an offshore company, registered in Malta.

- All the Beneficiaries under the Trust are not resident in Malta at the time the Trust is created.

A Trust may continue until the 100th anniversary of the date on which it was created, and will then terminate (unless terminated sooner). This provision does not apply to charitable Trusts.

As Malta does not have a long history of Trust law, unit Trusts will have the option of being governed by a foreign Trust law, while being managed from Malta, under the Recognition of Trusts Bill, 1994, and amendments to the Offshore Trusts Act, 1988.

Does Malta allow the formation of Captive Insurance Companies?

YES. Insurance Offshore Companies are subject to The Insurance Business Act (IBA), 1981, and The Banking Act, 1970. An Insurance Offshore Company may be:

- An insurance offshore Oversea company.
- An insurance offshore Subsidiary company.
- An insurance offshore Local company.
- Any other offshore company which expressly restricts its objects to the business of insurance. Such a company may be a captive insurance offshore company, which is defined as "*an insurance offshore company which restricts its business of insurance to risks originating with companies being members of a group of companies, of which it is itself a member, and having one parent or holding company.*"

The IBA, 1981, states that "*a company shall not be registered as an insurance offshore company unless the Authority is satisfied that the company is capable of properly conducting and supporting the business to be carried on, that it has the expertise and the financial resources for such purpose and that it will keep such resources in such assets and maintain where appropriate margins of solvency, as may be required by the Authority to be kept or maintained.*" Note that the IBA does not apply to an insurance broking offshore company or to a company whose business is exclusively the management of Insurance Offshore Companies.

Exemptions and amendments applicable to all Insurance Offshore Companies include:

- In order to carry on business as principals, insurance offshore companies (other than Oversea and captive companies) must have a minimum paid-up share capital of US$750,000.
- In the case of captive companies, the paid-up capital must amount to at least US$250,000.
- Insurance Offshore Oversea Companies are exempted from the requirement of keeping within Malta, and out of their own funds, paid-up capital assets.
- Insurance Offshore Companies are exempted from the requirement of transferring at least 25% of their net annual profits (before dividends) to a reserve fund, until the fund reaches the amount of the company's paid-up share capital (Insurance Offshore Oversea Companies are not required by the IBA to keep such a reserve fund).

Does Malta allow the formation of Banking Companies?

YES. Banking Offshore Companies are subject to The Banking Act, 1970, and amendments. A Banking Offshore Company may be:

- An offshore Oversea company, where a bank (which is recognized by the MIBA as being of international standing and repute) establishes a branch in Malta exclusively for offshore activities.

- An offshore Subsidiary company, where a bank forms and registers in Malta a private Subsidiary company exclusively for the business of offshore banking.
- An offshore local company, where a bank (which is licensed under the Banking Act, 1970 to carry on business in Malta) forms and registers in Malta a private subsidiary company exclusively for the business of offshore banking.
- Any other offshore company which expressly restricts its objects to the business of banking.

Requirements, exemptions and amendments applicable to all Banking Offshore Companies include:

- Must have a minimum paid-up share capital of US$1.5 million.
- Exempted from the requirement of transferring at least 25% of their net annual profits (before dividends) to a reserve fund, until the fund reaches the amount of the Bank's paid-up share capital.
- Banking Offshore Companies are exempted from the prohibition on commercial banks of the payment of dividends in certain circumstances.
- Banking Offshore Companies need not obtain Ministerial approval to use the word "bank" in the description or title under which they carry on business.
- Section 12 of the Banking Act prohibits commercial banks from carrying out certain transactions, such as the granting of credit facilities to any person to a value exceeding 25% of the Bank's paid-up capital and reserves.

Does Malta allow the formation of Shipping Companies?

YES. Non-Trading companies may operate as Shipping Companies which own or operate ships registered under any flag. The benefit of tax exemption applies equally to a Holding Company and to its subsidiaries, each of which may own or operate one or more ships. Malta encourages owners of all types of vessels, from pleasure yachts to oil rigs, to register their ships under the Maltese Flag.

The registration and operation of Maltese ships is regulated by a Merchant Shipping Act which is based mainly on United Kingdom legislation. There are no restrictions regarding the nationality of the crew, or the trading, sale or mortgaging of Maltese registered ships.

Financial institutions and contacts:

Bank of Valetta International Ltd.

Mr. Anthony Paris	356-249970	dial
86 South Street	356-222132	fax
Valetta, Malta VLT 11		

- Primary business activity: banking services.
- Private banking services and/or savings accounts.
- Consumer loans and credit facilities.
- Portfolio management of securities and mutual funds.

Deloitte & Touche Nominee Limited

Mr. Malcolm Booker	356-238829	dial
Director	356-220386	fax
21, Archbishop Street, Valetta, Malta VLT 07		

- Primary business activity: accounting services.
- Corporate services such as registered agent services.
- Company formation services are offered. Minimum formation fee Lm350 plus Lm500 license fee. Minimum annual fee Lm350.

Fenlex Nominee Services Ltd.

198 Old Bakery Street	356-241232	dial
Valetta, Malta	356-221893	fax

- Primary business activity: bank and trust services.

Malta Development Corporation

Mr. Joe V. Bannister	356-221431	dial
Chairman	356-606407	fax

House of Catalunya, Marsamxetto Road, Valetta, Malta

- Primary business activity: government services.

Malta International Business Authority

Mr. Marcel Cassar	356-344230	dial
Deputy Commissioner of Banking	356-344334	fax
Palazzo Spinola	1692 MIBA MW	telex

PO.Box St.Julians 29, Valetta, Malta STJ 01

- Primary business activity: government services.

Malta Trust & Nominee Ltd.

Wisely House, First Floor	356-223125	dial
206 Old Bakery Street	356-241301	fax
Valetta, Malta	1703 JENTI MW	telex

- Primary business activity: bank and trust services.

Mid-Med Bank (Overseas) Ltd.

15 Republic Street	356-249801	dial
Valetta, Malta VLT 04	356-249805	fax

- Primary business activity: banking services.

MONACO

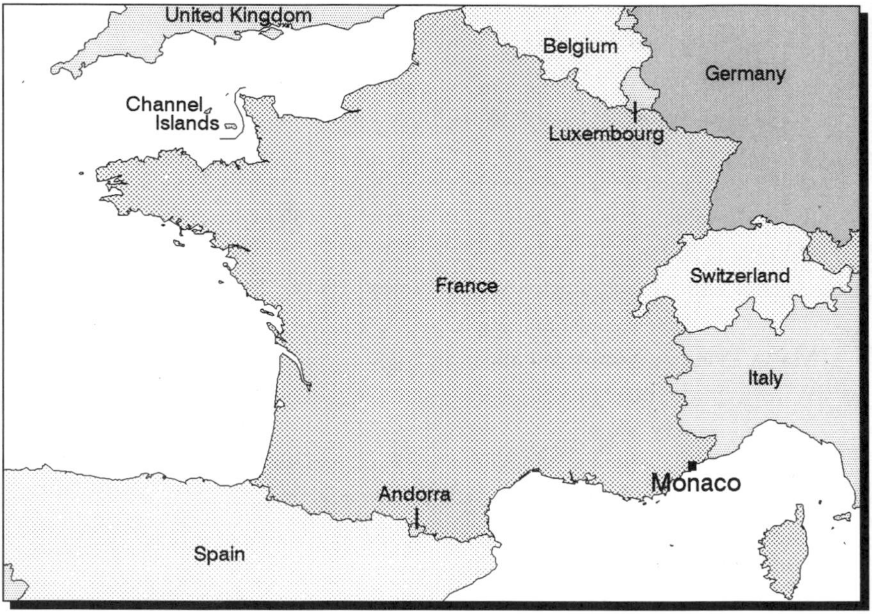

In Europe. In the heart of the French Riviera. At 0.073 square miles in size (465 acres) Monaco is the second smallest country in the world. Population is approximately 30,000. Main languages are French, English, Italian, and Monegasque. Climate is sub-tropical with relatively low humidity.

The Principality of Monaco has been the domain of the Grimaldi family since 1297, placing itself under French protection in 1861. During the 1800's, Prince Charles III saved the economy by introducing gambling. The government is a hereditary constitutional monarchy led by Prince Rainier III.

Cost of living is high. Connections to the rest of the world are excellent.

Does Monaco have a secrecy law?

N/A.

Is there any situation where bank secrecy can be lifted?

N/A.

Can foreign tax authorities obtain information on Monaco bank accounts?

N/A.

Is Monaco an independent country?

YES. Monaco is a stable, independent sovereignty that initially gained independence in 1489. The government is a hereditary constitutional monarchy led by Prince Rainier III.

Is the legal system based on English Common Law?

NO. The legal system is based on Monegasque law (similar to civil law) and is supplemented by French civil code.

Is there an income tax in Monaco?

YES. Companies pay a 35% income tax if more than 25% of their income is derived from Monaco. Companies that derive income from passive sources such as patents, licenses, or intellectual property rights pay profit taxes. There is no income tax for citizens of Monaco.

Are there any other taxes in Monaco?

YES. There are registration and stamp duties on the transfer of real estate.

There is no capital gains tax, gift tax, stamp duty, withholding tax, or estate tax for non-residents.

Are there any exchange controls in Monaco?

NO. There are currently no exchange controls in Monaco. The official currency is the French Franc.

Is there a tax treaty between the U.S. and Monaco?

NO. There is no double-taxation agreement between the U.S. and Monaco, although there is a tax treaty between France and Monaco.

Is there a tax treaty between Canada and Monaco?

NO. There is no double-taxation agreement between Canada and Monaco.

Does Monaco allow the formation of Limited Companies?

YES. Although Monaco supports the formation of a limited company known as the Société Anonyme Monegasque, in practice it is very difficult and time consuming. Incorporation can take up to 4 months, and requires prior government approval. If establishing a branch of a foreign corporation, audited financial statements must be filed for the previous 3 years. Minimum requirements include:

- Two shareholders and two directors. One director must be a legal resident.
- Minimum capitalization is FF500,000.
- Shares issued in kind are restricted from trade for two years.
- A registered chartered accountant must be appointed as auditor.

Does Monaco allow the formation of International Trusts?

NO. Civil law does not readily support the formation of International Trusts.

Does Monaco allow the formation of Captive Insurance Companies?

YES. Although Captive Insurance Companies can be formed in Monaco, there are other jurisdictions with lower costs and friendlier legislation.

Does Monaco allow the formation of Banking Companies?

YES. Although Banking Companies can be formed in Monaco, there are other jurisdictions with lower costs and friendlier legislation.

Financial institutions and contacts:

Ansbacher (Monaco) SAM
Ms. Lindsay Leggat-Smith 33-9350-9686 dial
Managing Director 33-9350-5344 fax
24 Boulevard Princesse Charlotte, Monte Carlo, Monaco 98000

- Primary business activity: bank and trust services.
- Safekeeping and custodian services.
- Portfolio management of securities and mutual funds.
- Company formation services are offered.
- Trust formation services are offered.

Banque de Placements et de Credit
Av. de Grande-Bretagne 2 33-9315-5815 dial
Monte Carlo, Monaco 469 955 telex

- Primary business activity: banking services.

Banque du Gothard (Monaco)

Le Monte-Carlo Palace	33-9350-6070	dial
9, boulevard de Boulin	33-9350-6071	fax
Monte Carlo, Monaco MC-98000	469 606	telex

- Primary business activity: banking services.
- Private banking services and/or savings accounts.
- Safekeeping and custodian services.
- Portfolio management of securities and mutual funds.
- Company formation services are offered.
- Trust formation services are offered.

Barclays Bank

31 Avenue de la Costa, Monte Carlo, Monaco

- Primary business activity: banking services.

Compagnie Monegasque de Banque

Les Terrasses, 2 Avenue de Monte Carlo, Monte Carlo, Monaco

- Primary business activity: banking services.

Credit Foncier de Monaco

17 Boulevart Albert 1er, PO.Box 6, Monte Carlo, Monaco

- Primary business activity: banking services.

Gordon S. Blair Law Offices

Mr. James W. Hill	33-9325-8525	dial
Associate	33-9325-7958	fax

3, rue Louis Aureglia, B.P. 449, Monte Carlo, Monaco MC 98011

- Primary business activity: law office.

Hoogewerf & Co. SAM

2 Avenue de Monte Carlo	33-9350-0820	dial
PO.Box 343	33-9350-2412	fax

Monte Carlo, Monaco MC 98006

- Primary business activity: banking services.

United Overseas Bank Geneve

Societe de Banque et d'Investissements		
Mr. Sylvain Mabilleau	33-9315-7474	dial
Directeur-Adjoint	33-9350-1537	fax
26, boulevard d'Italie	479464 MC	telex
B.P. 319, Monte Carlo, Monaco MC 98007		

- Primary business activity: banking services.
- Private banking services and/or savings accounts.
- Consumer loans and credit facilities.
- Portfolio management of securities and mutual funds.

MONTSERRAT

In the Eastern Caribbean. A 39.5 square mile island, 27 miles southwest of Antigua, population approximately 15,000. Main language is English. Climate is tropical with relatively low humidity, average temperature 76°F to 86°F.

Montserrat was discovered by Christopher Columbus in 1493 and named after that part of Spain for the similarity of the jagged mountain peaks. Colonized by the Irish in 1632, the island was long fought over by the French and British before being ceded to Britain in 1783.

During the 1980's Montserrat became plagued by money laundering activities related to illegal drug activities, theft and fraud. The U.S. Senate's report, *Crime and Secrecy: The Use of Offshore Banks and*

Companies and the Coopers & Lybrand *Survey of Offshore Finance Sectors of the Caribbean Dependent Territories* prepared for the British Government (known as the *Gallagher Report*) were especially damaging to Montserrat's international banking industry. Both reports expanded the "interpretation" of any activity considered a crime in Montserrat. After the release of the 1989 Gallagher Report, 259 of the 330 banks chartered in Montserrat had their bank charters revoked. Of the 259, most were organized by one company. Because of the world-wide publicity, it may be prudent to wait until the dust settles before using Montserrat for any type of banking operations requiring secrecy, privacy, and confidentiality.

Does Montserrat have a secrecy law?

YES. Montserrat's secrecy laws prohibit the unauthorized disclosure of information pertaining to a clients affairs to a third party.

Is there any situation where bank secrecy can be lifted?

YES. Montserrat's secrecy law allows the disclosure of confidential information relating to drug, theft, and fraud investigations. During the 1980's Montserrat became plagued by money laundering activities related to illegal drug activities, theft and fraud. In August 1985, the findings of the Permanent Subcommittee on Investigations of Offshore Banking were published in the U.S. Senate's report *Crime and Secrecy: The Use of Offshore Banks and Companies*. The report detailed money laundering activities in Montserrat. In 1990, the UK published its own version of events in a document referred to as the *Gallagher Report*. These reports have widened the "interpretation" of any activity considered a "crime" in Montserrat.

Can foreign tax authorities obtain information on Montserrat bank accounts?

NO. Confidential information relating strictly to taxation can not be released to foreign tax authorities.

Is Montserrat an independent country?

NO. Montserrat is a British dependency with a ministerial system of government and its own constitution. The government is headed by a resident British Governor.

Is the legal system based on English Common Law?

YES. The legal system is based on English Common Law and is supplemented by local statutes.

Is there an income tax in Montserrat?

NO. There is no income tax in Montserrat for income derived outside of Montserrat.

Are there any other taxes in Montserrat?

NO. There is no capital gains tax in Montserrat for capital gains derived outside of Montserrat. There is no gift tax or estate tax in Montserrat.

Are there any exchange controls in Montserrat?

NO. There are currently no exchange controls in Montserrat. The official currency is the East Caribbean Dollar.

Is there a tax treaty between the U.S. and Montserrat?

NO. There is no double-taxation agreement between the U.S. and Montserrat, although there is a double-taxation agreement between the UK and Montserrat. There are also double-taxation agreements with Denmark, Japan, Norway, Sweden, and Switzerland.

Is there a tax treaty between Canada and Montserrat?

NO. There is no double-taxation agreement between Canada and Montserrat.

Does Montserrat allow the formation of Limited Companies?

YES. Montserrat is a suitable jurisdiction for the formation of Limited Companies.

Does Montserrat allow the formation of International Trusts?

YES. Montserrat is a suitable jurisdiction for the formation of International Trusts.

Does Montserrat allow the formation of Captive Insurance Companies?

YES. Although Captive Insurance Companies can be formed in Montserrat, there are other jurisdictions with a more developed infrastructure.

Does Montserrat allow the formation of Banking Companies?

YES. Because of the U.S. Senate's report *Crime and Secrecy: The Use of Offshore Banks and Companies* and the UK's *Gallagher Report*, the requirements for chartering and operating an offshore bank in Montserrat have been considerably tightened. Although the restrictions place Montserrat in line with other jurisdictions, the Gallagher Report further suggested limiting offshore banking to branches or subsidiaries of recognized international banks and to applicants possessing impeccable references and financial resources.

A moratorium on new bank charters has recently been lifted.

Financial institutions and contacts:

Barclays Bank PLC

PO.Box 131, Plymouth, Montserrat, West Indies

- Primary business activity: banking services.
- Private banking services and/or savings accounts.

Canadian Credit Bank Ltd.

PO.Box 207, Plymouth, Montserrat, West Indies

- Primary business activity: banking services.

Kenneth Allen, Solicitor

Chambers

Plymouth, Montserrat, West Indies

- Primary business activity: law office.

Royal Bank of Canada

Ms. I.M. Meade	809-491-2426	dial
Customer Service Supervisor	809-491-3991	fax
Parliament Street	360-5713	telex

PO.Box 222, Plymouth, Montserrat, West Indies

- Primary business activity: banking services.
- Private banking services and/or savings accounts.

NAURU

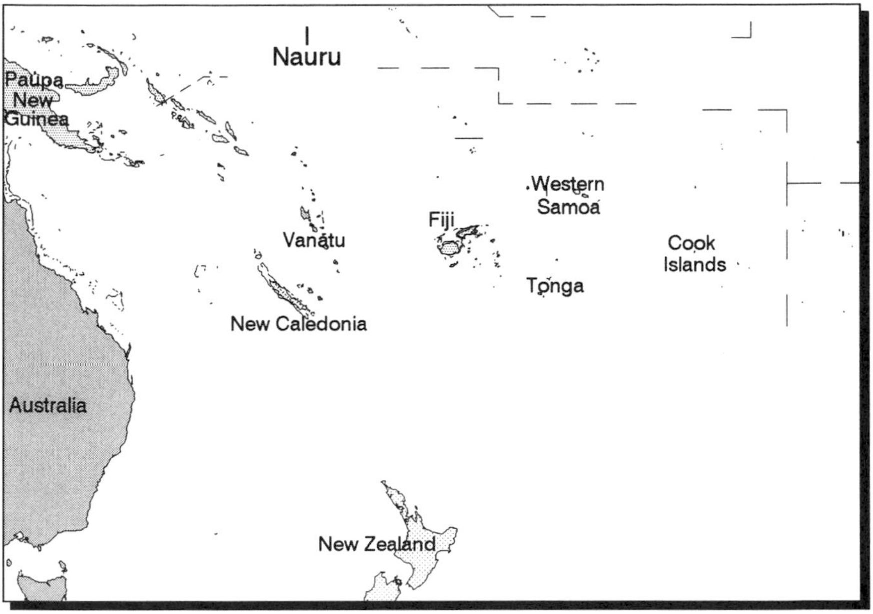

In the South Pacific. One of the smallest countries in the world, a 21 square km island 41 km south of the equator. Nauru is reachable only through Fiji and the Marshal Islands. Population is approximately 9,000. Main language is Nauruan and English. Climate is tropical with high humidity, average temperature 84°F.

The population is a mix of Polynesian and Melanesians that have been on Nauru for many generations. The island fell under German control in 1881, passing to Australia in 1914, and finally becoming independent in 1968.

Phosphate is the single natural resource, and is expected to be depleted early in the next century. Currently, every citizen receives over

$20,000 annually in royalties from the production and export of phosphates. To ensure the continuation of the Nauruan race, the government has established Trusts with the Nauruan people as Beneficiaries. The Trusts have over 4 billion dollars invested in Australian, Hawaiian, and other south Pacific real estate. Immigration is discouraged.

Does Nauru have a secrecy law?

YES. Nauru's secrecy laws prohibit the unauthorized disclosure of information pertaining to a clients affairs to a third party, although the interpretation of the law depends on the attitude of the Nauruan court officials at that particular time. Exercise caution.

Is there any situation where bank secrecy can be lifted?

NO. It appears that in the past, bank secrecy has been absolute. In the late 1980's, the New Zealand Serious Frauds Office claimed that Nauruan banks were being used for money laundering, although the New Zealand government could never obtain the information to prove their case.

Can foreign tax authorities obtain information on Nauruan bank accounts?

NO. Nauru will not cooperate with foreign governments when dealing with tax investigations. Generally, confidential information will remain confidential, although the interpretation of statutes is always at the discretion of the Nauruan court.

Is Nauru an independent country?

YES. Nauru became an independent sovereign state on January 31, 1968 and is an associate member of the British Commonwealth. The present constitution was adopted in 1968 and the Government is operated as a parliamentary democracy.

Is the legal system based on English Common Law?

YES. Modern company and Trust statutes have been enacted together with legislation to control the activities of banks, trust companies and insurance business, although the "interpretation" of the law may be at some times different than the "letter" of the law. Modern legislation, including the preservation of secrecy, has been specifically designed to meet the needs of tax planners.

Is there an income tax in Nauru?

NO. There is no income tax in Nauru.

Are there any other taxes in Nauru?

NO. There is no capital gains tax, gift tax, or estate tax in Nauru.

Are there any exchange controls in Nauru?

NO. There are currently no exchange controls in Nauru. The official currency is the Australian Dollar.

Is there a tax treaty between the U.S. and Nauru?

NO. There is no double-taxation agreement between the U.S. and Nauru.

Is there a tax treaty between Canada and Nauru?

NO. There is no double-taxation agreement between Canada and Nauru.

Does Nauru allow the formation of Limited Companies?

YES. Companies are governed by the Nauru Corporation Act 1972. Commercial law in Nauru recognizes the concept of "trading" and "holding" corporations with limited liabilities. Corporations are entitled to apply for licenses for establishment of trusts, banks and insurance companies.

Any individual or corporation may be a shareholder, secretary or director of a holding or trading corporation incorporated in Nauru. Every corporation must have a registered resident secretary. Nauru Secretaries Incorporated acts as the registered resident secretary for all corporations in Nauru. Presently any one of the following corporations may act as Registered Director:

- Nauru Nominee Corporation, PO.Box 300, Aiwo, Nauru
- Nauru Secretaries Incorporated, PO.Box 300, Aiwo, Nauru
- Buada Corporation, PO.Box 300, Aiwo, Nauru

Applications for incorporation must be routed through Registered Corporation Agents. Nauru Agency Corporation and Central Pacific Agency Corporation have been appointed as agents for this purpose.

Holding Corporation - A holding corporation is not authorized to trade, factor, broker, manufacture, or deal in goods. Certain exemptions and privileges apply to holding corporations as follows:

- A minimum of only one shareholder and one director are required.
- Corporations may be formed by the Nauru Government commercial authority on request by a person who would like to remain anonymous.
- May have any amount of share capital with no minimum or maximum limits prescribed by law.
- The identity of company owners can be kept discreet through bearer shares held anonymously or by nominees.
- May convert itself into a trading corporation.
- May not have more than 20 shareholders.
- May issue shares by way of gift without receiving any valuable consideration up to a par value of A$10.

- May not offer or issue debentures to the public.
- Need not have the accounts audited by a Registered Corporation Auditor.
- May have management and control anywhere in the world.

Trading Corporation - A trading corporation may trade, factor, broker, manufacture, or deal in goods, as long as these activities conform to the laws of Nauru or the laws of the country in which it operates. Certain exemptions and privileges apply to trading corporations as follows:

- A minimum of only two shareholders and two directors are required.
- May have any amount of share capital with no minimum or maximum limits prescribed by law.
- May issue bearer shares (with amended Articles of Association).
- May not convert itself into a holding corporation.
- Is not restricted to the number of shareholders.
- Is permitted to offer and issue debentures to the public.
- Is subject to public inspection of documents filed with the Registrar of Corporations; however, the records maintained by the Nauru Agency Corporation are not accessible to a third party without the permission of the sponsors of the corporation.
- May have management and control anywhere in the world.

The filing of an annual return is required for the renewal of incorporation at the end of each year, detailing changes in registered office, directors and secretaries, allotment of shares, and change in share capital.

Does Nauru allow the formation of International Trusts?

YES. Trusts are governed by the Nauru Trustee Corporation Act 1972, closely following the Trust laws of Britain, except where modified by the Foreign Trusts, Estates, and Wills Act 1972:

- The rule against perpetuities does not apply.
- There are no restrictions on directions for accumulation of income.
- Trusts may be of perpetual duration.
- Trusts established in Nauru are not required to be registered under Nauruan laws.

The Nauru Trustee Corporation Act 1972 established a Trustee corporation called the Nauru Trustee Corporation (NTC) with a statutory charter. It is permitted to act as Trustee for all types of Trusts, including purpose Trusts under the Foreign Trusts, Estates, and Wills Act 1972. No taxes or duties are payable in respect to any will admitted to probate in Nauru. At least one of the executors or administrators appointed by a foreign will must be a Nauruan Trustee Corporation, which is required to hold a Trustee license.

Does Nauru allow the formation of Captive Insurance Companies?

YES. Insurance companies are governed by the Insurance Act 1974. Captive Insurance Companies are required to conform to the same requirements as Banking Companies, as noted above.

Does Nauru allow the formation of Banking Companies?

YES. Banking Companies are governed by the Banking Act 1975. Banking licenses are granted only to "*persons who have a sound financial standing, are well reputed in commercial and financial circles, and have acquired sufficient expertise in banking, trade, and industry.*" To obtain a banking license, the bank must comply with the following conditions:

- The bank must have a minimum paid-up capital of US$100,000 within a period of two years from the date of issue of the license.
- The bank must furnish to the Registrar audited balance sheets and profit and loss accounts of each year within six months of year end.
- All the operations of the bank should be "in house" and should not accept deposits from the public.

The low capitalization, non-interference in operations, minimum administrative expenses and simplicity of the banking laws, rules and regulations are designed to provide incentive for entrepreneurs to seek banking licenses under the laws of Nauru.

Financial institutions and contacts:

Bank of Nauru
PO.Box 289, Nauru, Central Pacific

- Primary business activity: banking services.

Central Pacific Agency Corporation
PO.Box 302, Nauru, Central Pacific

- Primary business activity: company and trust formation services.

Nauru Agency Corporation
PO.Box 300 | 674-555-4011 dial
Aiwo, Nauru, Central Pacific | 674-444-3730 fax

- Primary business activity: company and trust formation services.
- Company formation services are offered. Minimum formation fee A$1,350 including license fee. Minimum annual fee A$810.
- Trust formation services are offered. Minimum formation fee A$2,800. Minimum annual fee A$2,260.
- Captive insurance company formation. Minimum formation fee A$2,550 including license fee. Minimum annual fee A$2,010.
- Banking company formation. Minimum formation fee A$2,550 including license fee. Minimum annual fee A$2,010.

PANAMA

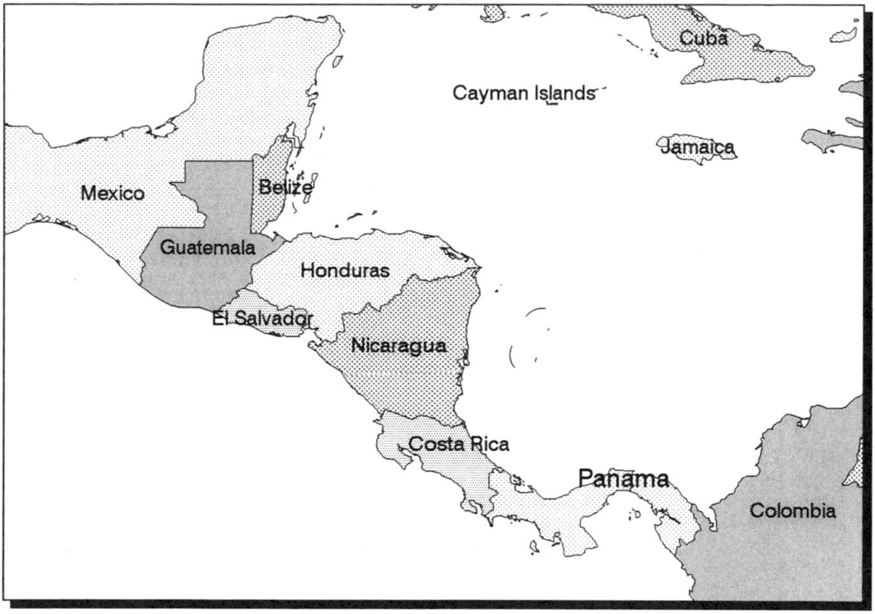

In Central America. Borders both the Pacific Ocean and the Caribbean Sea, between Costa Rica and Colombia. Population approximately 2.4 million. Main language is Spanish and English.

The province of Panama declared itself independent from Colombia in 1903 because the Colombian government had refused to sanction the construction of the Panama Canal, which was eventually completed in 1914. The U.S. held land flanking the Canal, but returned the land to Panama in 1979.

Stability has been compromised by the presence of drug dealers and arms smugglers, and the emergence of large scale money laundering operations.

Does Panama have a secrecy law?

YES. Panama's strict secrecy laws prohibit the unauthorized disclosure of information pertaining to a clients affairs to a third party, punishable by fines and jail sentences. The Bank Secrecy Law of the Republic of Panama has been designed to allow numbered (coded) accounts. No authority has the right to compel a bank to give any information concerning a coded account.

Banks will request that coded accounts have at least one proxy named, due to the fact that in the event of death of the only signing authority of the account, the Bank Secrecy Law does not allow them to give any information concerning the account, even to the courts.

Is there any situation where bank secrecy can be lifted?

YES. The U.S. government has been able to circumvent Panama's secrecy laws in the past, a notable example being former leader Manuel Noriega's bank records being made available to the trial held in the U.S. Officially, the only exception to bank secrecy is when an investigating authority is dealing with criminal proceedings. In this case the information is kept in "strict reserve" unless it is required to clarify the punishable facts under investigation.

Can foreign tax authorities obtain information on Panamanian bank accounts?

NO. Panamanian bankers have resisted foreign authorities attempting to gain access to confidential information. No bilateral treaty has been signed between Panama and any other country regarding disclosure of information for tax purposes.

Is Panama an independent country?

YES. The Republic of Panama is an independent country with elections held every five years. The three levels of government are executive, legislative, and judicial.

Is the legal system based on English Common Law?

NO. The legal system is based on Civil Law.

Is there an income tax in Panama?

NO. There is no income tax in Panama on income earned outside of Panama. Bank interest is not subject to taxation at source. Interest paid by Panamanian banks is exempt from Panamanian income tax.

Are there any other taxes in Panama?

NO. Income and capital gains from activities outside of Panama are not taxed. There is no gift tax or estate tax in Panama.

Are there any exchange controls in Panama?

NO. There are currently no exchange controls in Panama, with complete freedom in the movement of funds. Official currency is the U.S. dollar.

Is there a tax treaty between the U.S. and Panama?

YES. There is a double-taxation agreement between the U.S. and Panama covering shipping income.

Is there a tax treaty between Canada and Panama?

NO. There is no double-taxation agreement between Canada and Panama.

Does Panama allow the formation of Limited Companies?

YES. Company law in Panama is an adaptation of 1927 Delaware company law. Requirements and advantages include:

- Minimum number of directors is three.
- Officers can be non-resident.
- Shareholders meetings may take place in any jurisdiction.
- The identity of company owners can be kept discreet through bearer shares held anonymously.
- Companies are easily formed.
- Companies are required to use one of the following designations: Sociedad Anonima, Corporation, Incorporated, or their abbreviations.

Unless a company does business in Panama, no tax returns are required.

Does Panama allow the formation of International Trusts?

NO. Civil law does not readily support the formation of International Trusts.

Does Panama allow the formation of Captive Insurance Companies?

YES. Although Captive Insurance Companies can be formed in Panama, there are other jurisdictions with lower costs and friendlier legislation.

Does Panama allow the formation of Banking Companies?

YES. Although Banking Companies can be formed in Panama, there are other jurisdictions with lower costs and friendlier legislation.

Financial institutions and contacts:

Banco Nacional da Panama

PO.Box 5220, Panama 5

- Primary business activity: banking services.

Boliva International

Apartado 4508, Panama 5

- Primary business activity: company and trust formation services.

Caja de Ahorros

PO.Box 1740, Panama 1

- Primary business activity: banking services.

Chase Manhattan Bank, N.A.

Plaza Chase (507) 63-5319 dial

Urbanizacion Marbella, 8th Floor, Marbella, Panama 9A

- Primary business activity: banking services.
- Private banking services and/or savings accounts.
- Consumer loans and credit facilities.
- Safekeeping and custodian services.
- Portfolio management of securities and mutual funds.
- Company formation services are offered.
- Trust formation services are offered.

Edis Esquiral Gonzalez

Building 13, 2W Floor, Office 9, Via Espana, Panama City, Panama

- Primary business activity: law office.

First Incorporating Business

PO.Box 550142 (507) 69-1677 dial

Paitilla, Panama (507) 69-1037 fax

- Primary business activity: company and trust formation services.

Francis & Francis

PO.Box 8807N 7283 (507) 63-8555 dial

Eastern Building, 12th Floor, Panama 5

- Primary business activity: law office.

Hutchinson y Asociados
PO.Box 1290 (507) 27-5256 dial
Panama 9A

- Primary business activity: law office.

Interglobe Consultants, Inc.
PO.Box 6-1714
El Dorado, Panama

- Primary business activity: company and trust formation services.

Lamar, Westford & Assoc.
PO.Box 6-5879 (507) 27-2658 dial
El Dorado, Panama 6A (507) 33-3459 fax

- Primary business activity: company and trust formation services.

Management Services Overseas, Inc.
PO.Box 6-5879 (507) 27-2658 dial
El Dorado, Panama 6A (507) 33-3459 fax

- Primary business activity: company and trust formation services.

Mata & Pitti, Attorneys-at-Law
Mr. Francisco Mata (507) 64-5570 dial
Company Formation Agent (507) 64-6127 fax
PO.Box 87-1319, Calle Ricardo Acias, Banco Aliado Building, Panama 7

- Primary business activity: company and trust formation services.

Morgan y Morgan
Bancosur Building, 53rd Street, PO.Box 1824, Panama City, Panama

- Primary business activity: law office.

Mossack Fonseca & Co. Attorneys at Law
Ms. Anabella Acoca (507) 63-8899 dial
Attorney (507) 63-9218 fax
Arango-Orillac Building, PO.Box 8320, Panama 7

- Primary business activity: law office.

PanAmerican Management Services SA

PO.Box 7402, Panama 5

- Primary business activity: company and trust formation services.

Pardini & Assoc.

PO.Box 9654, Panama 4

- Primary business activity: law office.

Swiss Bank Corporation (Overseas) S.A.

Torre Swiss Bank		
Mr. C. de Maschkowski	(507) 63-7181	dial
Manager of Investment Services	(507) 69-5995	fax
Calle 53 Este	3166	telex
Marbella, Panama 9A		

- Primary business activity: banking services.
- Offers Private Credit Card (AMEX) backed by deposit.
- Private banking services and/or savings accounts.
- Safekeeping and custodian services.
- Portfolio management of securities and mutual funds. Minimum deposit US$200,000. Minimum annual fee 1/2% of assets or US$1,250 plus US$100 per transaction.

ST.KITTS & NEVIS

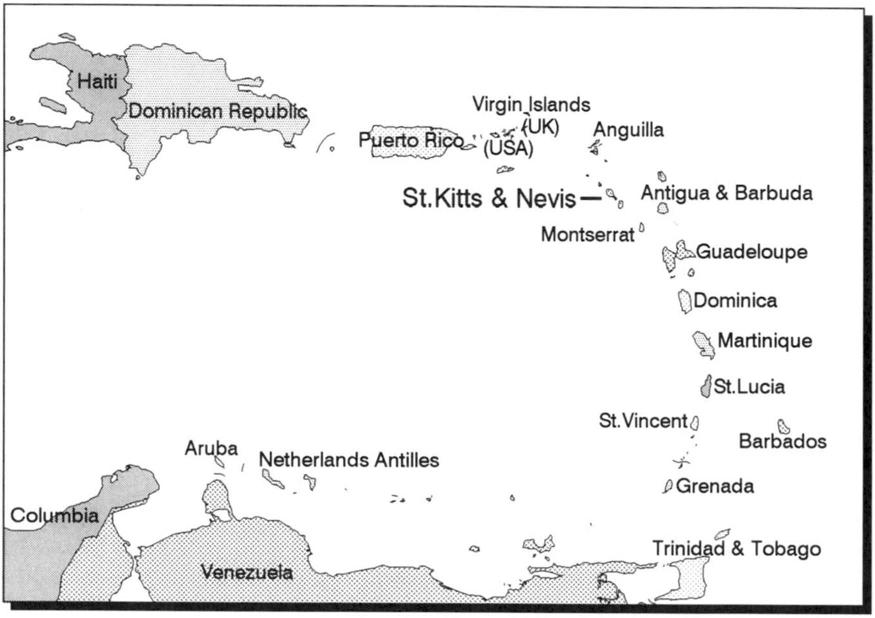

In the Caribbean (Lesser Antilles). St.Kitts & Nevis is located 1,200 miles southeast of Miami, 200 miles east of Puerto Rico. St.Kitts covers a land area of 68 square miles, while Nevis covers a land area of 36 square miles. They are separated by a channel two miles wide. Population is approximately 44,000. Main language is English. Climate is tropical with average humidity, average temperature is 79°F.

St.Kitts & Nevis (officially known as St.Christopher Nevis) was discovered by Columbus in 1493 and was colonized by Sir Thomas Warner in 1623, becoming the Mother Colony of the West Indies. St.Kitts & Nevis achieved Associated Status with Britain in 1967 and attained full political independence in 1983. The twin island destination enjoys a democratic government and is a member of the United Nations.

The government has recently upgraded their offshore financial centre in St.Kitts, fully computerizing the registration of companies and trusts. This continues the attempt to make St.Kitts & Nevis into one of the premiere tax haven countries in the world.

Does St.Kitts & Nevis have a secrecy law?

YES. The Confidentiality Relationship Act of 1985 prohibit the unauthorized disclosure of information pertaining to a clients affairs to a third party, punishable by prison sentence.

Is there any situation where bank secrecy can be lifted?

YES. Although St.Kitts & Nevis' secrecy law prohibits the unauthorized disclosure of information, the law does not apply to activities that are considered crimes in St.Kitts & Nevis, such as illegal drug activities, theft, or fraud.

Can foreign tax authorities obtain information on St.Kitts & Nevis bank accounts?

NO. Confidential information can only be released if there is a suspected criminal activity such as illegal drug activities, theft, or fraud, and is not available to foreign governments for tax investigations.

Is St.Kitts & Nevis an independent country?

YES. St.Kitts & Nevis achieved Associated Status with Britain in 1967 and attained full political independence in 1983. The twin islands are governed by a stable democracy. St.Kitts & Nevis is a member of the British Commonwealth and the United Nations.

Is the legal system based on English Common Law?

YES. The legal system is based on English Common Law and is supplemented by local statutes. The Island is served by the High Court of Justice and the Court of Appeal.

Is there an income tax in St.Kitts & Nevis?

YES. Local companies are liable to pay tax at a rate of up to 40% of net annual profits, paid annually. This tax does not apply to the profits of an approved enterprise which has been granted benefits under the Fiscal Incentives Act. Offshore companies doing business outside St.Kitts & Nevis are exempt from all forms of taxation.

Are there any other taxes in St.Kitts & Nevis?

NO. There is no capital gains tax, gift tax, or estate tax in St.Kitts & Nevis.

Are there any exchange controls in St.Kitts & Nevis?

NO. There are currently no exchange controls in St.Kitts & Nevis. The official currency is the East Caribbean Dollar.

Is there a tax treaty between the U.S. and St.Kitts & Nevis?

NO. There is no double-taxation agreement between the U.S. and St.Kitts & Nevis, although double-taxation agreements are maintained with Denmark, New Zealand, Norway, Sweden, Switzerland, and the United Kingdom.

Is there a tax treaty between Canada and St.Kitts & Nevis?

NO. There is no double-taxation agreement between Canada and St.Kitts & Nevis.

Does St.Kitts & Nevis allow the formation of Limited Companies?

YES. Non-resident domestic companies are governed by the Business Corporation Ordinance 1984, which has been modeled after Delaware and New York company law. St.Kitts & Nevis corporations offer the following advantages and benefits:

- Bearer shares or registered shares may be issued.
- Share capital may have a par value or no par value.
- Only one director and one shareholder is required.
- Directors and secretary may be corporate, and may be of any nationality.
- There are no nationality restrictions on beneficial owners.
- Shareholders and directors meetings may be held in any jurisdiction.
- Filing of annual returns is not required.
- It is not necessary to file the names of the directors, officers, or shareholders.
- Company records and principal office may be located in any jurisdiction.

Does St.Kitts & Nevis allow the formation of International Trusts?

YES. In April 1994 St.Kitts & Nevis introduced new Asset Protection Trust (APT) legislation. Unique features include a requirement that anyone starting an action against a St.Kitts & Nevis Trust must first post a bond of US$25,000.

Does St.Kitts & Nevis allow the formation of Captive Insurance Companies?

YES. St.Kitts & Nevis is a suitable jurisdiction for the formation of Captive Insurance Companies.

Does St.Kitts & Nevis allow the formation of Banking Companies?

YES. St.Kitts & Nevis is a suitable jurisdiction for the formation of Banking Companies.

Financial institutions and contacts:

Bank of Nevis Ltd.
Main Street 809-469-5564 dial
Charlestown, St.Kitts & Nevis, West Indies (NEVIS)

- Primary business activity: bank and trust services.

Bank of Nova Scotia
Fort Street 809-465-4141 dial
Basseterre, St.Kitts & Nevis, West Indies (ST.KITTS)

- Primary business activity: bank and trust services.

Bank of Nova Scotia
Main Street 809-469-5411 dial
Charlestown, St.Kitts & Nevis, West Indies (NEVIS)

- Primary business activity: bank and trust services.

Barclays Bank PLC
The Circus 809-465-2264 dial
Basseterre, St.Kitts & Nevis, West Indies (ST.KITTS)

- Primary business activity: bank and trust services.

Barclays Bank PLC
Main and Prince Charles Streets 809-469-5467 dial
Charlestown, St.Kitts & Nevis, West Indies (NEVIS)

- Primary business activity: bank and trust services.

M.Irvin Boncamper & Co.
A.F.M. Services Ltd. 809-465-4459 dial
PO.Box 281 809-465-5983 fax
Basseterre, St.Kitts & Nevis, West Indies (ST.KITTS)

- Primary business activity: company and trust formation services.

Ministry of Trade and Industry
Government Headquarters 809-465-2521 dial
Church Street, Basseterre, St.Kitts & Nevis, West Indies (ST.KITTS)

- Primary business activity: government services.

Morning Star Holdings Limited
Memorial Square 809-469-1817 dial
PO.Box 556 809-469-1794 fax
Charlestown, St.Kitts & Nevis, West Indies (NEVIS)

- Primary business activity: company and trust formation services.

N.S.B.A. Offshore Financial Consultants
Mr. Fred Barrett 800-685-3964 free
Managing Director
Charlestown, St.Kitts & Nevis, West Indies (NEVIS)

- Primary business activity: company and trust formation services.
- Company formation services are offered.
- Trust formation services are offered.

Nevis Cooperative Banking Co. Ltd.
PO.Box 60 809-469-5277 dial
Main and Chapel Streets 809-469-1493 fax
Charlestown, St.Kitts & Nevis, West Indies (NEVIS)

- Primary business activity: banking services.

Royal Bank of Canada (St.Kitts)
Corner Bay & Fort Streets 809-465-2389 dial
PO.Box 91 809-465-1040 fax
Basseterre, St.Kitts & Nevis, West Indies (ST.KITTS)

- Primary business activity: banking services.

St.Kitts-Nevis Chamber of Industry and Commerce
South Square Street 809-465-2980 dial
Basseterre, St.Kitts & Nevis, West Indies (ST.KITTS)

- Primary business activity: government services.

St.Kitts-Nevis-Anguilla National Bank Ltd.
Basseterre 809-465-2204 dial
St.Kitts & Nevis, West Indies (ST.KITTS)

- Primary business activity: bank and trust services.

St.Kitts-Nevis-Anguilla National Bank Ltd.
West Square Street 809-469-5244 dial
Charlestown, St.Kitts & Nevis, West Indies (NEVIS)

- Primary business activity: bank and trust services.

SWITZERLAND

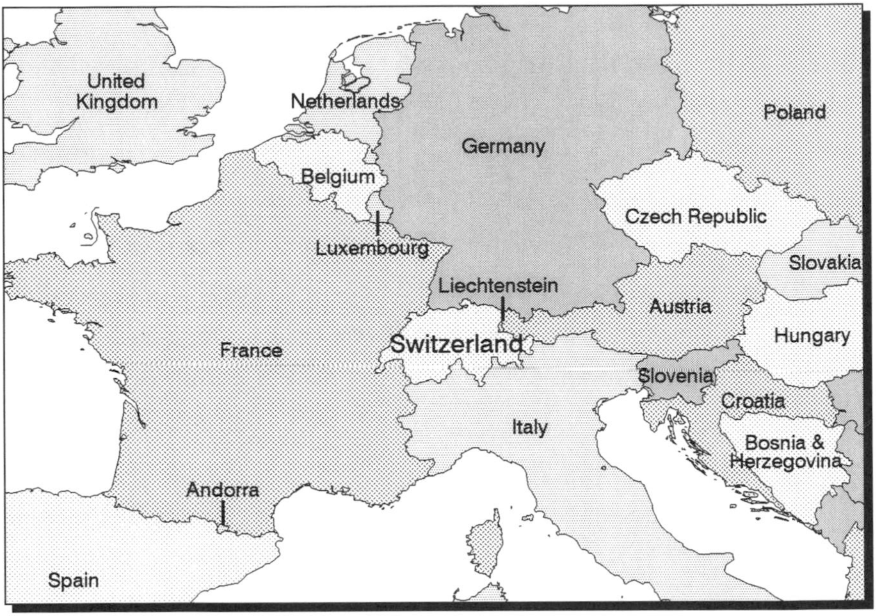

In Western Europe. Borders Austria, France, Germany, Italy, and Liechtenstein, and covers a total area of 15,940 square miles. Population is approximately 7 million. Main language is German, French, Italian, and Romansh.

The state of Switzerland traces its origins to a defensive alliance between Uli Schwyz and Unterwalden in 1291, and saw many wars in the early centuries of its existence. Since 1815 Switzerland has been neutral, with the European rulers deciding in Vienna on the recognition and protection of a lasting neutrality in Switzerland. The Swiss constitution of 1874 outlines the founding principles of federalism and democracy. In 1991 Switzerland proudly celebrated the 700th anniversary of its founding. Switzerland's currency has remained unchanged since the beginning of the century; a Swiss franc from 1900 is still accepted as legal tender today. Historically, the country has always enjoyed complete freedom in the import and export of capital.

The Swiss wrote their own banking laws to protect refugees fleeing Hitler and made it a serious offense, subject to heavy fine and imprisonment, for any bank or bank employee to reveal even the existence of a banking relationship. Bank secrecy faced an even greater challenge in the years after World War II. The allied governments believed that Nazi officials had deposited gold and other assets in Switzerland, demanding disclosure of bank records of all non-Swiss depositors. The Swiss refused to comply, stating that they had been neutral during the war, and respected the privacy of all individuals. Thinking that the Swiss would back down on their demands, the U.S. government seized all Swiss assets in the U.S. Switzerland remained firm and refused to offer any information. A compromise was worked out, and the Swiss government paid the U.S. approximately $60 million dollars for the return of Swiss assets. No bank information was ever released.

In May 1984 Swiss voters went to the polls to vote on a referendum that would have reduced bank secrecy in Switzerland. The voters rejected the proposal by a 3 to 1 margin. After the vote in 1984, the Federal Court expressly declared that bank secrecy would not be affected by revision of the 1934 Swiss Banking Law.

Swiss banks have agreed to provide U.S. investigators with the names of persons doing certain kinds of insider stock transactions through their facilities.

Does Switzerland have a secrecy law?

YES. Swiss bank secrecy is fixed in article 47 of the Swiss Federal Law Relating to Banks and Savings Institutions of November 8, 1934, as amended in 1970. It applies not only to everyone working within the bank, but also to members of its external auditors, even if the holders of private information are no longer working with the bank. Switzerland's bank secrecy law makes it a criminal offense for a bank or any of the bank's employees to divulge information of any kind to any individual, institution, public or private, with respect to any bank customer. Any infringement of the law can lead to criminal prosecution. The penalty for breaking bank secrecy is a minimum fine of SFr50,000 or six months in jail. If the act has been committed by negligence, the penalty shall be a fine not exceeding SFr30,000. The violation of professional secrecy remains punishable even after termination of the employment relationship.

Is there any situation where bank secrecy can be lifted?

YES. Bank secrecy can be lifted in cases of criminal activity. However, there must be a violation of Swiss *criminal law* (in Switzerland tax evasion is not a criminal offense, it is an administrative offense). A Swiss judge must sign a court order stating that there was a violation of Swiss law before bank secrecy can be lifted.

If a request for information is made by foreign authorities, they must be approved by the Federal Department of Justice, who will examine whether the request should be passed on to the judge in the bank's jurisdiction. Bank secrecy can also be lifted in favor of an heir in the event of a depositors death.

Can foreign tax authorities obtain information on Swiss bank accounts?

NO. Since tax evasion is not a crime in Switzerland, an inquiry by any foreign government would not be in accord with Swiss law, and therefore would not provide adequate grounds to have bank secrecy lifted (because tax evasion is not a crime in Switzerland). However, there is a test to determine if a banking transaction has been constructed to avoid taxes, and in certain extreme circumstances, bank secrecy may be compromised.

Is Switzerland an independent country?

YES. Switzerland is a stable, politically neutral country that proudly celebrated the 700th anniversary of its founding in 1991. The government consists of the Federal Council, the Federal Assembly, and the Federal Tribunal.

Is the legal system based on English Common Law?

NO. Swiss law is based on over 700 years of civil and commercial law. Switzerland's highest court is the Federal Tribunal, made up of 26 judges and 12 alternatives.

Is there an income tax in Switzerland?

YES. A corporation will pay less than 10% income tax, although corporations and banks are required to retain a 35% withholding tax on interest and dividends from Swiss sources. Swiss investment insurance products are completely exempt from Swiss taxes for non-residents.

Are there any other taxes in Switzerland?

YES. Swiss corporations are liable to pay a 3% stamp duty on capital stock upon incorporation. Each of Switzerland's 26 Cantons impose a different tax system on local residents.

Due to tax treaties, there are no taxes of any kind owed to the Swiss government by foreigners. If a non-resident purchases a Swiss life insurance policy, the insurance policy is protected by Swiss law against any collection procedures initiated by the creditors of the insured person.

Are there any exchange controls in Switzerland?

NO. There are currently no exchange controls in Switzerland. The official currency, the Swiss Franc, is by law 40% backed by gold.

Is there a tax treaty between the U.S. and Switzerland?

YES. There is double-taxation agreement between the U.S. and Switzerland. There are also double-taxation agreements with Australia, Austria, Belgium, Brazil, Canada, Denmark, Egypt, Finland, France, Germany, Greece, Hungary, Iceland, Indonesia, Ireland, Italy, Japan, Malaysia, Netherlands, New Zealand, Norway, Pakistan, Portugal, Singapore, South Africa, South Korea, Spain, Sri Lanka, Sweden, Trinidad and Tobago, and the United Kingdom.

Is there a tax treaty between Canada and Switzerland?

YES. There is a double-taxation agreement between Canada and Switzerland.

Does Switzerland allow the formation of Limited Companies?

YES. Switzerland's Laws of Obligation allow the formation of three types of companies; two types of Aktiengesellschaft (Private Company Limited by Shares or Public Limited Company), and the Gesellschaft mit beschrankter Haftung (Private Limited Company Without Shares).

Aktiengesellschaft (AG) - Private Companies Limited by Shares have the following statutory requirements:

- Issued shares may be either registered shares or bearer shares.
- A minimum of three shareholders are required.
- The incorporators may be nominees (to provide anonymity) and may be either individuals or corporations.
- Only one director is required, who must be a Swiss resident. The majority of directors (if more than one) must be Swiss residents.
- The directors of the AG must be stockholders, and directors and incorporators may be the same person or company.
- The minimum share capital is currently SFr50,000. Minimum par value is SFr100 per share.
- An annual audit is a statutory requirement.
- A withholding tax of 35% is imposed on dividends.

The memorandum must give details of the company's objectives. Upon incorporation a capital duty of 3% is payable.

Public Limited Companies are able to offer shares to the public after meeting the requirements of Swiss authorities and the Stock Exchange.

Gesellschaft mit beschrankter Haftung (GmbH) - A Private Limited Company Without Shares lists ownership in the Commercial Register instead of issuing shares. The incorporators may be nominees and may be either individuals or corporations. Only one director is required, who must be a Swiss resident. The majority of directors (if more than one) must be Swiss residents.

Does Switzerland allow the formation of International Trusts?

YES. Where a creditor proves beyond a reasonable doubt that an International Company or Trust was formed with the intent of defrauding a creditor, the Company or Trust is required to satisfy the claim out of the assets held. The statute of limitations on this type of action is 2 years.

Does Switzerland allow the formation of Captive Insurance Companies?

YES. Although Switzerland allows the formation of Captive Insurance Companies, other jurisdictions offer much friendlier legislation and lower formation costs.

Does Switzerland allow the formation of Banking Companies?

YES. Although Switzerland allows the formation of Banking Companies, the strict requirements make them impractical for tax planning purposes.

Financial institutions and contacts:

Ansbacher (Schweiz) A.G.

Mr. Urs Specker 41-61-252-1155 dial
Managing Director 41-61-251-4581 fax
Muhlebachstrasse 32, Zurich, Switzerland CH-8032

- Primary business activity: bank and trust services.
- Safekeeping and custodian services.
- Portfolio management of securities and mutual funds.
- Company formation services are offered.
- Trust formation services are offered.

Bank Ehinger & Co. Ltd.

Rittergasse 12 61-271-11-80 dial
4001, Basel, Switzerland

- Primary business activity: banking services.

Bank Institute Zurich

PO.Box 5138, Zurich, Switzerland CH-8022

- Primary business activity: banking services.

Bank J. Vontel & Co. Ltd.

Bahnhofstrasse 3, Zurich, Switzerland CH-8022

- Primary business activity: banking services.

Bank Julius Baer

Mr. M. Jauner	01-228-5111	dial
Managing Director	01-211-2560	fax
Bahnhofstrasse 36	823 865	telex
Zurich, Switzerland CH-8010		

- Primary business activity: banking services.
- Private banking services and/or savings accounts.
- Executor and administrator of wills and estates.
- Safekeeping and custodian services.
- Portfolio management of securities and mutual funds. Minimum deposit SFr250,000. Minimum annual fee 0.3% of assets or SFr250.

Bank of New York - Inter Maritime Bank

5, Quai du Mont-Blanc, PO.Box 1683, Geneva, Switzerland CH-1211

- Primary business activity: banking services.

Bank vonErnst & Cie AG

63-65 Marktgasse, 3001, Berne, Switzerland

- Primary business activity: banking services.

Banque Generale du Luxembourg (Suisse)

Rennweg 57	41-211-22-20	dial
Zurich, Switzerland CH-8023	41-211-99-08	fax

- Primary business activity: banking services.
- Private banking services and/or savings accounts.
- Consumer loans and credit facilities.
- Safekeeping and custodian services.
- Portfolio management of securities and mutual funds. Minimum annual fee 0.25% of assets.

Banque SCS Alliance

Mr. Guyon Krug	41-22-839-0100	dial
Vice Chairman	41-22-346-1530	fax

11, route de Florissant, Geneva, Switzerland CH-1206

- Primary business activity: bank and trust services.
- Safekeeping and custodian services.
- Portfolio management of securities and mutual funds.
- Company formation services are offered.
- Trust formation services are offered.

Barclays Bank (Schweiz) AG

Mr. Marcel Kengelbacher	1-221-13-35	dial
Branch Manager	1-211-54-26	fax

Schuetzengasse 21, Zurich, Switzerland CH-8001

- Primary business activity: bank and trust services.
- Offers private credit card backed by deposit.
- Private banking services and/or savings accounts.
- Consumer loans and credit facilities.
- Safekeeping and custodian services.
- Portfolio management of securities and mutual funds.
- Company formation services are offered.
- Trust formation services are offered.

Barclays Bank (Suisse) S.A.

Mr. Phillip Monks	22-310-65-50	dial
Branch Manager	22-310-64-60	fax

10 rue d'Italie, Geneva, Switzerland CH-1204

- Primary business activity: bank and trust services.
- Offers private credit card backed by deposit.
- Private banking services and/or savings accounts.
- Consumer loans and credit facilities.
- Safekeeping and custodian services.
- Portfolio management of securities and mutual funds.
- Company formation services are offered.
- Trust formation services are offered.

Barclays Bank (Svizzera) S.A.

Mr. Piero Pellandini	91-23-68-91	dial
Branch Manager	91-22-90-09	fax

2 Via Marconi, Lugano, Switzerland CH-6900

- Primary business activity: bank and trust services.
- Offers private credit card backed by deposit.
- Private banking services and/or savings accounts.
- Consumer loans and credit facilities.
- Safekeeping and custodian services.
- Portfolio management of securities and mutual funds.
- Company formation services are offered.
- Trust formation services are offered.

BFI Consulting AG

Mr. Urs Burkhard	41-1-980-4254	dial
President	41-1-980-4255	fax

Zurichstrasse 108, Ebmatingen, Switzerland CH-8123

- Primary business activity: insurance products & services.

Bilfinanz und Verwaltung AG

Gladbachstrasse 105	01-250-81-81	dial
PO.Box 832	01-252-51-78	fax

Zurich, Switzerland CH-8044

- Primary business activity: banking services.

Business Advisory Services SA

Mr. Arthur R. Moussalli	41-22-030540	dial
Managing Director	41-22-7860644	fax

7 Rue Muzy, 1207, Geneva, Switzerland

- Primary business activity: company and trust formation services.

Camafin Trust AG

PO.Box 506	41-1-715-2246	dial
Gartenstrasse 4	41-1-715-2243	fax

Zurich, Switzerland CH-8802

- Primary business activity: bank and trust services.
- Portfolio management of securities and mutual funds.

Chase Manhattan Bank (Switzerland) S.A.

63, rue du Rhone 41-22-787-9111 dial
Geneva, Switzerland CH-1204

- Primary business activity: banking services.
- Private banking services and/or savings accounts.
- Consumer loans and credit facilities.
- Safekeeping and custodian services.
- Portfolio management of securities and mutual funds.
- Company formation services are offered.
- Trust formation services are offered.

Commercial Bank of Basel

Aeschengraben 26, 4002 61-271-44-88 dial
Basel, Switzerland

- Primary business activity: banking services.

Confidesa AG

Mr. M. Weibel 41-12-213288 dial
Baarerstrasse 36 41-12-221049 fax
Zug, Switzerland CH-6300 86 4913 CONF CH telex

- Primary business activity: company and trust formation services.

Coutts & Co. (Lausanne) SA

Chemin de Chantermerle 14 021-653-2927 dial
PO.Box 112 021-653-5536 fax
Lausanne, Switzerland CH-1010

- Primary business activity: bank and trust services.
- Private banking services and/or savings accounts.
- Safekeeping and custodian services.
- Portfolio management of securities and mutual funds.
- Company formation services are offered.
- Trust formation services are offered.

Coutts & Co. AG

Talstrasse 50 01-214-5111 dial
PO.Box 8022 01-214-5396 fax
Zurich, Switzerland

- Primary business activity: bank and trust services.
- Private banking services and/or savings accounts.
- Safekeeping and custodian services.
- Portfolio management of securities and mutual funds.
- Company formation services are offered.
- Trust formation services are offered.

Coutts & Co. SA

13 Quai de l'Ile 022-319-0319 dial
Geneve, Switzerland CH-1211 022-28-3857 fax

- Primary business activity: bank and trust services.
- Private banking services and/or savings accounts.
- Safekeeping and custodian services.
- Portfolio management of securities and mutual funds.
- Company formation services are offered.
- Trust formation services are offered.

Coutts & Co. SA

Via Valdani 2 091-41-2002 dial
Chiasso, Switzerland CH-6830 091-44-5251 fax

- Primary business activity: bank and trust services.
- Private banking services and/or savings accounts.
- Safekeeping and custodian services.
- Portfolio management of securities and mutual funds.
- Company formation services are offered.
- Trust formation services are offered.

Credit Suisse

Paradeplatz 8, Zurich, Switzerland CH-8001

- Primary business activity: banking services.
- Private banking services and/or savings accounts.
- Executor and administrator of wills and estates.
- Safekeeping and custodian services.
- Portfolio management of securities and mutual funds.
- Company formation services are offered.
- Trust formation services are offered.

DeBerig SA

PO.Box 116, Geneva, Switzerland 1211

- Primary business activity: company and trust formation services.

Gotthard Bank

Mr. Giuliano Castelli	022-319-8222	dial
Senior Vice President	022-319-8120	fax
12, rue de Rive	422 383	telex

Geneva 3, Geneva, Switzerland CH-1211

- Primary business activity: banking services.
- Private banking services and/or savings accounts.
- Safekeeping and custodian services.
- Portfolio management of securities and mutual funds.
- Company formation services are offered.
- Trust formation services are offered.

Gotthard Bank

Mr. Gerhard Lortscher	01-225-1311	dial
Senior Vice President	01-221-1140	fax
Schutzengasse 22/24	817 198	telex

Zurich, Switzerland CH-8023

- Primary business activity: banking services.
- Private banking services and/or savings accounts.
- Safekeeping and custodian services.
- Portfolio management of securities and mutual funds.
- Company formation services are offered.
- Trust formation services are offered.

Gotthard Bank

Mr. Gunther Mack	021-341-5111	dial
Senior Vice President	021-341-5138	fax
1, avenue du Theatre	455 644	telex

Lausanne 2, Lausanne, Switzerland CH-1000

- Primary business activity: banking services.
- Private banking services and/or savings accounts.
- Safekeeping and custodian services.
- Portfolio management of securities and mutual funds.
- Company formation services are offered.
- Trust formation services are offered.

Gotthard Bank

Ms. Nicola Mordasini	091-28-1111	dial
Customer Relations	091-23-9487	fax
Viale S. Franscini 8	841 051	telex

Lugano, Switzerland CH-6901

- Primary business activity: banking services.
- Private banking services and/or savings accounts.
- Safekeeping and custodian services.
- Portfolio management of securities and mutual funds.
- Company formation services are offered.
- Trust formation services are offered.

H.Sturzenegger & Cie

St.Jakobsstrasse 46, Basel, Switzerland

- Primary business activity: banking services.

Hoogewerf Trust Co. SA

PO.Box 347	41-22-218393	dial
Geneva, Switzerland CH-1211	41-22-216407	fax

- Primary business activity: banking services.

JML Jurg M. Lattmann AG

Mr. Jurg Lattmann	41-1-363-2510	dial
President	41-1-361-4074	fax

Germaniastrasse 55, Zurich, Switzerland CH-8033

- Primary business activity: insurance products & services.

Jyske Bank (Schweiz)

Wasserwerkstrasse 12	41-1-362-7373	dial
Postfach 296	41-1-362-5150	fax
Zurich, Switzerland CH-8035	816-288	telex

- Primary business activity: banking services.
- Private banking services and/or savings accounts.
- Safekeeping and custodian services.
- Portfolio management of securities and mutual funds.

Midland Walwyn

Mr. Claude Oberson	41-22-310-4710	dial
General Manager	41-22-310-4704	fax

38 rue du Marche, Geneva, Switzerland CH-1204

- Primary business activity: fund or portfolio manager.
- Safekeeping and custodian services.
- Portfolio management of securities and mutual funds.

Mossack Fonseca & Co. Attorneys at Law

PO.Box 138	41-22-3290222	dial
40, rue du Stand	41-22-3290135	fax

Geneva, Switzerland CH-1211

- Primary business activity: law office.

Overseas Company Registration Agents

Mr. Urs Von Sury	41-61-261-6558	dial
Company Formation Agent	41-61-261-6534	fax
Spalentorweg 20	046-056-055	free

PO.Box 109, Basel, Switzerland CH-4009

- Primary business activity: company and trust formation services.
- Corporate services such as registered agent services.
- Company formation services are offered. Minimum formation fee US$5,000 plus license fee.

Riggs Valmet S.A.

14 Chemin Rieu	41-22-477575	dial
Geneva, Switzerland CH-1211	41-22-467241	fax

- Primary business activity: company and trust formation services.

Robeco Bank

16 Chemin des Coquelicots	41-22-341-1297	dial
Geneva, Switzerland CH-1214	41-22-341-1392	fax

- Primary business activity: bank and trust services.
- Portfolio management of securities and mutual funds.

Royal Bank of Canada (Suisse)

Mr. Jurg Hofer	022-311-1255	dial
Head of Private Banking Department	022-311-1595	fax
Rue Diday 6	422 147	telex
Geneva, Switzerland CH-1204		

- Primary business activity: bank and trust services.
- Private banking services and/or savings accounts.
- Consumer loans and credit facilities.
- Corporate services such as registered agent services.
- Safekeeping and custodian services.
- Portfolio management of securities and mutual funds. Numbered account SFr200 annual fee. Minimum annual fee 0.25% of assets or SFr250 plus SFr25 per transaction.
- Trust formation services are offered. Minimum formation fee SFr4,000. Minimum annual fee 0.8% of assets or SFr4,000.

Royal Bank of Scotland AG

Mr. John Read	411-224-6464	dial
Talstrasse 82	411-211-1550	fax
Zurich, Switzerland CH-8001		

- Primary business activity: banking services.
- Private banking services and/or savings accounts.

Royal Trust Bank (Switzerland)

Limmatquai 4	44-1-250-9111	dial
Zurich, Switzerland CH-8024	44-1-252-7940	fax

- Primary business activity: bank and trust services.
- Offers private credit card backed by deposit.
- Private banking services and/or savings accounts.
- Consumer loans and credit facilities.
- Safekeeping and custodian services.
- Portfolio management of securities and mutual funds.

SBC Portfolio Management Ltd.
Seehofstrasse 6 01-223-45-00 dial
Zurich, Switzerland

- Primary business activity: bank and trust services.

Seychelles Corporate Services AG
Limmatquai 52, Zurich, Switzerland

- Primary business activity: company and trust formation services.

Swiss Bank Corporation
1 Aeschenvorstadt, Basel, Switzerland CH-4002

- Primary business activity: banking services.

Swiss Bank Corporation
PO.Box 8010, Zurich, Switzerland

- Primary business activity: banking services.

Trade Administration Services AG
PO.Box 4818, Baarerstrasse 23, Zug, Switzerland CH-6304

- Primary business activity: company and trust formation services.

Uberseebank AG
Limiatquai 2, Zurich, Switzerland CH-8024

- Primary business activity: banking services.

Ueberseebank AG
PO.Box 8024, Limmatqual, Zurich, Switzerland

- Primary business activity: banking services.

Uptrend Treuhand Managementberatung
Schauenbergstrasse 12 41-13-711110 dial
Zurich, Switzerland 8046 41-13-711211 fax

- Primary business activity: company and trust formation services.

Volcon SA

Mr. T. Vollenweider	41-61-271-2100	dial
President	41-61-271-2144	fax

PO.Box 649, Basel, Switzerland CH-4010

- Primary business activity: insurance products & services.

VPB Finanz AG

Talstrasse 83	01-212-21-41	dial
Zurich, Switzerland CH-8001	01-212-00-31	fax

- Primary business activity: banking services.

TURKS & CAICOS

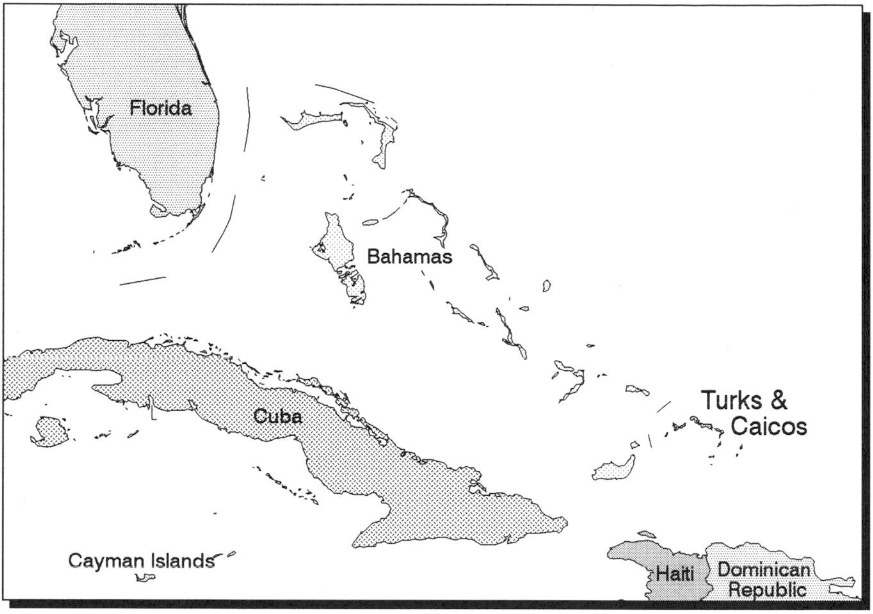

In the Caribbean. An archipelago of 40 islands and cays located 575 miles south east of Miami, 30 miles south east of the Bahamas and midway between Miami and Puerto Rico, north of the Dominican Republic and Haiti. The islands cover a land area of 193 square miles. The islands are each surrounded by a continuous coral reef. Population approximately 15,000. Main language is English. Climate is tropical with relatively low humidity, average temperature 83°F in summer and 77°F in winter.

The Arawak Indians were the first people to inhabit the Turks & Caicos Islands which were discovered in 1512 by Spanish explorer Juan Ponce del Leon, although the local belief is that the Islands were first discovered by Columbus on his first voyage in 1492. In 1678,

Bermudian immigrants settled on the islands of Salt Cay, Grand Turk and South Caicos where they established and developed a salt industry. The Bahamas tried unsuccessfully to annex the islands in 1700. During the next century the Turks & Caicos were invaded first by the Spanish and then by the French. British loyalists tried to establish cotton plantations in 1780. The Bahamas gained administrative control of the islands and governed them from 1799 to 1848, when the Turks & Caicos separated from the Bahamas, and were governed by their own council for over 20 years. The islands were placed under the administration of Jamaica from 1873 to 1962, the year that Jamaica gained her independence. In that year Turks & Caicos became a British Crown Colony, with a Governor appointed by the Queen of England.

Does the Turks & Caicos have a secrecy law?

YES. The Turks & Caicos have high client confidentiality. In addition to Part VIII of the Companies Ordinance 1981, professional relationships are protected by the Confidential Relationships Ordinance 1979 which provides for penalties of US$10,000 and imprisonment for up to three years for unauthorized disclosure of confidential information. Corporate bodies in breach of the Ordinance can be fined up to US$50,000.

Is there any situation where bank secrecy can be lifted?

YES. Due to the narcotics related Mutual Assistance Treaty with the U.S., confidential information can be released if there is a suspected criminal activity such as illegal drug activities, theft, or fraud.

Can foreign tax authorities obtain information on Turks & Caicos bank accounts?

NO. Confidential financial information is not available to foreign governments conducting tax investigations. Specific legislation states that judgements and requests for information in foreign tax cases are not enforceable in the Turks & Caicos.

Is the Turks & Caicos an independent country?

NO. The Turks & Caicos is a self governing British Crown colony, governed by an Executive Council of ministers appointed from the Legislative Council of elected members. A Governor appointed by Britain presides over the Legislative Council and Britain maintains responsibility for defense and foreign affairs. There is no desire for independence and the Islands are considered politically, economically, and racially stable.

Is the legal system based on English Common Law?

YES. The legal system is based on English Common Law and is supplemented by local ordinances. Commercial laws have been specifically designed to encourage offshore business.

Is there an income tax in the Turks & Caicos?

NO. There is no income tax in the Turks & Caicos. IBCs are guaranteed tax exempt status for 20 years from date of incorporation. It is unlikely that any taxes will be introduced in the foreseeable future as the prosperity of the Turks & Caicos depends on the success of the financial industry.

The Turks & Caicos government receives income from import duties of 30% and stamp duties, such as an 8% stamp duty on real estate transactions over US$50,000. Other sources of government income are hotel taxes, license fees, and a $15 departure tax.

Are there any other taxes in the Turks & Caicos?

NO. There are no direct taxes in the Turks & Caicos, no capital gains tax, no gift tax, no estate tax, and no death duties.

Are there any exchange controls in the Turks & Caicos?

NO. There are currently no exchange controls in the Turks & Caicos. The official currency is the U.S. dollar.

Is there a tax treaty between the U.S. and the Turks & Caicos?

NO. There is no double-taxation agreement between the U.S. and the Turks & Caicos. In fact, there is no tax treaty with any country.

Is there a tax treaty between Canada and the Turks & Caicos?

NO. There is no double-taxation agreement between Canada and the Turks & Caicos.

Does the Turks & Caicos allow the formation of Limited Companies?

YES. The Turks & Caicos Companies Ordinance of 1981 and subsequent amendments provide for the formation of the Ordinary Company, Exempted Company, Limited Life Company, and Foreign Company.

Minimum statutory conditions require that each company must have a registered office in the Turks & Caicos. An exempted company must have a local resident representative.

Ordinary Company - An ordinary company is used for conducting business within the Turks & Caicos. All information is a matter of public record, including names of shareholders, directors, and officers.

Exempted Company - An exempted company, which must carry on its business outside the Turks & Caicos, is free from the necessity to report to the Registrar changes in its shareholders and directors. Whereas an ordinary company files a detailed annual return, exempted companies file a simple form declaring that certain requirements of the Ordinance have been met and that the operations of the company continue mainly outside the Turks & Caicos.

Advantages and benefits of exempted companies include:

- Shares can be issued in bearer form.
- Shares may have no par value.
- There is no requirement to hold annual or general meetings.
- An exempted company requires only one shareholder and one director. Typically the owners of an exempted company would act as directors and shareholders.
- Directors and officers have no nationality restrictions and can be nominee corporations.
- Exempted companies require one secretary, who may also be a director.
- The register of shareholders is not required to be available for public inspection.
- No local auditors are required.
- The name need not contain the words Limited, Incorporated, Public Limited Company, Société Anonyme, or their abbreviations.

The Registrar's stated target is to incorporate companies on the day that documents are received. Providing that the Registrar approves the name, the necessary papers can be prepared and presented the same day, with the Certificate of Incorporation and Articles of Association being issued by the Registrar on the following day.

The annual government filing fee is US$250 for Ordinary Companies and US$300 for Exempted Companies. The Companies (Amendment) Ordinance 1993 allows the option of pre-paying annual Turks & Caicos government fees for a period of 5, 10 or

15 years at a substantial discount. For instance, by pre-paying for 15 years at a cost of US$2,000, you save US$2,500 in fees. This ensures the good standing of the company with a simple declaration each year. In addition, and as a further incentive, new IBCs incorporated between July 1 and December 31 will be excused from payment of the annual fee the following January.

Another provision in the 1993 Ordinance made it possible for Turks & Caicos IBCs to be limited by shares, limited by guarantee, have members with unlimited liability, or to have any combination of these three options. IBCs are guaranteed from any new taxation introduced during the 20 year period following incorporation.

Limited Life Company - The Companies (Amendment) Ordinance 1993 introduced the concept of a Limited Life Company. Minimum statutory conditions require that:

- The company has a minimum of two subscribers.
- The memorandum of association must limit the life of the company to less than 50 years.
- The company name must end with LLC or Limited Life Company.

Foreign Company - Foreign companies wishing to trade within the Turks & Caicos must submit to the Registrar of Companies the following:

- Memorandum of incorporation from the foreign company's home jurisdiction.
- Complete details on directors including name, address, and nationality.
- Name and address of local resident representative.

Does the Turks & Caicos allow the formation of International Trusts?

YES. Trusts are governed by the Trusts Ordinance 1990, which is similar to Jersey Trust law, with some refinements. The Trusts Ordinance recognizes Trusts formed in other jurisdictions. Advantages of Turks & Caicos Trust law include:

- No time restrictions - Trusts can continue indefinitely and are not limited to any set time period.
- The instrument creating the Trust can be executed in any jurisdiction.
- The Trust can specify that the laws of another jurisdiction are to apply to the interpretation and settlement of the Trust.
- The Trust is a private document and there is no requirement for it to be registered (unless the Trust holds Turks & Caicos land titles).
- Trustee Corporations are not required to be licensed under the Trustees (Licensing) Ordinance 1992 if the Trustee Corporation is acting for only one Trust, and is wholly owned by the Settlor or Beneficiary.

A Trustee is not required to reveal to any person, other than the Beneficiary of the Trust, any information regarding the forming or operating of the Trust, allowing for complete secrecy. A Turks & Caicos Trust can:

- Allow for the addition of future Beneficiaries.
- Exclude a Beneficiary from certain Trust assets.
- Require certain terms & conditions to be met before distributing Trust assets.

The Turks & Caicos Trusts Ordinance 1990 also allows the formation of an Asset Protection Trust, where if a Settlor (who is solvent at the time and not planning to become insolvent) transfers assets to the Trust and subsequently becomes insolvent, the Trust would not be declared void upon application by a creditor. An advantage of the Ordinance is that the intent of the Settlor in establishing the Asset Protection Trust is irrelevant to any attack against Trust assets.

Does the Turks & Caicos allow the formation of Captive Insurance Companies?

NO. No bank or insurance licenses have been issued since 1985, when the Turks & Caicos was hit by a banking scandal. Until new legislation is drafted, the Turks & Caicos may be closed to all but branches or subsidiaries of reputable international banks and insurance companies.

Does the Turks & Caicos allow the formation of Banking Companies?

NO. No bank or insurance licenses have been issued since 1985, when the Turks & Caicos was hit by a banking scandal. Until new legislation is drafted, the Turks & Caicos may be closed to all but branches or subsidiaries of reputable international banks and insurance companies.

Financial institutions and contacts:

Bank of Nova Scotia
Providenciales 809-946-4750 dial
Turks & Caicos, British West Indies

- Primary business activity: banking services.

Barclays Bank PLC

Butterfield Square	809-946-4245	dial
PO.Box 236	809-946-4573	fax
Providenciales	8418 BARPRO	telex

Turks & Caicos, British West Indies

- Primary business activity: banking services.

Barclays Bank PLC

PO.Box 61	809-946-2831	dial
Cockburn Town	809-946-2965	fax

Grand Turk, Turks & Caicos, British West Indies

- Primary business activity: banking services.
- Private banking services and/or savings accounts.
- Consumer loans and credit facilities.
- Safekeeping and custodian services.
- Portfolio management of securities and mutual funds.
- Company formation services are offered.
- Trust formation services are offered.

Bordier International Bank and Trust

Ms. Elise Hartshorn	809-946-4535	dial
PO.Box 5	809-946-4540	fax

Caribbean Place, Providenciales, Turks & Caicos, British West Indies

- Primary business activity: bank and trust services.
- Private banking services and/or savings accounts.

Business Accounting Services Ltd.

Mr. C. Ursu	809-946-4044	dial

184 Richmond Hill, PO.Box 303, Providenciales, Turks & Caicos, British West Indies

- Primary business activity: company and trust formation services.

Caribbean Management Services Limited

PO.Box 127	809-946-4732	dial
Town Centre Mall	809-946-4734	fax

Providenciales, Turks & Caicos, British West Indies

- Primary business activity: company and trust formation services.

Chancellor Securities Ltd.

Mr. Wayne Higgs	809-941-2689	dial
Account Manager	809-941-3688	fax

Leeward Highway, Caribbean Place
Providenciales, Turks & Caicos, British West Indies

- Primary business activity: licensed stock brokerage.

Coriat & Co.

Sabre House	809-946-2621	dial

PO.Box 171, Grand Turk, Turks & Caicos, British West Indies

- Primary business activity: law office.

First National Bank Ltd.

Mr. Iain Brown	809-946-4060	dial
PO.Box 58	809-946-4061	fax

The Arch Plaza, Providenciales, Turks & Caicos, British West Indies

- Primary business activity: banking services.
- Private banking services and/or savings accounts.
- Consumer loans and credit facilities.

Grand Turk International Trust Co.

PO.Box 61	809-946-2047	dial

Grand Turk, Turks & Caicos, British West Indies

- Primary business activity: company and trust formation services.

McLean & Associates

Mr. Hugh D. McLean	809-946-4277	dial
Barrister-at-Law	809-946-4484	fax

McLean Building, PO.Box 62, 2001 Leeward Highway
Providenciales, Turks & Caicos, British West Indies

- Primary business activity: law office.
- Company formation services are offered. Minimum formation fee US$2,775 plus US$300 government fee. Minimum annual fee US$1,500.

Misick and Stanbrook
MacLaw House, Duke Street 809-946-2476 dial
PO.Box 103 809-946-2173 fax
Grand Turk, Turks & Caicos, British West Indies
- Primary business activity: law office.

Morris Cottingham Assoc. Ltd.
Hibiscus Square 809-946-2504 dial
PO.Box 156 809-946-2503 fax
Grand Turk, Turks & Caicos, British West Indies
- Primary business activity: company and trust formation services.

N.S.B.A. Offshore Financial Consultants
Grand Turk 800-685-3964 free
Turks & Caicos, British West Indies
- Primary business activity: company and trust formation services.
- Company formation services are offered.
- Trust formation services are offered.

Northcote & Co.
PO.Box 164, Grand Turk, Turks & Caicos, British West Indies
- Primary business activity: law office.

Private Sector Development Office
Saber House 809-946-2732 dial
Front Street 809-946-2556 fax
Grand Turk, Turks & Caicos, British West Indies
- Primary business activity: government services.

Registrar of Companies
Grand Turk 809-946-2550 dial
Turks & Caicos, British West Indies
- Primary business activity: government services.

Savoy & Co.
Harbor House, Queen Street 809-946-2601 dial
PO.Box 157, Grand Turk, Turks & Caicos, British West Indies
- Primary business activity: law office.

Standard Private Trust Ltd.

Ms. Carla Cartwright	809-941-3300	dial
Manager	809-941-3301	fax

Leeward Highway, Caribbean Place
Providenciales, Turks & Caicos, British West Indies

- Primary business activity: company and trust formation services.
- Corporate services such as registered agent services.
- Safekeeping and custodian services.
- Portfolio management of securities and mutual funds.
- Company formation services are offered.
- Trust formation services are offered.

Superintendent of Offshore Finance

Finance Department	809-946-2937	dial
Grand Turk	809-946-2557	fax

Turks & Caicos, British West Indies

- Primary business activity: government services.

MARGINAL TAX HAVENS

The following countries, although not perceived as major tax havens, do offer certain attributes commonly found in tax haven jurisdictions.

Andorra

In Europe. A tiny haven in the eastern Pyrenees between France and Spain. Population is approximately 52,000. Main language is Spanish and French.

The independent state of Andorra has been independent since 1278, when rival powers of the region agreed on a compromise. Under the 700 year old agreement the state is ruled jointly between the Bishop of Urgel and the Count of Foix. As the estates of Foix have since passed to France, the present joint rulers are the Bishop of Urgel and the President of France.

Andorra's secrecy laws prohibit the unauthorized disclosure of information pertaining to a clients affairs to a third party, providing for criminal penalties or prison terms.

The legal system is based on Spanish Law. There is no income tax, capital gains tax, gift tax, or estate tax in Andorra. There are no exchange controls. Andorra has no currency of its own and instead uses Spanish and French currency. There is no exchange of information agreement between the Andorra and the U.S. or Canada.

Foreigners are not permitted to start a business, therefore incorporation is impractical.

Consult S.L.
Mr. Anthony Courtney — 33-628-29-190 dial
Chief Executive Officer — 33-628-29-783 fax
Carrer Dr. — 391 CONSULT telex
Nequi No.7, 3 er A, Andorra la Vella, Andorra

- Primary business activity: law office.

Aruba

In The Southern Caribbean. 12 miles north of Venezuela. Main language is Papiamento, English, Dutch, and Spanish.

Aruba's citizens are descendants of the peace-loving Arawak Indians, Dutch, Spanish and a blend of people from all corners of the world who came to the island in the twentieth century. Today there are over 40 nationalities living on the island.

No specific laws enforce bank secrecy, although according to Mr. E.J. Brion at Aruba Bank Ltd., "*the Bank Secrecy Act in Aruba provides that no information of the bank relationship can be given to third parties unless mandated by court order.*" No specific laws enforce bank secrecy, therefore bank accounts may be open to government inspection.

Aruba became independent on January 1, 1986, although Aruba is still a member of the United Kingdom of the Netherlands. The legal system is based on the Dutch legal system of civil and criminal law.

There is no income tax on an AEC (Aruba Exempt Company) or its shareholders.

Aruba Bank Ltd.
Mr. E.J. Brion 297-8-21558 dial
Investment Manager 294-8-29152 fax
Caya G.F. Betico Croes 41, PO.Box 192, Oranjestad, Aruba, West Indies

- Primary business activity: banking services.
- Private banking services and/or savings accounts.

Bahrain

Population approximately 500,000. Main language is Arabic. In 1882 the Emirate of Bahrain handed control of its foreign affairs to Britain, whose navy was in the process of suppressing the endemic piracy of the Arabian Gulf. In 1971 the Emir proclaimed Bahrain's independence, and soon after dismissed Parliament to rule the nation himself. Official currency is the Bahraini Dinar.

Chemical Bank Bahrain Branch
National Bank of Bahrain Building 973-214-816 dial
Government Road 973-251-568 fax
Manama, Bahrain

- Primary business activity: banking services.
- Private banking services and/or savings accounts.
- Safekeeping and custodian services.
- Company formation services are offered.
- Trust formation services are offered.

Swiss Bank Corporation
Bahrain Commercial Complex 973-533-303 dial
Sheraton Tower 8814 telex
Manama, Bahrain

- Primary business activity: banking services.

Campione

In Europe. Campione d'Italia ("sample of Italy") is on the shores of Lake Lugano, a little piece of Italian soil completely surrounded by Switzerland. Located in the Swiss canton of Ticino, about 16 miles from the Italian border and 5 miles from Lake Lugano, Campione is a tiny one square mile dot on the Swiss maps. As a separate country from Switzerland, Campione is not subject to Swiss laws, taxes, or tax treaties. Campione operates no border controls, so its approximately 2,200 residents travel freely.

Although officially Italian, residency in Campione brings many of the benefits of Swiss residency; including Swiss banking, postal, and telephone services, Swiss auto registration and driver's license, and the Swiss postal code CH-6911.

The legal system is based on Italian Law. There is no income tax, capital gains tax, gift tax, or estate tax in Campione imposed on non-residents.

There is no exchange of information agreement between Campione and the U.S. or Canada. Disclosure of information under a tax treaty between the U.S. and Switzerland is unlikely.

A corporation can be formed in Campione under Italian law with as little as US$1,000. The private limited liability company is known as an SRL (Societa Responsibilita Limitada). It takes longer to form a corporation in Campione than in Switzerland, but, unlike a Swiss corporation, a corporation formed in Campione can be entirely owned by foreigners. Shareholders have complete anonymity. Corporations formed in Campione have a number of advantages over Swiss corporations. They are able to use Swiss banking facilities. They have a mailing address that appears Swiss. They are not subject to Switzerland's high income and withholding taxes providing that business is done outside of Italy. The tax rate is SFr3,000 per employee per year. If no personnel are employed, taxes can be reduced to nearly zero.

Costa Rica

In Central America. South of Nicaragua, north of Panama. Main language is Spanish, some English. Moderate tropical climate. Costa Rica has had democratic politics, and has been independent since 1836. The present constitution has been in force since 1948.

Costa Rica's secrecy law provides total confidentiality and secrecy in bank transactions. The law also applies to attorneys. Costa Rica is a stable democratic republic, independent since 1836. The presidential head of state has full executive powers. The government is divided into executive, legislative, and judicial systems. The present constitution has been in force since 1948. Costa Rica is the only Latin American country to have no army. The legal system is based on Spanish civil law.

There is an income tax in Costa Rica for individuals and companies doing business in Costa Rica. There is also a withholding tax on dividends of non-resident shareholders. Income sourced outside of Costa Rica is not liable for income tax.

There are currently no exchange controls in Costa Rica. The official currency is the Cost Rican Colon. Although there is no tax treaty between the U.S. and Costa Rica, there is an exchange of information agreement that has been signed as part of the Caribbean Basin Initiative. No tax treaty has been signed between Canada and Costa Rica.

Banco Anglo Costarricense
Ms. Hilda Dengo 506-22-3322 dial
Directora 2132 telex
PO.Box 10038, Pensamos Como Usted, San Jose, Costa Rica 1863

- Primary business activity: banking services.
- Private banking services and/or savings accounts.

Banco Credito Agricola de Cartago
PO.Box 5572, San Jose, Costa Rica 1000

- Primary business activity: banking services.

Banco de Costa Rica
PO.Box 10035, San Jose, Costa Rica 1000

- Primary business activity: banking services.

Banco de Santander
PO.Box 6714, San Jose, Costa Rica

- Primary business activity: banking services.

Banco Nacional de Costa Rica
PO.Box 10015, San Jose, Costa Rica

- Primary business activity: banking services.

Central American Trust S.A.
Mr. Cecil E. Fisher 501-27-0815 dial
President
PO.Box 945, Suite 855
Centro Colon Office Building 1007, San Jose, Costa Rica

- Primary business activity: bank and trust services.

Citicorp (Costa Rica)
Edificio Plaza de la Artilleria
Avenidas Central y Primera, Calle 4, San Jose, Costa Rica

- Primary business activity: banking services.

Corporacion Internacional de Boston
PO.Box 6370, San Jose, Costa Rica 1000

- Primary business activity: banking services.

Corporation Francoamericana de Finanzas
Edificio Plaza de la Artilleria
Avenidas Central y Primera, Calle 4, San Jose, Costa Rica
- Primary business activity: banking services.

Costa Rica Stock Exchange
Mr. Rodrigo Bolanos 506-22-8011 dial
Director of Stock Exchange 506-22-0131 fax
PO.Box 1736-1000, San Jose, Costa Rica
- Primary business activity: government services.

Financial Engineering Consultants Inc.
Mr. R. Gonzalez 506-31-6575 dial
Director of Marketing 506-20-3470 fax
PO.Box 959, Centro Colon Towers 1007, San Jose, Costa Rica
- Primary business activity: company and trust formation services.
- Primary business activity: mail forwarding service

First Pennsylvania SA
PO.Box 528, San Jose, Costa Rica
- Primary business activity: banking services.

Global Consulting Group, Inc.
Dr. Stephen O. Williams 506-296-1525 dial
International Consulting 509-296-1511 fax
PO.Box 945, Suite 922, Centro Colon Tower 1007, San Jose, Costa Rica
- Primary business activity: newsletters, books, or information.
- Specific product: Financial Privacy News newsletter.

Ibero-Amerika Bank
PO.Box 5548, San Jose, Costa Rica
- Primary business activity: banking services.

Mr. Juan Edgar Picardo
Juan Edgar Picardo, Jr.
Apartado 2047, San Jose, Costa Rica
- Primary business activity: law office.

Cyprus

In the Eastern Mediterranean. Main language is Greek, Turkish, English. For centuries part of the Ottoman Empire, Cyprus passed to Britain as security for a loan that was never repaid. Cyprus gained independence in 1960 under a constitution designed to calm ethnic rivalries between the Greek and Turkish population. In 1974 a coup by the Greeks threatened to join Cyprus to Greece, and Turkey invaded to block the move. Today the island is divided between the Turkish northern third and the Greek southern section.

There are no exchange controls. Currency is the Cypriot Pound. Cyprus allows the formation of private insurance companies.

Gryphon Managers & Consultants Ltd.
Mr. Nicholas Larcos 357-249-8518 dial
Company Formation Agent 357-249-8824 fax
Suite 102, 8 Acropolis Avenue
Acropolis 139, PO.Box 8770, Nicosia, Cyprus

- Primary business activity: company and trust formation services.

Riggs Valmet International Ltd.
PO.Box 151 357-3-824508 dial
Paralimni, Cyprus 357-3-824508 fax

- Primary business activity: company and trust formation services.

Greece

In Southeast Europe. Main language is Greek. English, Italian, French, and German is also spoken.

There are no exchange controls. Currency is the Drachma. Greece imposes no taxes on offices or branches of foreign companies of any type dealing with management, agents, or operation of ships.

Global Money Consultants
2 Perikleous Street 30-1-896-2118 dial
Vouliagmeni 30-1-896-2152 fax
Athens, Greece 16671

- Primary business activity: newsletters, books, or information.

International Company Services Limited
85 Academias Street 30-1-361-6274 dial
Athens, Greece 10678 30-1-364-0565 fax

- Primary business activity: company and trust formation services.

Hungary

In Central Europe. Main language is Hungarian. German, some English, and some French is also spoken.

There are no exchange controls. Currency is the Forint. Bank deposits can be registered on a passbook system with no names recorded anywhere. This secrecy surpasses that available elsewhere, but means that if you loose the book, you've lost your money.

Overseas Company Registration Agents
Mr. Laszlo Kiss 36-1-266-3620 dial
Company Formation Agent 36-1-266-3619 fax
PO.Box 1244 Budapest Pf.785
Varmegye st. u. 3-5 V/1, Budapest, Hungary H-1052

- Primary business activity: company and trust formation services.

Ireland

Non-resident companies that do not conduct business within Ireland are exempt from corporation tax on income arising outside of Ireland.

Hill Samuel Bank Limited

Hill Samuel House	353-1-610444	dial
25/28 Adelaide Road	353-1-611413	fax
Dublin, Ireland 2		

- Primary business activity: bank and trust services.
- Private banking services and/or savings accounts.
- Consumer loans and credit facilities.
- Safekeeping and custodian services.
- Portfolio management of securities and mutual funds.
- Company formation services are offered.
- Trust formation services are offered.

International Company Services Limited

Front Suite, First Floor	353-1-661-8490	dial
56 Fitzwilliam Square	353-1-661-8493	fax
Dublin, Ireland 2		

- Primary business activity: company and trust formation services.
- Company formation services are offered. Minimum formation fee £195 plus £10 government fee. Minimum annual fee £10.
- Trust formation services are offered.

Riggs Valmet (Ireland) Ltd.

30 Lower Leeson Street	353-1-330180	dial
Dublin, Ireland 2	353-1-334526	fax

- Primary business activity: company and trust formation services.

Vitacom Company Services

Mr. Stephen P. Walsh-Hickey	353-51-386054	dial
65 Cliff Rd.	353-51-386921	fax
Tramore, Waterford, Ireland		

- Primary business activity: company and trust formation services.
- Company formation services are offered. Minimum formation fee £760 including government fee. Minimum annual fee £445.

Liberia

In Africa. The only tax haven in Africa, Liberia lies on the west coast between Guinea, the Ivory Coast and Sierra Leone. Population is approximately 2.5 million, with over 300,000 in the capital city Monrovia. The official language is English. Climate is tropical.

In 1822 an American group landed a party of freed slaves on the coast in Monrovia in an attempt to establish a haven for such people. In 1847 Liberia declared itself independent and adopted a constitution similar to that of the United States. Liberian offices in New York and Zurich assist in establishing operations.

The legal system is based on U.S. law, and is proclaimed in the Liberian Code of Laws of 1956.

Official currency is the Libyan Dinar. Liberia offers a zero tax rate to firms and Trusts externally owned and receiving all income from outside sources. No taxes are imposed on Liberian corporations provided that more than 50% of the stock is held by non-residents, and that no income is derived from trading within Liberia.

Liberia maintains tax treaties with Germany and Sweden. The identity of company owners can be kept discreet through bearer shares held anonymously or by nominees. Directors, shareholders, and officers may reside anywhere in the world. Registered office may be located in any jurisdiction. Shares may be bearer form. Because shares can be held in bearer form and changes in directors and shareholders need not be recorded after incorporation means that the beneficial owner can have complete anonymity.

Macao

In the South Pacific. A Portuguese colony attached by an isthmus to China. Maximum 15% tax.

Netherlands Antilles

In the Caribbean. The Leeward and Windward Islands, separated by 500 miles of Caribbean sea. The Leeward Islands (includes Curacao and Bonaire) are 35 miles north of Venezuela. The Windward Islands (includes St.Maarten, St.Eustatius, Saba) are 144 miles east of Puerto Rico. Total population approximately 200,000. Main language is Dutch, English, Papiamento, and Spanish. Climate is tropical with average humidity, average temperature 77 to 82ºF.

Curacao - A Spanish navigator, Alonso de Ojeda, a Lieutenant of Christopher Columbus, discovered Curacao in 1499. The Spaniards settled in the early 1500's. In 1634 Holland captured Curacao and founded a Dutch settlement. In 1954 the Netherlands Antilles achieved self-government.

Bonaire - Bonaire, inhabited by the Arawak Indians for centuries, was discovered by Amerigo Vespucci in 1499. He called the island Bonah or "Lowland." After a century of colonization, the Spaniards were dispossessed of the island by the Dutch in 1636. In 1639, Bonaire became a Dutch colony and the Dutch West India Company was formed developing Bonaire's salt production, corn, and livestock industries. During the early 1800's Bonaire was taken over by the British and the island suffered from the activities of French and British pirates. The Dutch regained control of the island in 1816. In 1954 Bonaire became an autonomous island territory with an elected Island Council Government as part of the Netherlands Antilles.

St.Maarten - St.Maarten was discovered by Christopher Columbus on November 11, 1493. The island was named after St.Martin of Tours, as the date of its discovery coincided with the feast of St.Martin. Though

Spain originally claimed St.Maarten, it was deserted when the Dutch set up an outpost in 1631. Ousted by Spain in 1633, the Dutch returned in 1648 to establish an accord with the French, dividing the island between them. The Dutch and French have co-existed peacefully in St.Maarten since then.

In 1954 the Netherlands Antilles achieved self-government as a sovereign island territory. The Governor represents the Royal Crown of the Netherlands. The legal system is based on the Netherlands legal system.

Companies pay an income tax of less than 5% in the Netherlands Antilles. There is no capital gains tax or gift tax in the Netherlands Antilles for companies. The tax treaty between the U.S. and the Netherlands Antilles was terminated in 1980. There is no exchange of information agreement between Canada and the Netherlands Antilles.

Algemene Bank Nederland NV
Pietermaai 17 599-9-611488 dial
Willemstad, Curacao, Netherlands Antilles

- Primary business activity: bank and trust services.

Banco di Caribe NV
Schottegatwey Oost 205 599-9-616588 dial
Willemstad, Curacao, Netherlands Antilles

- Primary business activity: banking services.

Banco Industrial del Venezuela CA
Heerenstraat 19 599-9-611621 dial
Willemstad, Curacao, Netherlands Antilles

- Primary business activity: banking services.

Curacao International Trust Co. NV
Handelskade No.8, PO.Box 812
Willemstad, Curacao, Netherlands Antilles

- Primary business activity: bank and trust services.

First Curacao International Bank NV
Breedestraat (0) 16, PO.Box 299
Willemstad, Curacao, Netherlands Antilles
- Primary business activity: bank and trust services.

Holland Intertrust (Antilles) NV
De Ruyterkade 58a, PO.Box 837
Willemstad, Curacao, Netherlands Antilles
- Primary business activity: company and trust formation services.

Maduro & Curiel's Bank NV
Plaza Jojo Correa 2-4 599-9-611100 dial
Willemstad, Curacao, Netherlands Antilles
- Primary business activity: banking services.

Touche Ross & Co.
Scharlooweg 41 599-9-614288 dial
PO.Box 809 599-9-613626 fax
Willemstad, Curacao, Netherlands Antilles
- Primary business activity: accounting services.

New Caledonia

In the South Pacific. A French territory. No income tax for residents.

Saint-Pierre and Miquelon

In the North Atlantic. French dependencies off the south coast of Newfoundland. Zero income tax to residents.

Tonga

In the South Pacific. A monarchy 800 km south of Samoa, 720 km southeast of Fiji. Highly developed infrastructure. New businesses receive long tax holidays. Legal system based on English common law.

Vanatu

In the South Pacific. A chain of 80 small tropical islands 2,250 km northeast of Sydney, Australia. Population is approximately 150,000 people spread out over a 1,300 km arc of the ocean. Main language is Melanesian, French, and English. Climate is tropical.

Vanatu (formerly New Hebrides) became independent in 1980. The present constitution was adopted on July 20, 1980 and the government is headed by an elected president. The government is divided into executivc, legislative, and judicial bodies. The legal system is based on English Common Law and is supplemented by local statutes influenced by the British prior to independence.

The island chain's capital, Port Vila, is the home of over 1,500 tax-exempt companies and over 90 tax-exempt banks. Connections through Australia. Allows the formation of private insurance companies. No significant taxes on anything. No tax treaties, no exchange control, nameplate banks are welcome.

There is no income tax, capital gains tax, gift tax, or estate tax in Vanatu. There are no exchange controls in Vanatu. The official currency is the Vatu. There is no exchange of information agreement between Vanatu and the U.S. or Canada.

ANZ Bank (Vanatu) Limited
Port Vila, Vanatu, South Pacific

- Primary business activity: banking services.

Barclays Bank
Port Vila, Vanatu, South Pacific

- Primary business activity: banking services.

Geoff Gee & Assoc.
PO.Box 782, Port Vila, Vanatu, South Pacific
- Primary business activity: law office.

Investor's Trust Limited

GPO.Box 211	678-2198	dial
Port Vila, Vanatu, South Pacific	678-3799	fax

- Primary business activity: bank and trust services.

KPMG Peat Marwick

PO.Box 212	678-2091	dial
Port Vila, Vanatu, South Pacific	678-3665	fax

- Primary business activity: bank and trust services.
- Specific product: booklet: "Vanatu - The Tax Haven of the Pacific."

Melanesia International Trust Co. Ltd.
Rue Pasteur, PO.Box 213, Port Vila, Vanatu, South Pacific
- Primary business activity: banking services.

Pacific International Trust Company Ltd

PO.Box 45	678-2957	dial
Port Vila, Vanatu, South Pacific	678-3405	fax

- Primary business activity: bank and trust services.
- Specific product: booklet: "Port Vila, Vanatu - The Pacific's Premier Financial Centre."

Wayne J.McKeague & Assoc.
PO.Box 140, Port Vila, Vanatu, South Pacific
- Primary business activity: law office.

Vatican

The Vatican is the smallest independent state in the world and exists solely as the residence of the Pope. The Pope ruled extensive areas of central Italy until 1860, when they were incorporated into the Kingdom of Italy, which invaded Rome itself in 1870 and confined the Pope to the complex of religious and administrative buildings known as the Vatican. In 1929 the Vatican was recognized as an independent state in return for the Pope relinquishing claims over Rome and surrounding territory. The official currency is the Italian Lira.

The Vatican Bank (the Institute for Religious Works) is famed for secrecy and has correspondent banks and agencies throughout the world.

Western Samoa

In the south Pacific. A group of Polynesian islands northeast of Australia and Fiji. Population approximately 180,000. Main language is Samoan and English.

Western Samoa has a bank secrecy law prohibiting the unauthorized disclosure of information pertaining to a clients affairs to a third party. Bank secrecy can be lifted in cases of illegal drug activities, theft, or fraud.

Western Samoa gained independence in 1962. The government is headed by a head of state, a prime minister, and a cabinet of ministers. Two major parties (both supporting offshore banking) are represented in parliament. The legal system is based on English Common Law and is supplemented by local statutes.

There is no income tax or capital gains tax in Western Samoa for companies. There is no exchange of information agreement between Western Samoa and the U.S. or Canada.

Apa & Enari
PO.Box 1129 685-22-234 dial
Apia, Western Samoa

- Primary business activity: law office.

Bank of Western Samoa

Beach Road	685-22-422	dial
PO.Box L-1855	685-22-595	fax
Apia, Western Samoa		

- Primary business activity: banking services.

Central Bank of Samoa

Registrar of Int'l & Foreign Companies	685-24-071	dial
PO.Private Bag	200SX 24100	telex
Apia, Western Samoa		

- Primary business activity: banking services.

Coopers & Lybrand Chartered Accountants

PO.Box 4463	685-24-336	dial
Apia, Western Samoa	685-21-316	fax

- Primary business activity: accounting services.

Drake & Company

PO.Box 757	685-24-280	dial
Apia, Western Samoa	685-24-370	fax

- Primary business activity: law office.

Epati, Stevenson & Nelson

PO.Box 210	685-21-751	dial
Apia, Western Samoa	685-24-166	fax

- Primary business activity: law office.

European Pacific Trust Company Limited

PO.Box 2029	685-21-758	dial
Apia, Western Samoa	685-21-407	fax

- Primary business activity: bank and trust services.

H.T.Retzlaff

PO.Box 1863	685-23-325	dial
Apia, Western Samoa	685-23-038	fax

- Primary business activity: law office.

Herota F.M.Luteru
PO.Box 1411 — 685-22-965 dial
Apia, Western Samoa
- Primary business activity: accounting services.

Kamu & Peteru
PO.Box 2949 — 685-20-799 dial
Apia, Western Samoa
- Primary business activity: law office.

Kruse, Vaai & Barlow
PO.Box 2029 — 685-21-758 dial
Apia, Western Samoa — 685-21-407 fax
- Primary business activity: law office.

Overseas Company Registration Agents
Level 1, loane Villamu Building — 685-21878 dial
PO.Box 3271, Falealili Street — 685-21869 fax
Apia, Western Samoa
- Primary business activity: company and trust formation services.
- Corporate services such as registered agent services.
- Company formation services are offered. Minimum formation fee US$500 plus US$300 license fee. Minimum annual fee US$300.

Pacific Commercial Bank
PO.Box 1860 — 685-20-000 dial
Apia, Western Samoa — 685-22-848 fax
- Primary business activity: banking services.

Pala Lima
PO.Box 173 — 685-21-953 dial
Apia, Western Samoa
- Primary business activity: accounting services.

Price Waterhouse & Company
PO.Box 1599 — 685-20-321 dial
Apia, Western Samoa — 685-23-722 fax
- Primary business activity: accounting services.

Sapolu & Company

PO.Box 4027	685-21-778	dial
Apia, Western Samoa		

- Primary business activity: law office.

Va'ai & Co.

PO.Private Bag	685-20-545	dial
Apia, Western Samoa	685-202 UNITEDCO SX	telex

- Primary business activity: law office.

Western Samoa International Trust Co.

Ioane Viliamu Building, Level 1	685-24-550	dial
Falealili Street, PO.Box 3271	685-21-837	fax
Apia, Western Samoa	SAMTRUST 2958 SX	telex

- Primary business activity: bank and trust services.

CHAPTER 7

QUICK REFERENCE GUIDE

QUICK REFERENCE #1 PRIVACY AND STATUTES

	Bank Secrecy?	English Common Law?	Independent Country?	Exchange Controls?
Andorra	yes	no	yes	no
Anguilla	yes	yes	no	no
Antigua	yes	yes	yes	no
Austria	yes	no	yes	no
Bahamas	yes	yes	yes	yes
Bahrein	---	---	yes	---
Barbados	no	yes	yes	no
Belize	yes	yes	yes	no
Bermuda	no	yes	no	yes
BVI	yes	yes	no	no
Campione	---	no	---	no
Cayman Islands	yes	yes	no	no
C.I. - Guernsey	no	no	yes	no
C.I. - Jersey	no	no	yes	no
Cook Islands	yes	yes	no	no
Costa Rica	yes	no	yes	no
Cyprus	---	---	yes	no
Gibraltar	yes	yes	no	no
Greece	no	no	yes	no

	Bank Secrecy?	English Common Law?	Independent Country?	Exchange Controls?
Hong Kong	no	yes	no	no
Isle of Man	no	yes	yes	no
Liberia	---	no	yes	---
Liechtenstein	yes	no	yes	no
Luxembourg	yes	no	yes	no
Macao	---	---	---	---
Malta	yes	yes	yes	no
Monaco	---	no	yes	no
Montserrat	yes	yes	no	no
Nauru	yes	no	yes	no
Netherland Antilles	---	no	yes	no
Panama	yes	no	yes	no
St.Kitts & Nevis	yes	yes	yes	no
Switzerland	yes	no	yes	no
Tonga	---	yes	---	---
Turks & Caicos	yes	yes	no	no
Vanatu	---	yes	yes	no
Vatican	yes	no	yes	no
Western Samoa	yes	yes	yes	---

QUICK REFERENCE #2 COMPANY DISCLOSURE

	disclosure to gov't of beneficial owners?	public disclosure of registered shareholders?	financial statements to be filed?	bearer shares possible?
Andorra	yes	---	---	---
Anguilla	---	---	---	---
Antigua	no	no	no	yes
Austria	---	---	---	---
Bahamas	no	no	no	yes
Bahrein	---	---	---	---
Barbados	---	---	no	---
Belize	no	no	no	yes
Bermuda	no	no	no	no
BVI	no	no	no	yes
Campione	no	---	---	---
Cayman Islands	no	no	no	yes
C.I. - Guernsey	yes	no	yes	---
C.I. - Jersey	yes	yes	no	no
Cook Islands	no	no	no	yes
Costa Rica	---	---	---	---
Cyprus	---	---	---	---
Gibraltar	yes	yes	no	no
Greece	---	---	---	---

	disclosure to gov't of beneficial owners?	public disclosure of registered shareholders?	financial statements to be filed?	bearer shares possible?
Hong Kong	yes	---	yes	no
Isle of Man	no	yes	no	no
Liberia	no	---	---	yes
Liechtenstein	no	yes	yes	yes
Luxembourg	---	---	---	---
Macao	---	---	---	---
Malta	no	yes	no	---
Monaco	---	yes	yes	no
Montserrat	---	---	---	---
Nauru	no	yes	no	yes
Netherland Antilles	---	---	---	---
Panama	no	yes	no	yes
St.Kitts & Nevis	no	no	no	yes
Switzerland	no	---	yes	yes
Tonga	---	---	---	---
Turks & Caicos	no	no	no	yes
Vanatu	---	---	---	---
Vatican	---	---	---	---
Western Samoa	---	---	---	---

QUICK REFERENCE #3
MINIMUM REQUIREMENTS

	minimum number of directors	minimum number of shareholders	directors may be corporate?	secretary may be corporate?
Andorra	---	---	---	---
Anguilla	1	1	---	---
Antigua	1	1	yes	yes
Austria	---	---	---	---
Bahamas	1	1 *	yes	yes
Bahrein	---	---	---	---
Barbados	---	---	---	---
Belize	1	1	yes	yes
Bermuda	2	1	yes	no
BVI	1	1	yes	yes
Campione	---	---	yes	yes
Cayman Islands	1	1	yes	yes
C.I. - Guernsey	1	2	---	yes
C.I. - Jersey	1	2	no	yes
Cook Islands	1	1	yes	no
Costa Rica	---	---	---	---
Cyprus	---	---	---	---
Gibraltar	1	1	yes	yes
Greece	---	---	---	---

* 2 shareholders required for incorporation.

	minimum number of directors	minimum number of shareholders	directors may be corporate?	secretary may be corporate?
Hong Kong	2	2	yes	yes
Isle of Man	2	1	no	no
Liberia	---	---	yes	yes
Liechtenstein	---	---	---	yes
Luxembourg	---	---	---	---
Macao	---	---	---	---
Malta	---	---	yes	yes
Monaco	2	2	no	yes
Montserrat	---	---	---	---
Nauru	1	1	yes	yes
Netherland Antilles	---	---	---	---
Panama	3	---	yes	---
St.Kitts & Nevis	1	1	yes	yes
Switzerland	1	3	no	yes
Tonga	---	---	---	---
Turks & Caicos	1	1	yes	yes
Vanatu	---	---	---	---
Western Samoa	---	---	---	---

CHAPTER 8

NORTH AMERICAN CONTACTS:

Company formation agents and law offices:

Corporate Service Center, Inc.
1280 Terminal Way, Suite 3, Reno, NV, USA 89502

- Primary business activity: company and trust formation services.
- Corporate services such as registered agent services.
- Company formation services are offered.

Corporate Management Services

Mr. Ralph W. Kydd	416-362-9949	dial
President	416-362-1628	fax

55 University Ave., Suite 900, Toronto, Ontario, Canada M5J 2P8

- Primary business activity: company and trust formation services.

David S. Lesperance Barrister Solicitor

Mr. David S. Lesperance	905-529-2700	dial
Barrister-at-Law	905-529-9071	fax
49 - 6A The Donway West	800-324-4565	free

Suite 2006, Toronto, Ontario, Canada M3C 2E8

- Primary business activity: law office.

Global-R

PO.Box 025216	011-506 32-0596	fax

Miami, FL, USA 33102-5216

- Primary business activity: bank and trust services.
- Primary business activity: company and trust formation services.

Harris & Harris Barristers & Solicitors

Mr. Paul R. LeBreux	416-798-2722	dial
Solicitor	416-798-2715	fax

190 Attwell Drive, Suite 400, Toronto, Ontario, Canada M9W 6H8

- Primary business activity: law office.
- Corporate services such as registered agent services.
- Executor and administrator of wills and estates.
- Safekeeping and custodian services.
- Company formation services are offered.
- Trust formation services are offered.

Laughlin Global Corporation Service, Inc.

Mr. Lewis E. Laughlin	702-883-8484	dial
Chief Executive Officer	702-883-4874	fax

2533 N. Carson Street, Carson City, NV, USA 89706

- Primary business activity: company and trust formation services.

N.S.B.A. Offshore Financial Consultants

Mr. Fred Barrett	407-283-7014	dial
Managing Director	407-223-9103	fax
1820 Jensen Beach Boulevard	800-685-3964	free

Suite 524, Jensen Beach, FL, USA 34957

- Primary business activity: company and trust formation services.
- Corporate services such as registered agent services.
- Company formation services are offered.
- Trust formation services are offered.

N.S.B.A. Offshore Financial Consultants

Mr. Fred Barrett	800-685-3964	free

Managing Director

101 - 1001 West Broadway, Suite 245, Vancouver, Canada V6H 4B1

2255-B Queen Street, Suite 850, Toronto, Ontario, Canada M4N 2L3

- Primary business activity: company and trust formation services.
- Corporate services such as registered agent services.
- Company formation services are offered.
- Trust formation services are offered.

Overseas Company Registration Agents

Mr. Kevin Mirecki	714-854-3344	dial
Attorney-at-Law	714-854-6967	fax

3501 Jamboree Road, Suite 2100, Newport Beach, CA, USA 92660

- Primary business activity: company and trust formation services.

Sabourin and Sun Inc.

Mr. Peter Sabourin	416-932-0305	dial
Managing Director	416-932-1879	fax

2221 Yonge Street, Suite 503C, Toronto, Ontario, Canada M4S 2B4

- Primary business activity: company and trust formation services.
- Corporate services such as registered agent services.
- Safekeeping and custodian services.
- Portfolio management of securities and mutual funds.
- Company formation services are offered.
- Trust formation services are offered.

Skinner, Sutton & Watson

Mr. Garrett Sutton	702-829-4400	dial
1325 Airmotive Way	702-329-3093	fax

Suite 370, Reno, NV, USA 89502

- Primary business activity: law office.
- Company formation services are offered.
- Trust formation services are offered.

Steven F. Stucker, Chartered

Mr. Steven F. Stucker	702-884-1979	dial
Managing Director	702-884-1938	fax

1802 N. Carson Street, Suite 208, Carson City, NV, USA 89701

- Primary business activity: company and trust formation services.

The Company Corporation

Mr. George Rohr	302-575-0440	dial
President	302-575-1346	fax
Three Christina Centre	800-542-2677	free

201 N. Walnut Street, Wilmington, DE, USA 19801

- Primary business activity: company and trust formation services.
- Corporate services such as registered agent services.
- Company formation services are offered.

The Consulting Group
The International Institute Companies
3601 S.E. Ocean Blvd. 407-220-4800 dial
Suite 103 407-220-4804 fax
Stuart, FL, USA 34996 800-922-1771 free

- Primary business activity: company and trust formation services.

The Offshore Incorporators
Mr. John Huxley 416-323-1786 dial
President 416-323-0825 fax
36 Castle Frank Road, Suite 101, Toronto, Ontario, Canada M4W 2Z7

- Primary business activity: company and trust formation services.
- Company formation services are offered.

Tom Pister, Barrister & Solicitor, CA
Mr. Tom Pister 416-962-8983 dial
Barrister-at-Law, Chartered Accountant 416-962-5369 fax
2 Bloor Street West, Suite 700, Toronto, Ontario, Canada M4W 3R1

- Primary business activity: accounting services.
- Primary business activity: law office.
- Company formation services are offered.
- Trust formation services are offered.

Turstra, Mazza
Mr. David Melnik 416-488-7918 dial
Solicitor 416-593-4559 fax
350 Lonsdale Road, Suite 311, Toronto, Ontario, Canada M5P 1R5

- Primary business activity: law office.

Government representative offices:

Anguilla Department of Tourism
271 Main St. 800-553-4939 free
Northport, NY, USA 11768 516-261-9606 fax

- Primary business activity: travel services or information.

Antigua and Barbuda Department of Trade and Tourism

Mr. Ambassador Hurst	212-541-4117	dial
Ambassador	212-757-1607	fax

610 Fifth Avenue, Suite 311, New York, NY, USA 10020

- Primary business activity: government services.

Antigua and Barbuda Embassy

Ms. Debbie Prosper	202-362-5122	dial
First Secretary	202-362-5225	fax
3216 New Mexico Ave. N.W.	7108 221130	telex

Washington, DC, USA 20016

- Primary business activity: government services.

Antigua and Barbuda Department of Trade and Tourism

Mr. Clarence Lord	416-961-3085	dial
Commissioner	416-961-7218	fax

60 St.Clair Ave. E., Suite 304, Toronto, Ontario, Canada M4T 1N5

- Primary business activity: government services.

Austrian Embassy

445 Wilbrod St.	613-563-1444	dial
Ottawa, Ontario, Canada K1N 6M7	613-563-0038	fax

- Primary business activity: government services.

Bahamas High Commission

360 Albert St.	613-232-1724	dial
Suite 1020	613-232-0097	fax

Ottawa, Ontario, Canada K1R 7X7

- Primary business activity: government services.

Bahrain Embassy

3502 International Dr. N.W.	202-342-0741	dial

Washington, DC, USA 20008

- Primary business activity: government services.

Barbados Industrial Development Corp.
800 Second Ave. 212-867-6420 dial
New York, NY, USA 10017
- Primary business activity: government services.

Barbados High Commission
151 Slater St. 613-236-9517 dial
Suite 210 613-230-4362 fax
Ottawa, Ontario, Canada K1P 5H3
- Primary business activity: government services.

Belize High Commission
112 Kent St. 613-232-7389 dial
Suite 2005, Tower B 613-232-5804 fax
Ottawa, Ontario, Canada K1P 5P2
- Primary business activity: government services.

Channel Islands Tourist Board
Taurus House 416-485-8724 dial
512 Duplex Ave. 416-267-7600 fax
Toronto, Ontario, Canada M4R 2E3
- Primary business activity: travel services or information.

Costa Rica Republic Embassy
408 Queen St. 613-234-5762 dial
Suite 200, Ottawa, Ontario, Canada K1R 5A7
- Primary business activity: government services.

Cyprus Republic High Commission
2211 R. St. N. W. 202-462-5772 dial
Washington, DC, USA 20008 202-483-6710 fax
- Primary business activity: government services.

Greece, Embassy of
76-80 MacLaren St. 613-238-6271 dial
Ottawa, Ontario, Canada K1S 2A9 613-238-5676 fax
- Primary business activity: government services.

Hong Kong Tourist Association
Mr. Terence Fu 212-869-5008 dial
Director - United States 212-730-2605 fax
590 Fifth Avenue, 5th floor, New York, NY, USA 10036-4706
- Primary business activity: travel services or information.

Hong Kong Tourist Association
Mrs. Lily Shun 416-366-2389 dial
Director 416-366-1098 fax
347 Bay St., Suite 909, Toronto, Ontario, Canada M5H 2R7
- Primary business activity: travel services or information.

Hungary, Embassy of the Republic of
7 Delaware Ave. 613-232-1711 dial
Ottawa, Ontario, Canada K2P 0Z2 613-232-5620 fax
- Primary business activity: government services.

Liberia, Embassy of the Republic
160 Elgin St. 613-232-1781 dial
Suite 2600 613-563-9869 fax
Ottawa, Ontario, Canada K1N 8S3
- Primary business activity: government services.

Luxembourg, Embassy of
2200 Massachusetts Ave. N. W. 202-265-4171 dial
Washington, DC, USA 20008 202-328-8270 fax
- Primary business activity: government services.

Monaco, Consular Representatives
1800 McGill College Ave. 514-849-0589 dial
14 floor, Montreal, Quebec, Canada H3A 3K9
- Primary business activity: government services.

Montserrat Tourist Office
775 Park Ave. 800-646-2002 free
Huntington, NY, USA 11743 516-425-0903 fax
- Primary business activity: travel services or information.

Netherlands Foreign Investment Agency
Mr. Paul van Schaik 312-616-8400 dial
303 East Wacker Drive, Chicago, IL, USA 60601
- Primary business activity: government services.

Netherlands, Royal Netherlands Embassy
275 Slater St. 613-237-5030 dial
3rd floor 613-237-6471 fax
Ottawa, Ontario, Canada K1P 5H9
- Primary business activity: government services.

Panama, Permanent Mission of
2862 McGill Ter N. W. 202-483-1407 dial
Washington, DC, USA 20008 202-483-8413 fax
- Primary business activity: government services.

Peru, Embassy of
170 Laurier Ave. W. 613-238-1777 dial
Suite 1007 613-232-3062 fax
Ottawa, Ontario, Canada K1P 5V5
- Primary business activity: government services.

Saint Kitts and Nevis High Commission
112 Kent St. 613-236-8952 dial
Suite 1610 613-236-3042 fax
Ottawa, Ontario, Canada K1P 5P2
- Primary business activity: government services.

Saint Lucia High Commission
112 Kent St. 613-236-8952 dial
Suite 1610 613-236-3042 fax
Ottawa, Ontario, Canada K1P 5P2
- Primary business activity: government services.

Saint Vincent / Grenadines High Comm.

112 Kent St.	613-236-8952	dial
Suite 1610	613-236-3042	fax
Ottawa, Ontario, Canada K1P 5P2		

- Primary business activity: government services.

Seychelles High Commission

820 2nd Ave.	212-687-9766	dial
Suite 900F, New York, NY, USA 10017		

- Primary business activity: government services.

Sierra Leone High Commission

1701 - 19th St. N. W.	202-939-9261	dial
Washington, DC, USA 20009		

- Primary business activity: government services.

Singapore Republic High Commission

Two United Nations Plaza	212-826-0840	dial
25th floor	212-826-2964	fax
New York, NY, USA 10017		

- Primary business activity: government services.

Solomon Islands High Commission

820 - 2nd Ave.	212-599-6194	dial
Suite 800B, New York, NY, USA 10017		

- Primary business activity: government services.

Switzerland, Embassy of

5 Marlborough Ave.	613-235-1837	dial
Ottawa, Ontario, Canada K1N 8E6	613-563-1394	fax

- Primary business activity: government services.

United States of America Embassy

100 Wellington St.	613-238-5335	dial
PO.Box 866, Station B, Ottawa, Ontario, Canada K1P 5T1		

- Primary business activity: government services.

Financial contacts:

Bank of Nova Scotia

One Liberty Plaza	212-225-5000	dial
26th Floor, 165 Broadway	212-225-5286	fax
New York, NY, USA 10006		

- Primary business activity: banking services.
- Private banking services and/or savings accounts.
- Consumer loans and credit facilities.
- Safekeeping and custodian services.

Bank of Nova Scotia

1st Mezzanine Floor, Scotia Plaza	416-866-5000	dial
40 King St. W.	416-866-5005	fax
Toronto, Ontario, Canada M5H 1H1		

- Primary business activity: banking services.
- Private banking services and/or savings accounts.
- Consumer loans and credit facilities.
- Safekeeping and custodian services.
- Portfolio management of securities and mutual funds.

Chemical Bank Private Banking

Ms. Vilma Ciaramicoli	212-270-3359	dial
Vice President	212-687-0967	fax
270 Park Avenue, 46th Floor, New York, NY, USA 10017-2070		

- Primary business activity: banking services.
- Private banking services and/or savings accounts.
- Consumer loans and credit facilities.
- Safekeeping and custodian services.
- Portfolio management of securities and mutual funds.
- Company formation services are offered.
- Trust formation services are offered.

Union Bank of Switzerland

Mr. Thomas D. Brunner	212-715-3000	dial
Assistant Vice President	212-715-3946	fax
299 Park Avenue	MCI 620317 UBS UW	telex
New York, NY, USA 10171-0026		

- Primary business activity: banking services.
- Private banking services and/or savings accounts.
- Consumer loans and credit facilities.
- Safekeeping and custodian services.
- Portfolio management of securities and mutual funds.
- Specific product: Worldwide Directory of International Banks.

EUROPEAN CONTACTS:

Company formation agents and law offices:

International Company Services Limited

Mr. D. Dentith 441-71-493-4244 dial
Director 441-71-491-0605 fax
Suite 1C, Standbrook House
2-5 Old Bond Street, London, UK W1X 3TB

- Primary business activity: company and trust formation services.
- Company formation services are offered. Minimum formation fee £150 plus £32 government fee. Minimum annual fee £32.
- Trust formation services are offered.

Jordan & Sons Ltd.

20-22 Bedford Row 441-71-400-3333 dial
London, UK WC1R 4JS 441-71-400-3366 fax

- Primary business activity: company and trust formation services.
- Corporate services such as registered agent services.
- Company formation services are offered. Minimum formation fee £300 plus £32 licence fee. Minimum annual fee £132.

Overseas Company Registration Agents

Mr. Peter Sidney 441-71-355-1096 dial
Company Formation Agent 441-71-495-3017 fax
72 New Bond Street, London, UK W1Y 9DD

- Primary business activity: company and trust formation services.
- Corporate services such as registered agent services.
- Company formation services are offered. Minimum formation fee £95 plus licence fee.

Financial contacts:

American Express Europe Limited

International Dollar Card	441-273-548-427	dial
PO.Box 77	441-273-563-650	fax
Prestamex House, Brighton, UK BN2 1YX		

- Primary business activity: banking services.
- Offers private credit card backed by deposit.

Bank Julius Baer

Bevis Marks House	441-71-623-4211	dial
Bevis Marks	441-71-283-6146	fax
London, UK EC3A 7NE	887 272	telex

- Primary business activity: banking services.
- Private banking services and/or savings accounts.
- Safekeeping and custodian services.
- Portfolio management of securities and mutual funds.

Bank of N.T. Butterfield & Son Ltd.

Mr. Ian R. de Leschery	441-71-814-8800	dial
Senior Manager	441-71-814-8821	fax
24 Chiswell Street	8812016 BNTBLN	telex
London, UK EC1Y 4TY		

- Primary business activity: banking services.

Bank of Nova Scotia

West End	441-71-491-4200	dial
10 Berkeley Square	441-71-629-9362	fax
London, UK W1X 6DN		

- Primary business activity: banking services.
- Private banking services and/or savings accounts.
- Consumer loans and credit facilities.
- Safekeeping and custodian services.

Barclays Bank Private Banking

54 Lombard St. 441-71-626-1567 dial
London, UK EC3P 3AH

- Primary business activity: bank and trust services.
- Portfolio management of securities and mutual funds.

Barclays Private Trust Limited - Headquarters

Mr. David Beale 441-71-487-2000 dial
Director 441-71-487-2050 fax
49 Grosvener Street, London, UK W1X 9FH

- Primary business activity: bank and trust services.
- Offers private credit card backed by deposit.
- Private banking services and/or savings accounts.
- Consumer loans and credit facilities.
- Safekeeping and custodian services.
- Portfolio management of securities and mutual funds.
- Company formation services are offered.
- Trust formation services are offered.

Coutts & Co.

440 Strand 441-71-753-1000 dial
London, UK WC2R 0QS 441-71-240-0265 fax

- Primary business activity: bank and trust services.
- Private banking services and/or savings accounts.
- Safekeeping and custodian services.
- Portfolio management of securities and mutual funds.
- Company formation services are offered.
- Trust formation services are offered.

Lloyds Bank Private Banking

Bolsa House 441-71-248-9822 dial
80 Cheapside 441-71-489-3230 fax
London, UK EC2V 6EE

- Primary business activity: bank and trust services.
- Portfolio management of securities and mutual funds.

Seymour Pierce Butterfield Limited

Mr. Christopher Honeyborne	441-71-814-8700	dial
Chief Executive	441-71-814-8711	fax
24 Chiswell Street	8811530 SPBLTD	telex
London, UK EC1Y 4TY		

- Primary business activity: bank and trust services.

Swiss Bank Corporation

66 Hanover Street	441-31-225-9186	dial
Edinburgh, UK EH2 1HH	7-2567	telex

- Primary business activity: banking services.

WORLDWIDE CONTACTS:

Company formation agents and law offices:

Overseas Company Registration Agents
International Management Mauritius Ltd.
Ms. Suzanne Gujadhur 230-212-9800 dial
Company Formation Agent 230-212-9833 fax
Les Cascades Building, 5th Floor
Edith Cavell Street, Port Louis, Mauritius

- Primary business activity: company and trust formation services.
- Corporate services such as registered agent services.
- Company formation services are offered. Minimum formation fee US$450 plus US$100 licence fee. Minimum annual fee US$100.

Derks & Partners
PO.Box 9230, 3506 Ge Utrecht, Netherlands

- Primary business activity: law office.

Government representative offices:

Gulf Investment Corporation
PO.Box 3402 965-2-431911 dial
Safat, Kuwait 13035 965-2-448894 fax

- Primary business activity: government services.

Financial contacts:

ABN Bank
32 Vijzelstraat 31-20-29-3249 dial
Amsterdam, Netherlands

- Primary business activity: banking services.

Bank Mees & Hope NV

548 Herengracht, PO.Box 293, Netherlands 1000 AG

- Primary business activity: banking services.

Cook Islands Trust Corporation Limited

The Rocks, 29 George Street

PO.Box 4858 GPO, Sydney, Australia

- Primary business activity: bank and trust services.

Jyske Bank Private Banking

Vesterbrogade 9	45-33-787878	dial
Copenhagen, Denmark DK-1780	45-33-787833	fax

- Primary business activity: banking services.
- Private banking services and/or savings accounts.
- Portfolio management of securities and mutual funds.

Bank of Nova Scotia

Ocean Building, #15-01	65-535-8688	dial
10 Collyer Quay	65-532-2440	fax

Singapore 0104

- Primary business activity: banking services.
- Private banking services and/or savings accounts.
- Safekeeping and custodian services.
- Portfolio management of securities and mutual funds.

Barclays Private Banking

Ms. Julie Teo	65-224-8555	dial
Director	65-221-9624	fax

50 Raffles Place, 21-01 Shell Tower, Singapore 0104

- Primary business activity: banking services.
- Offers private credit card backed by deposit.
- Private banking services and/or savings accounts.
- Consumer loans and credit facilities.
- Safekeeping and custodian services.
- Portfolio management of securities and mutual funds.
- Company formation services are offered.
- Trust formation services are offered.

Coutts & Co. AG

50 Raffles Place, No. 05-05	65-223-3132	dial
Shell Tower	65-223-5098	fax
Singapore 0104		

- Primary business activity: bank and trust services.
- Private banking services and/or savings accounts.
- Safekeeping and custodian services.
- Portfolio management of securities and mutual funds.
- Company formation services are offered.
- Trust formation services are offered.

Overseas Company Registration Agents

Mrs. Diana Bean	65-535-3382	dial
Company Formation Agent	65-535-3991	fax

24 Raffles Place, 26-05 Clifford Centre, Singapore 0104

- Primary business activity: company and trust formation services.
- Corporate services such as registered agent services.
- Company formation services are offered. Minimum formation fee US$3,750 plus licence fee.

Royal Trust Bank (Asia) Ltd.

#19-01 Shell Tower	65-224-9111	dial
50 Raffles Place	65-225-3809	fax
Singapore 0104		

- Primary business activity: bank and trust services.
- Offers private credit card backed by deposit.
- Private banking services and/or savings accounts.
- Consumer loans and credit facilities.
- Safekeeping and custodian services.
- Portfolio management of securities and mutual funds.

Swiss Bank Corporation

Mr. Nicholas L. Wood	65-224-2200	dial
Associate Director	65-531-3444	fax
6 Battery Road	RS 24140 SINSUIS	telex
#35-01, Singapore 0104		

- Primary business activity: banking services.

Swiss Bank Corporation
1704 Kyobo Building, 1, 1-ka — (82) 2-720-61-97 dial
Chongro, Chongro-ku — K 32290 telex
Seoul, South Korea 110-121

- Primary business activity: banking services.

KmG Klynveldkraayenhof & Co.
Prinses Irenestraat 59, Amsterdam, Netherlands 1077 WV

- Primary business activity: banking services.

Nederlands Middenstandsbank NV
Eduard van Beinumstraat 2, PO.Box 1800
Amsterdam, Netherlands 1077 XT

- Primary business activity: banking services.

Nederlandsche Credietbank NV
Heregracht 458, PO.Box 941, Amsterdam, Netherlands 1017 CA

- Primary business activity: banking services.

Rabobank Nederland
Croeselaan 18 — 4-0200 telex
3521 CB Utrecht, Netherlands

- Primary business activity: banking services.

Riggs Valmet Trust Management B.V.
148 Westblaak — 010-413-7372 dial
Rotterdam, Netherlands 3012 KM — 010-733-3178 fax

- Primary business activity: company and trust formation services.

Swiss Bank Corporation Nederland N.V.
Mr. C.J.M. Bierman — 31-20-6-510-510 dial
Chief Executive — 31-20-6-961-671 fax
Hoogoorddreef 5, Postbus 2333 — 1-1386 telex
1100 DV Amsterdam Z-O, Amsterdam, Netherlands

- Primary business activity: banking services.

Notes

Notes

TAX HAVEN ROADMAP

Now that you own the most authoritative tax haven directory ever published, ensure that it always remains up-to-date.

Tax Haven Roadmap will be updated annually with new tips and strategies, as well as with the latest contact names and addresses.

By reserving your copy now, you will be guaranteed to receive each annual update long before it hits the bookshelves.

In addition, Uphill Publishing Ltd. will send out periodic tax bulletins to annual subscribers. These bulletins will be sent to subscribers in the United States and Canada, at no additional cost. You have no continuing obligation and may cancel your standing order at any time.

If you wish to receive the annual updated version of *Tax Haven Roadmap* please complete the information below and send us a copy. Your VISA Credit Card will be billed $19.95 each year (includes all taxes) plus $2.95 shipping (in the Continental United States and Canada). Prices for all Canadian orders in Canadian Dollars and prices for all U.S. orders in U.S. Dollars.

Yes, I would like to receive the annual updated *Tax Haven Roadmap,* and any pertinent fax bulletins relating to international tax havens.

Please bill my VISA, Credit Card No.: ______________________

Expiry: ______________________

Full Name: ______________________

Address: ______________________

City: ______________________

State/Province: ______________________

Country: ______________________

Zip/Postal Code: ______________________

Telephone No.: ______________________

Fax No.: ______________________

Signature: ______________________

Please return to:

UPHILL PUBLISHING LTD.
190 Attwell Drive, Suite 400
Etobicoke, Ontario
M9W 6H8

or by fax to: (416) 798-2715